GROWING
THROUGH THE
STORMS

A Love Letter From God

ESTHER ABIJAH

WESTBOW
PRESS*
A DIVISION OF THOMAS NELSON
& ZONDERVAN

WestBow Press books may be ordered through booksellers or by contacting:

WestBow Press
A Division of Thomas Nelson & Zondervan
1663 Liberty Drive
Bloomington, IN 47403
www.westbowpress.com
844-714-3454

Because of the dynamic nature of the Internet, any web addresses or
links contained in this book may have changed since publication and
may no longer be valid. The views expressed in this work are solely those
of the author and do not necessarily reflect the views of the publisher,
and the publisher hereby disclaims any responsibility for them.

Any people depicted in stock imagery provided by Getty Images are
models, and such images are being used for illustrative purposes only.
Certain stock imagery © Getty Images.

ISBN: 979-8-3850-0152-1 (sc)
ISBN: 979-8-3850-0154-5 (hc)
ISBN: 979-8-3850-0153-8 (e)

Library of Congress Control Number: 2023911610

Print information available on the last page.

WestBow Press rev. date: 10/26/2023

To the reader of this book.

I Pray that nothing shifts you from your purpose. May God's glory shine in your life as you obey Him and allow Him to set you apart for His kingdom work. May the strength of God keep you running the good race despite the storms you pass through.

CONTENTS

Every storm we face is a lesson that can turn into beauty. What we go through breaks us physically so we can evolve spiritually.

INTRODUCTION

Have you realized that sometimes, in life, the more we run away from something, the more that thing also runs after us? The more we try to avoid something, the more we find ourselves sinking deep into it —this is what the call of God does. That phone rings until you answer, and your mind becomes restless when you fail to do so. The story of life happens in such a way that giving up can be easy— but we are the only ones who can narrate what we go through with authenticity. Once you tell someone your story and they pass it on, it becomes a second-hand story. Although the person may be familiar with your story, they have not *felt* the experience. It takes grace and compassion to *understand* the pain of someone's experience without having to walk in the person's shoes yourself.

Growing Through the Storms is a love letter from God to me and to all who engage in this book. It is a love letter that the Holy Spirit directed me to write. As I obeyed and started writing, a still, small voice whispered healing words, and growth began manifesting. Through this letter, He helped me navigate the challenges of my life and view life from a different perspective.

You may have gone through or *will* go through pivotal moments that will push you in the direction God wants for you and to the destination He has prepared for you. A pivotal moment for me was the challenges I faced in 2018—being judged and misunderstood by those I once called sisters in Christ, resulting in rejection, false accusations, and gossip—This made me feel as if my life was falling apart, only for me to realize that God was putting together the life He had destined for me. In all the misunderstandings and rejection, God wanted my attention. He told me, "Write!"— a strong, directive voice that is hard to ignore. So, I obeyed and did just that. God wanted to reposition me. It was time to pick up my cross and focus solely on Him and the task He had called me to accomplish.

I remembered that my soul thirsted for more of Him in those days. I felt as if something was missing, and the call from Him was getting deeper and deeper. It was a call I had to answer, and hard to resist. I realized the loneliness and rejection were not due to what was going on in my life but rather a strong pull from God. The voice of God amid the storms of my life has always been strong. His voice does not confuse. It assures and liberates. God constantly speaks and writes through me to the heart of His children. He is always speaking to my heart, and it has been a privilege and honor to be an instrument used to proclaim His deep love and thoughts on how to navigate the matters we face in everyday life—bringing hope into the lives of His children. Picking up my cross and walking in my purpose has not been an easy journey, as the work of God comes with opposition. Still, it has been one of the most fulfilling and exhilarating journeys I have ever walked on.

You may be at a point where the call of God has gotten louder, and the repositioning season has begun. I want to assure you that no matter how heavy the cross gets, bear with it and never give up the race. Press on to reach the end of the race and receive the heavenly prize for which God, through Christ Jesus, is calling you (Philippians 3:14).

1

NEW BEGINNINGS

*God has a "next" for you—and moving forward is the
only way to discover it. Keep moving forward.*

God gives us a new beginning or a fresh start every day. He desires
that we leave behind past disappointments and strain toward the
prize He has in store for us, facing the unknown with a renewed
mind. You may have had an awful yesterday, last week, or year;
you may have had a good one. Whatever it may be, never forget
the lessons you learned and the many blessings and achievements
you obtained from God. In this season, let the promises of God
continue to be your source of strength and guide you through the
difficulties. Every day brings on its disappointments, but there are
also many lingering blessings. It may be hard to let go of what was,
but you must turn the page to experience a new world of possibilities.
Explore, grow, and discover all God has in store for you.

Sometimes, letting go of the old can be challenging because we
may feel we're exactly where we should be. No! God wants to offer
you more, and His purpose for your life is much more than what you
leave behind. He wants you to experience the absolute best through
Jesus Christ. Moving on may be scary, especially if you do not know
what's ahead. But God wants to guide you through the uncertainties,
and you can be sure that wherever He takes you is perfect.

You may be reluctant to turn the page because of what you may
have to give up, even if those things no longer serve a purpose in
your life. But that chapter is over, and staying will only rob you of
experiencing the most incredible things ahead. Moving on means

you're ready to face what God has in store for you; it means you're prepared to face the magnitude of the blessings that await you. Trusting God to lead you into your next chapter is never in vain. The first step is always the hardest, but once taken, the rest will begin to unfold, and in the end, you will know why you need to turn the page. 'For I know the plans I have for you,' declares the Lord, 'plans to prosper you and not to harm you, plans to give you hope and a future" (Jeremiah 29:11). God's plans lead us to where He has destined us to be.

Let's revisit the story of Sodom and Gomorrah, taken from the book of Genesis. Lot's wife hesitated and disobeyed God's instructions not to look back at Sodom, which resulted in her turning into a pillar of salt (Genesis 19:26). We wouldn't want that to happen to us, would we? It was hard for her to let go of the past as she thought about Everything she had left behind. When God tells you to let go—trust Him! He will never ask you to leave something behind if He isn't going to replace it with blessings that surpass. So, you must keep going, forgetting what is behind you and moving toward what lies ahead. God loves you so much, and even if the previous season of your life was not your best, know that He is on your team in every chapter. You are where you are today for a reason, and there is a reason He is taking you where you are heading. What you need does not lie in your past. It is not where you've stepped away from; it is where God is taking you. Trust the journey, trust the process, and keep moving in faith. The best part of life is yet to come.

Prophet Isaiah gave the Lord's people something to be hopeful about after they had such a terrible experience during their captivity in Babylon. He wanted them to know that God wanted to do something new. The only way was to forget their humiliating experiences and focus on the future as a nation (Isaiah 43:19). Like the Israelites, God wants to create rivers in your dry wastelands. He can't do that if you are still camping in your wasteland. What God will do cannot compare to the things of the past. Forget the former things. He will do something new, unbreakable, unshakeable, and unspeakable. He has already begun. Can you not see it? Can you not feel it? Where you lack, He will provide. Where Everything seems complicated and impossible, He will make a path. He will close every opposing door and open heaven's gate for you. The old things are gone; the new has come. Give thanks to the Lord, for He is about to pour abundant blessings into your life—new and exciting things! You will see the old no more as you prepare to receive His overflow of goodness.

Why are you worried? Why are you downcast? Our God is faithful and does all things beyond our expectations. Are you wondering when that situation will take a turn for the better? Are you wondering when your finances will come through for that project you've been dreaming of accomplishing? That spouse you've been praying to have? That breakthrough? Life may seem bleak right now, the sky may look gray, and the chances of a sunny day may seem impossible. The new beginning and the break you have been praying for seem like a never-ending story. Many come and go with their golden plaques. You stand there and wonder when your turn will come. But I encourage you to praise His name throughout the questions. Never doubt His goodness in your life. He is love, and love He pours out. Blessings He pours, abundance He gives. He has brought us this far through His faithfulness, love, grace, and mercy. God knows you are tired; He sees your tears and wants you to cry no more. He wants you to come to Him, to seek Him in all your ways.

Do you believe the Lord can change your life and give you the new beginning you have been praying for? He is with you through the transitions, the bumps, and the turbulences. He is the God of the impossible; nothing is too big or small for Him to do. The apostle Paul tells us in Philippians to rejoice in the Lord always (Philippians 4:4). Lift your head and look forward to that new beginning. May God strengthen you to leave what's not for you and grant you the patience to wait for His blessings.

The Unmerited Favor of God

"Surely, Lord, you bless the righteous; you surround them with your favor as with a shield" (Psalm 5:12). This scripture tells us the favor of God acts as a shield. No one can nullify God's favor in our lives. God's unmerited favor is *grace*—given to us not because of what we have done but because of who He is. This favor was displayed when God decided to make man in His likeness (Genesis 1:27). We are in Him. He is in us. His favor was shown through Christ, the Son of the living God, and what He did for us on the cross.

Difficult times are inevitable, but believers in Christ have the comfort of knowing they don't have to go through them alone. Going through the storms of life creates doubts and disappointments. It challenges us in ways that our strength alone cannot handle. When things are hard to bear, we wonder if God will ever come through for us. But the reality is that He always does and always has from the beginning. This act is the unmerited favor of God—grace.

When the unmerited favor of the Lord is upon your life, you will find yourself in places you never imagined. You will go from zero to a hundred in seconds without working for it. The amazing things that never crossed your mind will begin to manifest. Promotions you were never expecting will knock on your door. You will be the light in all the rooms you never thought you would enter—that is what God's unmerited favor does. It places you on the front line and leaves you and others puzzled. People will wonder how you went from the bottom to the top so quickly. No, it is not by magic, luck, or your power but by God's grace. People who witness the unmerited favor of God's hands in your life will be in awe of Him. All will be amazed at how your story has suddenly changed, how God showed up for you when everyone else turned their backs on you.

The Bible tells us that those who find the Lord find life and receive favor from Him (Proverbs 8:35)— this is favor He gives us without having to work for it. We must never stop seeking God, as it is through Him we have life. God's unmerited favor changes Everything. The great news is that it is available to all who accept Christ as the Son of God and diligently seek Him daily. We did not earn the blood of Jesus. God gave it out of His love for us. His favor is already upon us; we must seek Him to experience it, believing and accepting it faithfully. How can we enjoy what we do not know we have? We have God's unmerited favor—grace. It's only by His grace we are who we are today. His Word says, "His favor lasts a lifetime; weeping may stay for the night but rejoicing comes in the morning" (Psalm 30:5). Today, I encourage you to keep walking in His favor through faith in Christ.

A Time and a Season

Elevation Church pastor Steven Furtick once said, "The only thing harder than waiting for God's time is wishing you had." The theme of Ecclesiastes explores the meaning of life. King Solomon makes us understand that there is a time for Everything and a season for every activity under the heavens (Ecclesiastes 3:1). He also believed that life's true meaning is having an intimate relationship with God, fearing Him, and obeying His commands (Ecclesiastes 12:13). But that is not always the case for us. Even though we may have a relationship with God, we often complain about many things that happen to us. I don't know about you, but I have been guilty of this, wondering when His promises would manifest. I have been mad at God, unhappy with situations in my life, and questioned why He watched me go through certain things and if He would ever come through.

Like me, you may ask God repeatedly when something will happen for you. You may try making moves you usually wouldn't make to get what you want more quickly—disobeying God by chasing what He wouldn't want for you. Pause! Stop taking matters into your own hands, stop questioning His timing—and start trusting Him instead. Although we wish things would happen sooner, we must remember that God does not make mistakes. Every good thing worth having is worth waiting for; everything God wants to do for us is great! We may pray for that promotion and expect it to happen tomorrow; we may pray for breakthroughs and expect an overflow of good things the next day. Patience has always been something I struggle with; I hate to wait. Even after exercising patience daily, I still wondered when God would finally come through.

It's okay to wonder when His time will come, but you must never allow yourself to sit in the questions and replay them repeatedly because those questions will not get you the answers—trusting God will. We must remember that when God makes us wait, it is not to punish us. He cares too much about us to grant us things He knows we are not ready to handle. Waiting on Him is not about how long the wait is but what we do while we wait.

Do you frequently complain about what is not right in your life? Do you often blame God or people for unfortunate situations in your life? Never allow the enemy's lies to dishearten you into giving up or thinking God will not do what He has promised. In your waiting, you will be tested and tried. You will be required to stand firm in your faith. This season, you must prove your faithfulness and trust in God. In this season, you must accept His plans for your life. Ask God to strengthen and equip you for what is ahead. Praise Him with a heart of gratitude while you wait and seek Him more.

In such a season of my own, I sat and swung up and down in my mind. It was a season when I felt that God was silent. In that silence, He led me to Habakkuk 2:3— "This vision is for a future time. It describes the end, and it will be fulfilled. If it seems slow in coming, wait patiently, for it will surely take place. It will not be delayed" (NLT). This verse was uplifting, as it was the same reply God gave Habakkuk in his time of distress as he wondered and complained about why God was taking so long to bring justice to His people. Why was He so silent as the Babylonians continued their wicked ways? God promised Habakkuk that He would do something new, which would be hard for him to believe, and this new thing was for an appointed time. The Lord promised to bring destruction to His people's enemies. Still in his waiting, Habakkuk questioned God's time for him. He wondered why God was taking so long to intervene. Habakkuk could have given up, but he settled and waited on the Lord in solitude, even in his distressed and confused state. He never gave up on God, knowing God would never give up on him. Every question he had drew him closer and closer to God for answers.

Often, we know what and how things should happen for us, but we are not the ones with the last Word. Waiting to hear from God is hard; waiting in patience can be more challenging—this is a strengthening test you must pass to move on to the next level in your life. It is easy to give up hope when we feel God is silent. It is easy to feel discouraged and drift from God's presence, but what we need to remember as children of God is that the Bible tells us never to forget that "a day is like a thousand years to the Lord, and a thousand years is like a day" (2 Peter 3:8 NLT). So imagine waiting for God to answer you for five years when it's only been two minutes in His eyes, or imagine waiting for a minute when it's been years in His eyes. No one knows when the time of the Lord will come because He is not bound by time and lives in eternity. He does not go by our January-to-December timeline.

So the question is not, "Will God answer me?" "Will He show up on time for me?" or "Is He hearing me?" but rather, the question should always be, "Am I willing to wait patiently on a trustworthy God's time?" "Am I willing to trust Him with what I can't control?" We are children of God not because of what He can offer us but because of who He is and whom He has proven to be in our lives. God's promises should anchor hope in our waiting—hope that pushes us to keep going no matter what is in front of us. It is not in God's nature to lie. He is not a man that He should lie, not a human being that He should change His mind (Numbers 23:19). His time is unpredictable but perfect. It might be slow in coming, but it's perfect! God moves when we least expect it. He is never early, never late, but always right on time. We can rest knowing He does what He promises at the right time.

We can see the waiting period as a time of lessons and thanksgiving rather than sadness, torture, and misery. We can still be happy and move about this season, enjoying all the blessings without getting stuck in the future. In your stillness, praise Him and be firm in your faith. If we could fast-forward our lives and see what God has prepared for us, we would see what a waste it is to stress and worry. But right now, we obviously can't fast-forward time; this is what having faith and trusting God is all about—not knowing what the future holds but trusting the one who holds it. Keep persevering through faith and find comfort in knowing that even though it may feel as if God has forsaken you, He is right here with you. At the same time, He is preparing a table for you in the future—this is a glimpse of His sovereignty. Because of His omnipresence, we are never alone. He is our endless supporter. In a vision, I saw a young man instructed by a bus driver to sit quietly at the back of the bus, explaining that he could move to the front seat when it was time. Then, I saw two scenarios. In the first scenario, he disobeyed and fought his way up with all his strength. It was not easy, as he got knocked down by those ahead. He fought hard and got trampled on, trying to get to the front when he knew it was not his turn yet. It was not a comfortable journey, and even though he made it to the front, he continually worried that someone would come and attack him from where he now sat.

In the second scenario, he humbly listened and sat there with his hands between his legs, waiting patiently for his turn. Though the wait was long, he remained humble and hopeful. Because of his obedience, he found favor with the driver. At one of the bus stops, the driver took his hand and moved him to the front of the bus. The people ahead of him tried to fight him. They were mad and jealous and didn't understand why he was being moved to the front when it "wasn't his turn" yet. But the driver protected him, hovering over him and slowly and gracefully guiding him to the front seat. The man never worried about losing His place to another as he sat there because he knew the driver had his back.

This vision came to me as I started writing this topic. The Spirit of God says the moral of this vision is that if God asks you to wait, it's for a good reason, one that you may not understand now but will one day. Moving toward a direction with forced hope when it's not time may cause you pain, trauma, and wasted strength. Whatever plans God has for you will come to pass if you wait for Him patiently and in humility and obedience. He knows best, and His time is perfect for you.

Our obedience to God speaks volumes—it tells Him that we trust His words and that He can count on us. King Solomon said, "Whatever God does is final. Nothing can be added to it or taken from it. God's purpose is that people should fear him" (Ecclesiastes 3:14 NLT). When the favor of the Lord is upon your life, absolutely no one can move you from your place of honor.

At a point in life, you will have to go through a season of waiting. What do you do in your waiting? Do you seek God's direction in your waiting? How is your attitude in your season of waiting? Do you frequently complain? The Word of God tells us that none of the promises God made to the Israelites was left unfulfilled (Joshua 21:45). Waiting for God to act can be mentally and physically draining if you're not doing so with purpose. Do you look forward to God in humility, obedience, patience, and praise, or do you wait in manipulation—trying to make things go the way you want? You must remember that God is the only one with the power to restore your fortunes. Yes, it is not easy to wait. It can be irritating, but all it takes is one move from God when it's time, and you'll sing a new song. He is faithful and will complete what He's started in the lives of those who seek Him (Philippians 1:6).

God is a God of breakthroughs and impossibilities. Maybe you are waiting for Him to give you a financial breakthrough, healing mercies, a spiritual breakthrough, a God-given spouse, a dream job, or a house. Maybe you've been waiting for admission to that dream school, fulfilling that business plan, or receiving the fruit of the womb. Whatever breakthrough you are waiting on God for, rest assured that it will come to pass. Don't be discouraged by what is not happening. Stay encouraged by who God is. Keep trusting Him, depend on Him, pray, and never lose faith.

2

THROUGH THE UNCERTAINTIES

*When doubts filled my mind, your comfort
gave me renewed hope and cheer.*
—Psalm 94:19 NLT

Have you ever been in a situation and wondered when "this too shall pass"? Have you ever been at a crossroads and didn't know which way to go? One of the hardest things in life is being uncertain about what's ahead. We sink ourselves in the what-ifs and what-will, allowing our questions to hold us back. However, we have a light in Jesus, so we don't have to walk in that darkness alone or be stuck there. We can confidently walk boldly forward, trusting God with our blind spots, knowing that a package awaits us at the end of the tunnel.

It can be frustrating when you don't know where to go or what to do. Still, we must continually remind ourselves of God's promises. We must use His Word as the lamp to guide our feet and the light for our path. As children of God, we are offered Christ as our light when we go through the darkness. His light helps us keep going when unsure of what we may encounter. We must keep going because we know that whatever we run into, God has already given us victory. God has promised through His Word to be with us through life. When we pass through the waters, He is with us; when we pass through the storms, He is with us. Through trials and tribulations, He is with us. When we pass through the valleys of the shadows of death, we can rest in His peace that transcends all understanding. Never be afraid of the unknown, stand in the strength of God, and be courageous, knowing He is with you every step. Life's journey is never for you to figure out, but it is the Lord's to lead and you to follow.

When you allow God to guide you, you'll walk to freedom, peace, and unbreakable joy. Whether emotional, mental, financial, or circumstantial problems, seeking God first is the solution. God is the only one who knows what lies ahead; He is the only one who can help you distinguish your right from your left. We must stop relying on ourselves and the people around us for what God alone can give us. We may not understand what is happening in our lives and around us. We may be uncertain about many things. Still, we can always depend on God through the uncertainties; He will never lead us mindlessly. Do not be alarmed by what is ahead. When God raises His hand in our lives, the results will surpass our expectations. Allow God to be your driver and trust that He knows exactly where your destination is. We must enjoy the ride and allow Him to help us endure the storms, bumps, and swerves.

To trust God is to be free from the bondage of fear. Being afraid indicates that we do not trust God or doubt His power and capabilities. God promises us in His Word that we never need to be afraid because no matter what comes our way, He is always with us and will hold us up with His righteous right hand (Isaiah 41:10). Everything that has a beginning has an end, except God—so whatever circumstances you face in your journey will surely pass. Do not lose hope if things take a long time to make sense. Don't let it discourage you; instead, let it be a push to keep holding on in faith.

Feeling Unease

The feeling of anxiety can sometimes crush our world in ways we never expected. Not knowing what life will bring our way can bring unease, discomfort, fear, and panic. Are you currently in this season of your life—facing anxiety? Are life's many hardships unsettling you and not knowing what to do or where to turn? So many times, we face situations in life that leave us stranded in our minds. And in these moments, we must realize that the only answer to whatever we may be going through is looking to God! He is the antidote to our fear and anxiety. Jesus Christ gives us hope and assurance amid our confusion.

When we look around the world today, we see negativity and chaos. It only reminds us that things could worsen. It gives us little assurance. But as always, God intervenes and proves otherwise when we think all hope is lost. The mighty hand of God in our lives is where our comfort resides. The apostle Paul reminds us not to be anxious about anything, but in all situations, with prayer, petition, and thanksgiving, make our requests to God (Philippians 4:6). Believing in God's promises gives us peace and helps us stand tall in times of brokenness.

It is so easy to be anxious and burdened by the problems in our lives that sometimes we find the days moving too slowly, wondering how we will get through the day, the week, the month, or the year. When we hit the unexpected, our first instinct is to panic. Fear starts creeping in, and we start doubting ourselves and our capabilities. Worst of all, we start questioning the power of God. The battles get too hard; everywhere we turn, there seems to be no way out, and feeling stuck and worrying becomes fundamental. Life circumstances steal our joy day and night as we suffer sleepless nights and thoughts of discouragement. The enemy places these in our lives to confuse us and make us think there is no way out. He makes us believe the worst about ourselves and our situation.

So today, I want to encourage you to stop playing word games in your mind repeatedly. Life is given to us to enjoy (Ecclesiastes 2:24). God promised never to leave or forsake us (Deuteronomy 31:6). Yes, we may feel that He is far away during such times. Still, we can rejoice in knowing that He sees us and is right there with us in every way and turn. The enemy has no hold on you. Victory is on your side always—dwell on that. Start believing in the power of God and make choices based on who you know Him to be and not on your circumstances. The Word of God tells us that when we seek God, we will find Him when we do so with all our hearts (Jeremiah 29:13).

The advantage we have as children of God is that our heavenly Father is always there when we need Him. The amazing part about being hit with the unexpected is that we have a mighty God who goes before us to ensure our safety and always prevails no matter how big our problems may seem. God did not promise us a problem-free life. We will go through problems whether we prepare for them or not. If anything, Christians face more challenges because the enemy knows what we possess as children of God. Satan hates anything good, and our God is good all the time. Everything God wants for us is perfect; therefore, we are a massive threat to Satan. He attacks us the most because he feels endangered by us.

But our God is faithful. In Him, we can stand against all oppositions. He gives us the strength to overcome all our battles, become strong enough to hold on to the joy offered freely and withstand every adversity. We must have an intimate relationship with God; we must get closer and closer to Him. That is the only way to gain the strength we need to endure and fight off anxiety and fear. We can't find joy in our social lives, degrees, careers, and so on. We can experience it only by surrendering our all to God and allowing Him to be there.

Knowing When to Ask for Help

"I lift my eyes to the mountains—where does my help come from? My help comes from the Lord, the Maker of heaven and earth" (Psalm 121:1). As children of God, we must remember that we are not obligated to do life alone. In our efforts, we must realize that we are made strong in our weaknesses and sufferings. It is easy for us to feel defeated in a world filled with many problems, but we must learn to approach our storms with a proper mindset because we are believers in Christ.

Why should we allow ourselves to feel defeated? Has God not promised us eternity (Romans 6:23)? Has He not assured us a prosperous future (Jeremiah 29:11)? Has God ever said and not done? Has He ever promised and not fulfilled? Did He not promise us in His Word that all things work together for the good of those who love Him (Romans 8:28)? The feeling of defeat can be terrifying—a feeling that brings about the thoughts of losing at life; it leaves you second-guessing yourself, and worse, it leaves you second-guessing God's infinite power. While this is a normal feeling during adversities, you must never forget who you are in this season. Yes, you may feel defeated sometimes, but as a child of God, are you dominated by your problems? The lies the enemy injects into our minds can seem real, but they are all part of his deceptive way of making us believe we are incapable.

Bear in mind that the feeling of defeat comes about only when you forcefully try to control the things God is supposed to regulate in your life. This feeling should indicate that you are trying too hard, doing something not cut out for you—mentally or physically. You have a Father whose power is beyond what the human mind can understand, a Father who has never failed you. You are where you are today because of His grace.

Imagine a child trying to open a water bottle as hard as possible. What happens when they fail to open it? The child may get frustrated, angry, and discouraged. Now, a child willing to surrender, realizing that it is impossible to do it with their faint strength, will ask for help from their parents. This child will not keep trying to open it when their strength proves inadequate.

That is the same with God and us. We are to surrender to Him and recognize that it is never by our strength but by His. Just as our parents will never turn us away when we ask for help with opening a water bottle, the same way our heavenly Father will never turn His back on us when we ask Him for help. You might keep trying yourself through stubbornness, pride, and disobedience, trying to force things to happen. When they don't, you feel defeated and broken, not knowing when to drop Everything and say, "God, help me."

Letting go and freeing yourself from gripping tightly to your storms means you acknowledge you need God's help. When you fail to let go of the things you cannot control, you miss the chance to allow God to do His work in your life. God is faithful, good, merciful, and most importantly, He has rescued us before and will do it again.

Why do you allow yourself to feel defeated? Because you seek help in the wrong places, you listen to many voices, including the voice of the enemy. Jesus promises to give us rest (Matthew 11:28)—which can happen only when we accept His invitation to surrender it all to Him. Paul puts it this way, "We now have this light shining in our hearts, but we ourselves are like fragile clay jars containing this great treasure. This makes it clear that our great power is from God, not from ourselves. We are pressed on every side by troubles, but we are not crushed. We are perplexed but not driven to despair. We are hunted down, but never abandoned by God. We get knocked down, but we are not destroyed" (2 Corinthians 4:7-9). We serve a mighty God and can overcome all things through Him. You will always feel defeated by what is beneath you until you realize you are a treasure of light that can not be dominated.

The enemy wants you to believe that you have failed, but God wants you to believe in His unconditional love and faithfulness. God has not forsaken you in your situation. He is greater than the reasons you may feel defeated. Accept His invitation to cast your burdens on Him so He can sustain you. I declare and decree that the Spirit who raised Christ from death helps you rise above your circumstances, helping you feel better, stronger, and wiser.

His Promises Still Stand

In the book of Hebrews, Paul encourages us to have great confidence in the hope that lies before us, as God's promise and oath to us are unchangeable because He is a God of His Word (Hebrews 6:18). In the book of 2 Corinthians, Paul also assures us that God has identified us as His own and placed the Holy Spirit in our hearts as the first installment that guarantees everything He promised (2 Corinthians 1:22). God's promises made between Him and humanity stand no matter what! The promises of God are there for us before time. We see He kept and fulfilled every promise He made to His people throughout the Bible. Today, you and I are enjoying the benefits of His promises to Abraham. This act shows how our God is a God of His Word. His promises keep us going when all hope is lost.

The psalmist wrote, "He will rescue you from every trap and protect you from deadly disease. He will cover you with his feathers. He will shelter you with his wings. His faithful promises are your armor and protection" (Psalm 91:3–4 NLT). Rest in this promise today, knowing that though many weapons may be formed against you in life, you have a mighty God who promises to protect you from every enemy trap.

The Spirit of God has been reminding me lately of the importance of leaning on the promises of God. He has told me that the only way I can enjoy the benefits of God's promises is through obedience. Sometimes, amid the storm, we may forget His promises, turn to other sources, or lean on our strength and understanding. Amongst the promises of God come knowledge and wisdom. The Word of God says, "If you need wisdom, ask our generous God, and he will give it to you. He will not rebuke you for the asking" (James 1:5).

The wisdom of God helps us with decision-making. Still, we sometimes find ourselves leaning toward our own will amid adversities—this is not what God wants for us. Through my experiences of relying on and navigating my life based on His will,

I have learned that operating on my understanding screams a lack of trust in God. It screams foolishness and lack of intelligence. "The way of fools seems right to them, but the wise listen to advice" (Proverbs 12:15)—in this context, the advice of God through the Holy Spirit. We must allow the Holy Spirit to bring to our understanding what the word of God says so that we are not making the mistake of living based on our human reasonings.

We have all been to a place where we sought our ways, knowledge, and wisdom during challenges. I can attest through my past experiences that a route in that direction calls for destruction. With the wisdom of God, we know that we fight life's battles "not against flesh and blood, but against the rulers, against the authorities, against the powers of this dark world and against the spiritual forces of evil in the heavenly realms" (Ephesians 6:12). As I began surrendering, I could hear the Spirit of God teaching me, directing me, and helping me through my circumstances. Seeking God's wisdom instead of my own helped me to stand still even when I wanted to move. It kept me silent when I wanted to speak and kept me from falling when the enemy kept pushing me. His wisdom is full of love and mercy; when we seek it, we yield good fruits, "impartial and sincere" (James 3:17). Through His wisdom, we are reminded of His promises. His promises are your armor. You must wear them around your heart to help you stand and face your storms. When we stand on the promises of God through faith and prayers, we have automatically shielded ourselves with armor that causes what the enemy throws at us to bounce right back. When we stand on God's promises, it shifts us onto a firm foundation. Our faith in God shields us from the enemy's fiery arrows and makes us waterproof to our afflictions. We become strong and resilient amid the storms.

Dwelling on the promises of God and staying obedient to Him opens many doors of blessings in our lives. As the Scriptures say, "All people are like grass, and all their glory is like the flowers of the field; the grass withers and the flowers fall, but the word of the Lord endures forever" (1 Peter 1:24–25). The Word of God is constant and true; it is everlasting and final. "It is alive and active. Sharper than any double-edged sword, it penetrates even to dividing soul and spirit, joints and marrow; it judges the thoughts and attitudes of the heart" (Hebrews 4:12).

Our spouses, parents, friends, and children may make promises and take them back or fail to follow up. The Word of God, which reveals God's promises, is the one thing no one can take away from you. It helps us move toward what is right, teaching and preparing us for God's good work (2 Timothy 3:16–17). Our lives and possessions are fleeting, but the promises of God remain eternal. The Promises of God are the only reliable source we can depend on through life's journey. Our joys will be temporary if we lack a connection with the source of life. Life does not come with a manual, but as children of God, before we entered this world, our heavenly Father had already set aside a manual to help us navigate life's journey—the Bible! That is our navigation system.

In John's gospel, Christ compares Himself to a vine, God the Father to the gardener, and us to the branches, and those who remain in Him will produce much fruit (John 15:5). The only way branches produce fruit is to connect to a vine. Jesus Christ is the living Word; if we want to live a fruitful life, we must never disconnect ourselves from Him. The Word of God is the most valuable yet priceless possession you will ever have. It is available to all to guide us through life's journey. God's Word instructs us to continually study and meditate on it, obeying everything written in it so that all we do will be successful (Joshua 1:8). God is faithful in all His ways. He keeps all His promises for all who love and seek Him. As believers, we can rest in knowing that whatever God says in His Word concerning us is final. "Though the mountains be shaken and the hills be removed, yet my unfailing love for you will not be shaken, nor my covenant of peace be removed,' says the Lord, who has compassion on you" (Isaiah 54:10).

God made a covenant with Noah never to destroy the world with a flood and marked His promise with a rainbow as a reminder to His children. And generations later, God made a covenant to Abraham to make him and his descendants a mighty nation—the father of many. "God took an oath in his own name, saying: 'I will certainly bless you, and I will multiply your descendants beyond number.' Then Abraham waited patiently, and he received what God had promised" (Hebrews 6:13–15 NLT). "Abraham waited patiently"— the part we all seem to struggle with occasionally, *waiting*. Even though Abraham initially did not see how God's promise to him was possible as he was childless, God proved His promise by blessing him with a son, Isaac. God gave Abraham and his descendants the land extending from the border of Egypt to the great Euphrates River (Genesis 15:18–21) because He is a God of His Word. We see He reminded Abraham's son, Isaac, of this covenant, then to Isaac's son, Jacob (Genesis 26:3; 28:13).

Our God is a covenant-keeping God, and we can rest knowing nothing about Him changes. He has a blessing for each of us with our name on it, extending far beyond what our minds can fathom.

Every generational curse becomes a generational blessing when God comes through for us. His love for us is so pure and true, a love we never have to fight to have. Our emotions may come and go, and our problems may come and go, but the love of God can never be taken away and is beyond comparison. How does it feel to know that His covenant of blessings will never be broken?

Every morning you wake up, it is for a purpose. God has so much for you in store. He is not done with you yet. Not even your mistakes can make God withdraw His promises. He has a *next* for you; you must wait a little longer to see it. As Abraham waited, I pray that the Lord will grant you the patience to wait for every promise He has made concerning your life.

Blessings for Obedience

The Word of God tells us in 1 John that we are now the children of God, and what we will be has not yet been made known. But we know that when Christ appears, we shall be like him, for we shall see him as he is. All who have this hope in him purify themselves, just as he is pure. (1 John 3:2–4). Jesus Christ came to save us from our sins, so our lives represent freedom. Live your life as a child of God who has been bought and freed by the blood of Jesus. John tells us that if people keep sinning, it shows they belong to the devil. But the Son of God came to destroy the devil's plans. Being in Christ means no practice of sin. The children of God are determined by their life of righteousness and love for others (1 John 3:8–10).

God plans to return and take us so we can be with Him for eternity. Jesus Christ has made this possible—and our acceptance of Him and living our lives through Him will open the promised heaven for us— a life of abundance through Jesus Christ. As John said, being in Christ and loving one another means "we have passed from death to life" (1 John 3:14). The reward we reap on earth by living and obeying God is a promised heaven. Through our obedience to God, we stand for the life God wants for us. The Word of God says, "You will keep in perfect peace all who trust in you, all whose thoughts are fixed on you!" (Isaiah 26:3 NLT). We live a life of peace through Christ.

God also promised us joy—the fullness of joy. The psalmist said, "You will show me the way of life, granting me the joy of your presence and the pleasures of living with you forever" (Psalm 16:11 NLT)—not only joy and peace but also everlasting love. We gain heaven when we see Him, and He has also promised us heaven on earth when we live our lives through Christ, His Son. Deuteronomy 28:1–14 gives us a breakdown of all the blessings we stand to gain by obeying God's commands. I love using the story of Noah as an example of obedience. God instructed Noah to build an ark to save him and his family from the great flood. He obeyed God's instructions, and in the end, his obedience to God saved him and his family (Genesis 7:1-5). Noah followed God's instructions not because he knew what would happen—he followed God's instructions because *he trusted God*. As with Noah, God will direct you on a path you never expected. Many around you will not understand, but never let that divert your attention from what the Lord asks you to do. Never let that cause you to withdraw. We must always try to remain still for God so that even in the middle of all the noise and distractions, we may be able to hear His voice because it is in the silence we hear Him the loudest. Stay obedient to God, no matter how overwhelming life may seem.

One of the lessons life has taught me is that some things should strictly remain between you and God. When He shows you a vision, it is a mistake for you to broadcast it or try to make others understand it. This is how many dreams have ended before their manifestation. Your God-given vision does not require the approval of others. You are to hold it within your heart and do your part in manifesting that vision. The only way to see the will of God manifest in your life is to walk hand in hand with God through obedience —obey His decree and follow His regulations (Ezekiel 20:11). God will never point you in a direction and not lead you there.

I once heard a story about a group of missionary men in a village somewhere on the continent of Africa. One day, during a prayer session, the Spirit of God revealed a danger coming their way and directed them to flee. When the men made this known to others, some men said they were not going anywhere as they chose to stand firm in faith and fight against any danger that may come their way. Unfortunately, some wicked men invaded the area moments later, killing many people, including the missionary men who chose to stay behind. When people heard of this, they questioned God and wondered why He did not save these men of God from danger. This story got me thinking—what if God sends me help or the Holy Spirit directs me to one path, and I choose to do something else that looks like God's will when it is actually my own will? We must learn to discern the voice of God and obey it. We must stand on guard and never miss "A Watchman moment" from God (Ezekiel 33:1-9).

How do you know what is from God and your own will? What if God wants you to launch that business, but you want to tidy up a few things first, causing you to miss a big break? What if God wants you to hop on that bus, but you are sure He is sending a private jet, so you wait and wait? I am sure we've all been to a place where deciding seemed like a never-ending road. In these moments, we must heed the voice of God than our voices and the voices of others so we're not leaning toward our own will and understanding. When God instructs, it doesn't matter what people say, and it doesn't matter how foolish they think you look for obeying. God will always lead you through; He will never abandon you halfway. Many benefits come with obedience, and just as when a child obeys their parents, they stand to gain favor in their sight. The same goes for all of us and what we stand to gain with God as we yield to His decrees and regulations.

Unlike our earthly parents, who may cut us off from disobeying them at any time, God is merciful and gives us more chances than we deserve to come to our senses and run back to Him. The benefits of obeying God are the blessings promised in Deuteronomy 28. "Wherever you go and whatever you do, you will be blessed" (Deuteronomy 28:6 NLT). "They will attack you from one direction, but they will scatter from you in seven!" (Deuteronomy 28:7 NLT). "The Lord will establish you as his holy people as he swore he would do. Then all the nations of the world will see that you are a people claimed by the Lord, and they will stand in awe of you" (Deuteronomy 28:9–10 NLT). Verse 11 says that the Lord will prosper you. He will bless your works and cause rain to fall where it is dry. Through your obedience, God will cause you to lend to many nations but never be the one to borrow. He will make you the head and never the tail, and you will always be at the top and never at the bottom (vv. 12–13).

God never lies. His words are certain. No one can do for you in years what God can do for you in seconds. And if all you must do is surrender and obey Him, what more could you ever ask of Him? We are human and imperfect. Sometimes, we may drift off here and there, but God is merciful and faithful. He never shuns a child who goes to Him with a heart of repentance. Jesus told His disciples after the Last Supper, "If you love me, keep my commands" (John 14:15). We've all struggled to keep some if not all of His commands, as our flesh is constantly battling against our spirit. But the question is not about what you've failed to do. Now, how do you plan to get back in line with God? Nothing screams, "I love you!" to God more than a person choosing to put his or her own will aside and follow God's will. Jesus said, "If you keep my commands, you will remain in my love, just as I have kept my Father's commands and remain in his love" (John 15:10).

One may ask, what are His commands? Apart from the Ten Commandments God gave Moses (Exodus 2:1–17), God can at any given moment instruct us to do something that falls in His will for our lives. God's greatest command is to love Him with all our heart, soul, mind, and strength, and the second is to love each other just as He loved us (Matthew 22:37). God considers us His own through Jesus Christ. He does not want us to love or worship other gods but Him.

As a parent, it frustrates me when I see my children fighting with each other. This makes me think about how God feels when we fight, gossip, backbite, knock each other down, and hold grudges against each other. We are all guilty and have fallen short of His glory. And God, at a point, has been super disappointed in us. Still, we are so blessed to have a Father who never holds our wrongs and mistakes against us, but rather, He engineers them into His plans for us. He is not a God of retraction. He stands by His Word and gives to us in abundance. We would usually rather walk away from what He has to offer. Jesus said that He no longer calls us servants but friends (John 15:15). We did not choose Christ—He chose us.

Therefore, it breaks His heart when we turn away from Him. What happens when you turn against God? "The Lord will send on you curses, confusion and rebuke in everything you put your hand to until you are destroyed and come to sudden ruin because of the evil you have done in forsaking him" (Deuteronomy. 28:20). In Deuteronomy 28:20–68, the Word of God lists all the consequences of disobeying God. Choosing to turn against God is choosing curses and destruction. But surrendering in obedience brings us blessings upon blessings!

Restore My Fortunes, O Lord

"Restore our fortunes, Lord, as streams renew the desert. Those who plant in tears will harvest with shouts of joy. They weep as they go to plant their seed, but they sing as they return with the harvest" (Psalm 126:4–6 NLT). We pass through many seasons in life—the planting, rainy, stormy, and harvesting seasons: the ups, the downs, and the calm. Sometimes, going through these seasons brings on confusing emotions. One minute, we are happy; the next, we are angry, afraid, sad, depressed, or even lost when life gets hard and impossible to comprehend. When things hit hard, everything seems to fall apart.

There are days we wish to stay in bed, and days we don't feel like speaking to anyone. But regardless of all our mixed emotions, we still must get up and move. We still must go to work, take the kids to school, do the house chores, make that critical phone call, go for that appointment, prepare that meal for the family, and so on. We still get up to do the work! With sadness in our hearts, we see things are not going as we wished they would or planned. We push through and get up to sow the seeds regardless—because we believe in brighter days. We believe there is a mighty God who will come through for us. We believe all our hard work will pay off one day, so we keep going and never quit.

I don't know what you are going through now, but I do know that life can sometimes be challenging. During these times, we must never forget that victory always belongs to the children of God and that these clouding times are not permanent but a sign that brighter days are ahead. We must never forget we belong to a God who restores and strengthens; He makes all things new and beautiful at the right time. Whatever we feel we've lost, God will give back in doubles. So often, we may want to give up. The more we try, the more things get worse. I want to encourage you not to give up. God has promised to give you rest as you place all your burdens in His hands (Matthew 11:28). The enemy targets those He feels threatened by. You are a child of God, making you a target, which is also your power. God is in your corner; you are more than a conqueror. He sees all your hard work. He sees all you go through and all you have lost. Do not give up before enjoying the reward of all your hard work. No matter what you are facing or how hard life knocks you down, keep getting up, ask God for the drive to do the work, and remember that He is a God who refines. As you get up every morning to plant your seeds, may the work of your hands never be in vain. Get ready for the season of great harvest! When the storms of life threaten to drown and overwhelm you, God will sustain you, and you will sing songs of joy again.

More than We Ask

The Word of God tells us, "He who did not spare his own Son but gave him up for us all, how will he not also, along with him, graciously give us all things?" (Romans 8:32). God gives us more than we ask or work for during our harvest times. We might not always get what we want, but God always gives us what we need. Trust me when I say this. Look at it from this point of view: Would you always give your children whatever they ask of you? I believe your answer is *no!*—because parents know what's best for their children. I love my children too much to give them less than they deserve. Sometimes, what we want is not always good for us; a good parent wants what's suitable for their children.

We serve a loving Father whose love for us is overwhelming. We must trust Him just as we would trust our earthly parents to have our backs. God wants what's best for us. When we ask Him for certain things, we should never be discouraged when things don't turn out how we want them to because, in the end, when we yield to Him, things turn out way better than expected. He always goes beyond what we ask. "What no eye has seen, what no ear has heard, and what no human mind has conceived, the things God has prepared for those who love him" (1 Corinthians 2:9). God will never give you something that He knows will harm you along the way. He always gives us what will last for a lifetime, not what we can find happiness and pleasure in for a moment.

For example, when you pray for a life partner and suddenly the current one you are courting breaks it off with you, do not assume that God did not listen to your prayers. When you pray for God to give you a better job and you lose your current job instead, do not be quick to count God's faithfulness out just yet. When you pray and ask Him to remove all the things in your life that are not serving you, suddenly, random things start happening in your life in which people are walking out of your life, and things are just not adding up—do not assume God is punishing you, and do not listen to your prayers because—oh, my dear—He does; you were just not ready for the answers, which is fine. It is a process; embrace it. His answers may surprise us and are not what we expect, but they are always good for us.

When the time is right, He will bring you that fantastic mate who fits you perfectly, who will love and cherish you the way He wants you to be cherished. He will bring around the best group of people in your life who will build and ride for you through all seasons. You will land that job you have always dreamed of but never thought was possible. We may not get what we want because God does not offer less than the best and does not work in our time, but according to His timetable—we can rest and trust Him. He is an on-time God and does what He promises; His no is an answer to a better yes. Never be discouraged. All the hardship we go through in life strengthens and prepares us for what He has in store. Ask Him to help you bear the spiritual fruit of patience because when the harvest finally comes, you will exult and rejoice for never giving up. Trust in His time. Trust in His process.

When You Get to the Top

God is faithful and always gives us more than we ask, but what happens after He blesses us with all we ask and more? Will we still remember the Giver, or will we be taken over by the blessings He has given us? On His way to Jerusalem, Jesus met ten men with leprosy. In the distance, the men called out to Him, "Jesus, Master, pity us!" (Luke 17:13). After Jesus healed and cleansed them of their sickness, only one of them (a Samaritan) came back in praise to God. "He threw himself at his feet and thanked him" (v. 16). Jesus was saddened by the other nine lack of appreciation and gratitude. Just like these men, we will walk through storms, and as children of God, we have a solid foundation in Christ, whom we can trust to always look out for us. When we call on Him, He hears our cries and comes to our aid. Now, Do we remember to show a heart of gratitude? Do we go back to Him with a heart of praise and worship for all He has done for us—or just like the nine lepers, we forget and go about our lives, only to come back again when we find ourselves in deep waters?

It is hard to extend a helping hand to others when we show no gratitude toward where our help is from. Apart from going to God with a heart of praise and thanksgiving, another way of showing God how grateful you are for all the blessings He pours into your life is by being gracious to others in humility as God has been to you, and that is hard to do when we forget primarily where our help comes from. We forget about who placed us on top. We forget the God who has done it all for us. We become so boastful and prideful of our blessings as if we acquired them with our own strength.

In the book of Deuteronomy, we are reminded never to forget the God who blesses us and to keep His commands even when we get to our promised land (See Deuteronomy 8:1–20)—this was a reminder and advice to the Israelites as God delivered them from the hands of slavery, and one that pertains to you and me as well. It is through Christ we acquire all we have. While he was in prison, Paul put it this way: "I can do everything through Christ, who gives me strength" (Philippians 4:13 NLT).

We are often so forgetful as we're always wrapped up in our busy schedules, circumstances, and the storms of life. We forget the position we once were in and start looking down on those who are where we used to be, and worse, we forget the God who delivered us from our valleys. God does not bless us so we can forget, boast, and claim all the glory. God blesses us so we can glorify Him, acknowledge His goodness, and stay humble. This opens a gateway for more incredible blessings. "He gave you manna to eat in the wilderness, something your ancestors had never known, to humble and test you so that in the end, it might go well with you. You may say, 'My power and the strength of my hands have produced this wealth for me'" (Deuteronomy 8:16–17). God blesses us so we can remember Him and attest to His goodness.

I understand that society sometimes makes it hard to proclaim all God has done for us. Fearing what others might say and think often keeps us in a bubble where we would rather keep all the amazing things God has done for us to ourselves because we're afraid people will think we are boastful. But God wants us to reach out; He wants us to glory His name and bless others. Rendering blessings to someone can come in many forms, such as giving advice, being a voice of encouragement, and providing a helping hand—financially, socially, and so on. We must remember God in our promised land because He gave us strength, provided the right opportunities, and pointed us the right way. He controls the elevator in our lives.

The story of Samson, found in Judges 16:1–31, is one of my favorites in the Bible. There is a bit of everything in it. What I like the most is that it shows what a person can accomplish when he or she has God's favor and obeys His commands. However, it also shows how it can all come crashing down when a person disobeys God, turning their back on Him and doing their own thing. God wanted to use Samson mightily to defend His people from the Philistines. So He gave Samson super strength, which was out of this world and would be well attained only through God's rules.

For years, Samson obeyed God and was a strong leader. But some time later, He got careless with the blessings and tasks God trusted Him with. He fell in love with a Philistine woman named Delilah, got surrounded by the wrong people, and drifted more toward the enemy (the Philistines) and farther and farther away from God. He breached God's rules and followed Delilah, a Philistine woman. Because of this, the Philistines planned to capture him through Delilah as he trusted her with his greatest secret (Judges 16:15–21). But God, who is kind and genuinely wants us to succeed, never turns His back on us. Samson cried out to God to restore His strength, and God listened to him and gave him the strength to finish the task (Judges 16:28–30). God is always willing to forgive us and give us a chance to redeem ourselves if we are eager to go to Him in repentance.

Samson's story is quite old but still relevant today. We see a resemblance to his story today all the time as we watch people rise to the very top of their professions only to forget the purpose for which they are there. Samson ended up breaking all his vows. He didn't take God's rules for him seriously, but being the God He is, the Lord still used Samson to defeat the Philistines.

Samson could have done so much more if he had obeyed or remembered who gave him the gift He possessed. Before God uses us, He tests us to see the position of our hearts toward the little He has entrusted us. This is just as God promised Solomon that if he obeyed His commands, decrees, and regulations, he would establish the throne of his dynasty over all of Israel forever, as He promised David (1 Kings 9:4–5).

This same promise stood for Samson, and this same promise stands for you and me. But what happens when we turn our faces away from God, disobeying His commands and forgetting that He placed us where we are? Just as He has the power to bless, so does He also have the power to take it all away. Just as He has the power to make, so does He have the power to destroy when we turn our backs on Him. One day, God will take you to the top. He will bless you beyond your wildest imagination. My prayer is that when you get up there, you realize and accept that you are there not for yourself only but for others as well, and most importantly, for God's glory. My husband once said, "Our reign on the top has an expiry date, but our impact can last forever."

It is not about the flashes of lights. It is not about the comfort we acquire in life. It is about the difference we make in the lives of others with what God has blessed us with that counts. May His abundant blessings enable us to extend those blessings down to others instead of keeping them all to ourselves in silence. May we never cease to acknowledge God for all He has done but testify of His continuous goodness in our lives. May we change and be there for others with the same mercy and grace God has shown us.

3

CONTENTMENT VS. COMFORTABILITY

Godliness with contentment is great gain.
—1 Timothy 6:6

Contentment is when a person is satisfied or happy with what he or she has, and comfortability is settling in whatever condition he or she is in with the refusal to move. The difference is in the mindset because a person who is content with what they have can shift to comfort if not careful. Content people know not to settle because life can improve, so they move but simultaneously are satisfied with what they have. People who are comfortable with where they are, even though they know there is better ahead, choose to stick with what feels familiar and, therefore, stay. We often find ourselves having difficulties differentiating the two.

Paul expresses his secret to living a life filled with praise as being content with what he has despite adversities (Philippians 4:11–12). What happens when we confuse being content with being comfortable? How do you know when you have become too comfortable in your contentment? As the Word of God tells us, "Godliness with contentment is great gain" (1 Timothy 6:6)—this means that in our contentment, we praise, we worship, and we carry an attitude of gratitude for what God has blessed us with. We have hope that Christ is always with us. This is what Paul meant when he said he had found the secret to being content in all circumstances—because he depended on God for his tomorrow and not whatever situation he found himself in.

Sometimes, we find it hard to be content with what we have and embark on a forced journey to seek more earthly wealth. We believe true contentment comes after acquiring as much as possible, but that is far from the truth. In your contentment, you believe that no matter where you stand, God will provide every need as He promised us in His Word. He told us not to worry about everyday life because if He can provide for the birds in the sky, why not you, His beloved child? (See Matthew 6:25–34).

Not being comfortable in your contentment comes when, even though you are happy with what you currently have, you still strive and look to God for the better. This motivates us to move forward with the hope that whatever God has for us will come to pass as we continue seeking Him first in all we do. No matter how long it may take, we never settle but work hard for the greatness promised.

Being comfortable, on the other hand, is when you become relaxed wherever you find yourself. You park and sit, not because you do not believe there is more for you but because you have become too comfortable to realize that you deserve more, and you have lost the zeal to grab onto hope; therefore, you refuse to move and strive for what God has for you ahead. The comfort zone is a lovely place to be, a place of relaxation, a paradise for many—but the reality is that you will never uncover your full potential there. The fear of moving keeps us relaxed—being afraid to try new things, take risks, mess up our comfortable arrangements, or even leave loved ones out of our next equation.

In 2017, I started praying about God's will in my life. This prayer opened a new door in my life, involving the shedding of the old and building the new. In 2018, the Spirit of God led me to leave my childhood church, which I had been in for over twenty years. It was not an easy decision. I almost disobeyed and stayed. But I felt strongly within my soul a push that wouldn't subside. I questioned why the sudden urge to leave came when I wanted God to use me more for His glory—but I felt He did indeed want me to leave, to break out of my comfort zone and reach for greater heights. He wanted to do more in my life, and I had this unexplainable hunger. I wanted more. I wanted spiritual growth and God to use me in the most uncomfortable and unimaginable ways. I did not see myself acquiring that where I was at the time. It felt too comfortable and too relaxed for me, but also, at the same time, I felt gated, as if I were wasting away my potential, one that I knew would be impactful. I prayed, I cried, and I sought God about it. Sometimes, I wanted God to give me a sign to change my mind about leaving. The more I asked, the more He gave me reasons (through dreams and the random unexplainable events that were going on around me) to leave and strive for more. I was unsure what God had in store for me, but I felt it was amazing and challenging. It required my attention, dedication, intentionality, and obedience to Him, which would help fulfill the vision He had revealed to me.

So I left, even though it was one of the hardest decisions I had ever had to make. The next phase was to accept the reality of what might happen next. I made a bold decision to walk, even when I did not know what I was walking into—but I knew it was not something to harm me. I knew that greatness would be achieved only by making the sole decision to walk and strive for it, even though I was blind to what was ahead. I made a move God was compelling me to make.

Growth requires tough decisions. It requires our willingness to be vulnerable regardless of how the world may see us, growing through the storms, irrespective of how big the storms are. I have realized that vulnerability is even more beautiful when exposed to the right people. Through the storms of life, you will learn that not everyone will understand you or your story through the storms of life. Not everyone will have the eyes to see you the way God sees you. Sometimes, that can be a painful pill to swallow when those you love and surround yourself with are the ones who can't see you or see the "help" in your vulnerable moments. You will also learn that wherever God directs us, He provides what we need. He provides the destiny helpers, the strength, and the resources required to get by in all seasons. Sometimes, when God shows us a way, it may seem strange to those around us. But, if you know that God is directing and repositioning you on a certain path, you do not need approval from others to make that move. Our purpose is to go on this life's journey alongside God, live for Him, bring glory to His name, and reach out and proclaim Him to the world. And our reward for that is the gifts of blessings we reap along the way and the future glory that awaits us. Jesus Christ reminds us in His Word to seek first the kingdom and righteousness of God, and all other things shall be added (Matthew 6:33). We seek God, not people or our interests.

Sometimes, what God shows you is for you alone to understand because the reality is that many people around you will not understand the calling on your life. They will come with their speculations and reasons for choosing your paths. Never become other people's speculations, never become their assumptions, never become what the negative talks and gossip are about, but rather focus on God and stay true to yourself and the journey ahead. Focus on the task He has for you. Holding tightly to God's promises, obeying His commands, and following His directions helps fade the distractions. We each have our race to run. We each have a task we must complete; we each have a specific impact we are to make. And the faster we realize, the quicker we will reach the end of our race and receive our heavenly prize, which God calls us toward through Jesus Christ (Philippians 3:14). God will never lead you to a place that is not for you.

Sometimes, bringing ourselves to take the first step is difficult, and God knows this. He knows we won't get up and leave unless situations force us out of our comfort zones. Sometimes, it may take people we meet to hold our hand through a season in our lives. But when it's time to let go of their hand, we must let go and lean toward more; otherwise, we stand to miss all the opportunities ahead or, worse, miss our calling.

Parting ways with where you feel comfortable is never a goodbye, but it is your realizing that "Hey—I am thankful for this comfort level and what it contributed to my life, good or bad. But I was created for more than this, for exceptional and not just comfort." As you journey through life, you must be careful not to overlap comfort with contentment—this means that you do not allow your contentment to become a comfort zone, whereby you stop reaching for the abundance God wants for you. Being content is a test for more. In our comfort zone, we become lazy—reluctant to move forward, too relaxed, and afraid to realize we deserve more.

We all love to be where we feel comfortable or around what's familiar, but familiarity and comfort are not God's destination for you. You must break out of that shell! What the comfort zone does is cripple you. It keeps you stagnant. What happens when you remain stagnant for a long time? You start breaking down, stop functioning, and eventually question your existence. You can't be comfortable and expect God to use you. God uses the willing heart, ready to break free from the norm and to pass through the uncomfortable for God's glory. After the Israelites escaped Egypt, they desired to return to Egypt even though their lives were not pleasant. They were too comfortable with their life in Egypt and refused to see they deserved better. When Moses led them out of Egypt, they constantly complained, wishing they had stayed in Egypt, even if it meant suffering to death. They said, "If only we had died by the Lord's hand in Egypt! There we sat around pots of meat and ate all the food we wanted, but you have brought us out into this desert to starve this entire assembly to death" (Exodus 16:3).

Comfort causes us to settle, even in our sufferings. But when we open ourselves up for God and suffer for Him, He will give us comfort that surpasses the one we are stuck in (See 2 Corinthians 1:3–7). You must be okay with facing discomfort because it is through the discomfort you uncover the path to your purpose (See

James 1:2–4). Never lean toward discontentment. Why? Because an attitude of discontent causes you to worry about what you do not have, making you overlook the blessings in your life. In worse cases, causing you to make moves illegally, rushed, or greedily to get to a level that suits your satisfaction—this only leads to your ruin and destruction. Paul instructs Timothy to pursue righteousness and a godly life with faith, love, perseverance, and faithfulness, holding firm to the eternal life God has called him (See 1 Timothy 6:11–12). Being comfortable pushes your need for faith. Faith can work only through the mess, challenges, and uncertainties. We move out of our comfort zone by faith, believing God is our eyes looking toward where we are going. And by faith, we are content with what God has blessed us with, believing He will supply every other need when the time is right.

Make the decision today to step out of your comfort zone. As the apostle Paul said to Timothy, "Pursue righteousness and a godly life, along with faith, love, perseverance, and gentleness. . . . Hold tightly to the eternal life to which God has called you" (1 Timothy 6:11–12 NLT).

God Comes Through in Power!

When Pharaoh and his troops were behind, catching up to the Israelites right before they crossed the Red Sea, The Israelites panicked and cried out to God. They even blamed Moses for bringing them this far so they could die in the desert. But Moses said to them, "Do not be afraid. Stand firm, and you will see the deliverance the Lord will bring you today" (Exodus 14:13).

God is all-powerful and not limited by anything that limits humans. He holds the entire world in His hands, including our circumstances. He helps us conquer all the attacks of the enemy. He guarantees a blessing in everything we do according to His will.

The amazing thing about God is that you will never see Him coming. But when He does, it will make a statement—not just for you to see but also for those around you to see and witness His glory. Habakkuk reminds us of this in His prayer to God. He said, "When He stops, the earth shakes, and when He looks, the nations tremble" (Habakkuk 3:6 NLT). He also prayed, "The sun and the moon stood still in the sky, as your brilliant arrows flew and your glittering spear flashed" (Habakkuk 3:11 NLT). God leaves a footprint that can never be erased or forgotten. He changes our situation in a way we could never have imagined possible. He is the God of the impossibilities (Matthew 19:26; Luke 1:37). Mighty is He, and marvelous are the works of His hands. He fulfills all that He promises. He is the only one who gives us rain when we are too dry to function. He gives strength to the weary (Isaiah 40:29). He never abandons us (Hebrews 13:5; Psalm 138:8). He guides us (Proverbs 16:9). God is the source of His power. He is a God who creates by words (Psalm 33:9).

Pastor Phil Kniesel of Hope City Church in Edmonton, Alberta, once said, "God's goal is to make our lives into an advertisement to a watching world about how everyone needs the hope that comes through Jesus Christ." The things God will reveal in our lives are not only for our eyes but also for the world to witness how beautiful and powerful our God is.

Life is not about the absence of problems or being surrounded by everything that makes us happy, but about living for God. It is about the faith we stand on that cannot be broken even by the strongest storms we face. In the Bible, we see Jesus performing many miracles. Those same miracles can be your portion through the storms. We see God's power displayed throughout the Bible in the lives of believers. His power saved Daniel from the lion's den (Daniel 6); His power saved Shadrach, Meshach, and Abednego from the blazing furnace (Daniel 3:1–30); His power saved David from Goliath (1 Samuel 17:1–51); His power led Gideon and his men in defeating the Midianites (Judges7:1–25); His power parted the

Red Sea (Exodus 14:21-29). Only God can do the impossible and free us from the shackles of the enemy.

Praise Him through your storms. No matter what happens, whether positive or negative, praise Him! Have faith and watch His mighty hand in your life. He has the power to open or shut all doors. He is not ordinary, nor is everything He does. He comes through in power! As He did for the Israelites, for David, the three brothers, Daniel, and others throughout the Bible, He will also come through in power for you. Your situation is not out of His reach. It is not a surprise to Him. Don't let your storms cloud your judgment of who God is and what He can do. Remain still, trust Him, keep persevering, and watch Him make way for you where there seems to be none.

All power and authority belong to God, and when we receive His Son, Jesus Christ, we have that same power working in us and through us to overcome every attack and circumstance. God's Word tells us that though troubles surround us, His hands reach us and save us from the plans of our enemies (Psalm 138:7). What a beautiful and mighty God we serve! Stay encouraged and know that your situation will soon change through His power.

His Grace Is Sufficient

Grace gives us undeserving blessings. It is God's unmerited favor—to all believers! God showed His love through grace by cleansing us from our sins and giving us solid reasons to hold on to our faith in Him. Have you ever heard the phrase "By the grace of God, I'm doing well"? —This is a common statement made by many. Sometimes, it's made by a person on the verge of giving up but still manages to keep smiles on their faces through the grace of God. Should we be doing fine with all the weight of life? Nope! Not at all. But because God is who He says He is, His grace is sufficient, even though we do not deserve it. He makes us strong when we find ourselves battered by the worries of life. His grace has been proven countless times in the lives of His Children.

The grace of God moves sinners from the back of the line to the front of the line. The grace of God is for all, bringing salvation to all people (Titus 2:11). This means that no one must work hard for it. We do not have to prove ourselves to gain God's grace. His grace is about who He is, not what we do to achieve it. God assured the apostle Paul that His grace was enough for him when he was battling with what he called a thorn in his flesh (See 2 Corinthians 12:8–9).

Knowing and leaning on God's grace in your life is to delight in afflictions, for you know His grace opens heaven's gate for you when hell is dragging you dry—not because you deserve to enter through the gates of heaven but because God is compassionate and merciful. His grace strengthens us in our weakness. It keeps us dependent on His divine power, making us look at our circumstances through brighter lenses.

With the battles of the flesh, the struggle against the world, and the wars the enemy wages at us, we are blessed to be where we are today—alive and thriving. Life is pleasant in our eyes, not because we have it all but because God's grace makes everything beautiful and possible. Even as he faced prison time, Paul tolerated his thorns and gave us one of the best motivating verse: "I can do everything through Christ who gives me strength" (Philippians 4:13). This verse assures us and encourages us to keep going no matter what we face in life. Paul was a man who was passionate about God and lived solely for Him, even in storms. Through the grace of God, you can also stand for Christ and be a vessel of encouragement to others. God is at work daily; even if we do not see it now, we will realize it later.

Be reminded that what we do in life is not done by our strength but by God's grace. The salvation we have through Christ is by the grace of God. We cannot take credit for the good things in our lives. They happen because we serve a God whose grace comes in abundance and changes everything in and around us! A God whose grace turns all things around for our good. He is faithful when we're not, gracious when we are wrong, and loves us even when we are unlovable. Rest in the fact that His grace is enough for you, and His power takes control where you are weak.

Stressing over the storms of life leads to exhaustion and will never fix your problems. Being a Christian is an open door for the enemy to attack. Still, it also qualifies us to be victorious by default. It offers a much bigger doorway to the abundance of blessings available to God's children. Even though His grace is for all, it may look different in each person's life as we go through different problems at different times. And even though we all go through storms, our fingerprints are different from each other. One may say, "By the grace of God, I slept in the comfort of my bed." Someone else may complain that he or she slept on a mat. What about the guy on the street who slept near the dumpster? He may also complain that he slept near a dumpster on a cold night. What about his fellow neighbor who was dragged and killed while sleeping by another dumpster?

We all go through life's unfortunate storms, and in every situation we find ourselves, someone's case may be worse than ours, but one thing we can all attest to is that we all push through our weight by the grace of God. We can't compare the level of someone's life to ours because we are journeying through different routes and heading to different destinations. Still, one thing we all have in common is the transportation of God's grace ——which is sufficient for all of us. Through every storm, we must recognize His grace at work.

Wouldn't it be great to have a problem-free life? Of course, that is not possible. There will always be difficult moments, even when we do not chase after them. We will still go through the storms. Our journey as Christians is one of faith—to stand firm amid the storms in our lives so that what God has said concerning us will prevail.

God will never allow us to pass through the stormy rain without covering us with His wings—His *grace!* The storms of life can throw us off, making us forget that we are saved, cleansed, and redeemed by grace through Jesus Christ. Take comfort in this.

A Prepared Table

"You prepare a table before me in the presence of my enemies. You anoint my head with oil, my cup overflows" (Psalm 23:5). Let me ask, how many times have you recited Psalm 23 only to rush to the part where He prepares a table for you in the presence of your enemies.? We all want God to prepare a table for us in the presence of our enemies. But do we also ask God to *prepare us* for that table.? Yes, the preparation stage is not fun, but you can never know how to maintain the value of where God is taking you if you've not been equipped or prepared for it.

God is always preparing beautiful things for you, but before He hands them to you, He ensures you are equipped to handle them. Just as you wouldn't want a half-cooked meal, you wouldn't want a half-prepared table. In preparation, you will cross seasons that might make you feel as if all hope is lost and you are headed toward failure, especially after you have had so many conversations with God through prayer and nothing is happening. Recall the goodness of God, and allow that to be your motivation. His silence means wait —Wait for Him to speak before you move.

The feeling that you are stuck while waiting for God to act is a lie the enemy wants you to believe. When you are in Christ, you constantly move toward greatness, even when time seems to stand still. Those still moments are when God makes His most significant moves in your life. A big breakthrough is about to be launched. When you ask God for something, realize that it will possibly not arrive as you expect it to. God comes through in His time, and His delivery causes all to be in awe of Him. Sometimes, your answers may not show up in the beautiful way you imagined but may come in the form of an earthquake, not to harm you but to reshape the ground you walk on.

When you pray for God to prepare a table for you, you also must ask Him to prepare *you* for that table. Sometimes, what we have in mind is not even close to what God has for us. His thoughts and ways are above ours. You must learn to surrender and trust God continuously. You are not facing your trials alone, and when they come, they are to serve a purpose in your life. Even if the enemy sent them your way, God causes them to work for your good (Romans 8:28). Nothing goes out without passing by God's desk. The enemy can not destroy the handwork of God. Everything God does has its purpose, and the goal is never to harm but to lift us.

The answers to our prayers are not dependent on us. It's not about what we wish for that will happen but what God's will is. Have an open mind and look to God in all things. Trust God, and believe that whatever you ask for in prayers, He will do more than you expect —this means you must follow His regulations and wait for Him to prepare you for the table He has set for you.

Great things take time and require your patience. The Bible tells us to be joyful in hope, patient in affliction, and faithful in prayers (Romans 12:12). To enjoy God's great blessings, you must faithfully wait for His perfect time, even if the situation looks terrible. God is preparing a table for you in the presence of your enemies (Psalm 23:5). Whatever God is involved in never crumbles; it may come as a storm, but eventually, it calms. Be still, zoom in on His voice, learn to rest in Him, and allow Him to direct your steps toward your purpose. Everything works together for our good when we put God in the center of our plans.

Sometimes, God blocks certain things— moves we try to make because He knows that making those moves will put us on the wrong path. We then start thinking that our plans and dreams are delayed but remember: sometimes what we see as a delay is God's protection in disguise. God knows when you will be ready for the table He has set for you. Rushing your plans based on how fast someone is running or how far ahead someone is can make you end up at the wrong table. A table God did not prepare for you, risking the one He has designed particularly for you.

Stay faithful in your prayers, and never allow your circumstances to redirect you or steal your joy. No matter where you are in life, you are not late. You are not early. You are right where you are supposed to be, and God Himself will propel you to greater heights when the time is right. Allow God to do His work in your life, even if you've waited long for that breakthrough. Learn to endure to enjoy a well-prepared meal served on a table solely for you.

In the meantime, keep making boss moves and learn to lie back a bit. Be constant in prayer and find rest in knowing that the storms of life cannot stop the provision of God in your life. If He intends it, nothing or no one can prevent it. I know that whatever table God prepares for you is not one with a broken leg. It is a perfect table.

Worth More than Many Sparrows

"Are not two sparrows sold for a penny? Yet not one of them will fall to the ground outside your father's care. And even the very hairs of your head are all numbered. So, don't be afraid; you are worth more than many sparrows" (Matthew 10:29–31). We've all been to a place where we've questioned God's involvement in our lives. The minute things shift toward negativity, we wonder if God sees what is happening.

The world we know today can be a scary place. With so much going on around us, it is possible to feel stuck, alone, and uncertain of what tomorrow holds. It is so easy to feel as if you are stuck in a web and that God is out of reach, but in all things; we must hold on to the hope we have in Christ. Many blessings are hidden in the unseen; just because we do not see them immediately doesn't mean they are not there.

When no one knows and sees what we go through, we choose to keep it private, not because we want to but because of how judgmental the world can be. We often choose to keep it all in, but one thing is for sure—God sees all. He sees you at your broken point. He sees you at the point of your "Red Sea." He stands as a mediator between you and the enemy to give you victory. We often see obstacles, but He sees victory. He sees opportunities. He sees and knows all we go through when no one else does. He sees our nightly cries. "The Lord's eyes are on the righteous, and his ears are attentive to their prayers, but the face of the Lord is against those who do evil" (1 Peter 3:12).

The stubborn situations in your life that refuse to cease no matter what you do, trust! God sees! When help seems far away, when friends and family abandon you, God is beside you. Pastor Steven Furtick once said in his sermons, "It feels good when God shows up just in time, but the greatest feeling is when you realize that He never left you." As hard as it is to believe at times, God never leaves us; He is always there. You are not invisible to Him. He sees you when no one else does. When you can't cross the road to the other side because of all the weight you carry, He sees you! He knows your heart. He knows your burden. He knows what you are going through or have been through. He knows other people's motives toward you. He knows when you are stuck with the feeling of suffocation. He loves you so much and wants you to know He sees you and will always step in to make way for you.

Going through life's unwanted situations is never fun. At some point in life, we may have been wronged and abused by the people we once trusted. We become guarded when all we've ever experienced is being misunderstood and left out. When life hits us left and right with unpleasantness, we build a wall so no one can get close enough to hurt us again. We become afraid to love and trust and sadly become withdrawn from a community we once knew as family, from what once seemed normal. The past pain keeps us caged, stranded, and discouraged, and we ask ourselves, "What now? Where do I go from here? How do I move on from this terrible nightmare?"

Today, I want you to know that God sees you. Allow yourself to love, trust, and feel again. There are great people and great opportunities God has prepared just for you. He has the best for you; what you have gone through does not change that. Stay encouraged, knowing that your storms are not your destination and do not define you. We can never control what life throws our way, but we can control how we react toward them. Not all the situations we go through need our attention because some are thrown to distract us. If you know yourself and know the power of the God we serve, you will not fear what anyone can do to you. Speaking about our past experiences, especially the terrible and sad moments, can be hard and painful. But because we have a God who is always by our side and watches over us in all things, we somehow get to a point at which we can tell our story to others and be an encouragement to them without having the urge to break down but instead feel the presence of God around us.

Despite all the disappointments, we are blessed to serve a merciful and gracious God. Going through the sad parts of life is never easy. It is challenging and can break us badly if we allow them to. These are not moments in life we look forward to. But with the strength of God, we can rise and keep going. By His grace, we can link our words to tell our story to encourage and help others find hope.

I have always admired those who have gone through unspeakable heart-wrenching situations but still owned up and dared to lay bare, allow God in, and inspire others. I am proud to stand with such a group. We need God's grace, wisdom, and peace to move on without hate and bitterness toward the unfortunate situations we've gone through. The enemy wants us to give up, but God wants us to have freedom, a sound mind, and live life in the fullness of His glory. God sees what has been done in the dark. The world might be blind to what you have gone through, but God saw them. God knows the details of your life in every aspect. Turn your mind away from what keeps you second-guessing your existence and run your race. The word of God tells us that God's "eyes are on the ways of mortals; He sees their every step" (Job 34:21).

May you find rest and encouragement, knowing you do not have to hide behind closed doors or allow yourself to be drained so much that you forget you have a big God. Let your scars remind you that you are strong and are made to conquer. They are a reminder that if God took you out the last time, He will surely do it again this time around. Arise and shine! God sees you—and He is for you.

4

LEAD US NOT INTO TEMPTATION

⚬⚬❦⚬⚬

Lead us not into temptation, but deliver us from the evil one.
—Matthew 6:13

Google defines *temptation* as "the desire to do something, especially wrong or unwise." Temptation is one of the fights we face daily as children of God. Whether small or big, temptation can be a hard fight to win. Even Jesus was tempted, and because of this, the Word of God tells us that He is the right person who can relate to those tempted (Hebrews 2:18).

Temptations can come in many forms —being drawn to eat that delicious big piece of apple pie when you've made a vow to go on that weight loss journey or, while fasting, tempted to retaliate toward those persecuting you. Tempted to quit on an assignment God is trusting you to accomplish, or when you're thinking of watching a movie with sexual themes, and so on. We are blessed to have the Holy Spirit, who is near and constantly reminds us of who we are and what path to take. With Jesus's help, we can resist all temptations.

Sin is desirable because we wrestle against the flesh, and the lies the enemy tells make us believe there is nothing wrong with sinning. When we dwell in the presence of God and allow the Word of God to take residence in our hearts, we can break free from temptations. The Word of God instructs us to think of "excellent and praise-worthy things" (Philippians 4:8). God's Word is the daily bread that strengthens us spiritually and weakens our flesh. The enemy wants you to believe or go after the things that are not pleasing in the sight of

God —The things that stifle the Holy Spirit in you. His job is to lie, steal, and destroy, but God wants you to have life in full (John 10:10).

Thinking of pure things makes it hard for the enemy to get into your mind. When he cannot trace his qualities in you, it is hard for him to use them against you. Refuse to be defeated; refuse to be a victim of his plans and schemes. I understand that sometimes the burden and temptation to have your way in life can be very heavy to break. Still, you must also realize that choosing to live on your terms leads to a destructive path. Through Jesus, we are redeemed; it is no longer us who live, but Christ who lives within us (Galatians 2:20). The power in you is greater than any plans the enemy has up his sleeve. With that, you can win the battle of saying no to the temptations he entices you with.

Pray for God's help daily. Each new day comes with a fresh start, and though it may come with its problems, we are more than conquerors through Christ. Seek the Lord for control over the things you struggle to give up. He alone can give you the strength to move forward, leaving the old behind.

Our heavenly father is always on the watch out for us; when we allow Him in, He will help us overcome our struggles. Through Jesus, we are liberated. Through the Holy Spirit, we hold the power to overcome.

A City with Broken-down Walls

"A person without self-control is like a city with broken-down walls" (Proverbs 25:28 NLT). The Word of God teaches us that self-control is the crowning fruit of the Holy Spirit (Galatians 5:23), the fruit a believer must bear to benefit from God's excellent plans and blessings. When we choose to exercise self-control, not only do we benefit from its gifts, but those around us also benefit.

Is it always easy to control ourselves? Of course not. In the heat of the moment, pain is dominant. One of the things I struggled to change about myself to enjoy God's fullness was my actions through pain. Aside from the fact that I started writing this entire book through some of my life's most painful and challenging moments, I have also allowed my pain to get the best out of me when I felt misunderstood and wrongly judged. Oh, boy—it never ends smoothly when you take matters into your own hands! We serve a God who sees all things, so never feel the need to prove your innocence to others because that will only make you look bad. Though God can use our circumstances to birth our greatness, the enemy can also use them to bring out the worst in us. God has given us the spirit of self-discipline (2 Timothy 1:7)—this means we can control ourselves from things that are not pleasing in His sight —things that not only tint our spirit as children of God but also misrepresent God's image in us.

God said, "Rule over the fish in the sea and the birds in the sky and over every living creature that moves on the ground" (Genesis 1:28)—this means God has given us the power over anything that hinders our walk with Him. It is hard to be a leader when you lack self-discipline. As I have grown through the storms of life, God has taught me that a true leader can control his or her behavior and feelings. How? How do we make this fruit dominant in our lives? How do we handle temptations, addictions, and habits we struggle to overcome? We acknowledge our weaknesses and ask for God's help through self-discipline! God cannot fulfill His will in us if we lack self-control. The Word of God is a powerful weapon when fighting temptations. When we lack the sense to control ourselves, we give way to the enemy to step in any time he pleases because our walls are broken down, and this is all he needs to step in and do as he wants.

I know that everything in our lives is well navigated through one power—that of the Holy Spirit. The power that lives in us helps us rise above challenges and walk on a straight path. In all our ways, acknowledging God will help keep our walls up, leading us on the path God has designed for us. The ability to control our fleshly urges is the beginning of a beautiful journey. We tend to live so backward that we worry and burden ourselves with the things of the world. The practice of self-control means knowing when to retract from anything that is not beneficial to you or anything detestable to God. Disciplining ourselves is what God requires of us. God has not given us a spirit of timidity and fear but rather a spirit of power, love, and self-discipline (See 2 Timothy 1:7).

We can do it. We can win the war against the flesh, the world, and Satan. Our flesh will constantly battle us to do the opposite of what God requires of us because we fight against dark forces in the spiritual world, but God's supernatural power allows us to beat all odds and rise above the challenges. Through God's Holy Spirit, we can discipline ourselves and exercise self-control. Lean toward God's yoke, for His yoke is easy and His burden is light (Matthew 11:30).

Free Will

"The secret things belong to the Lord our God, but the things revealed belong to us and to our children forever so that we may follow all the words of this law" (Deuteronomy 29:29). I once read a statement someone made on an Instagram post: "If God is an all-knowing God, that means He knew that Eve was going to be tricked by the serpent. And if this is so, why did He allow it to happen? Wouldn't that mean He tricked Adam and Eve as well?" Reading this got me thinking about the free will God has given to humanity. It wasn't that God was tricking them, but God was being God—who gives us the free will to choose. God will not control how we respond if we have been told not to do something. He gives us the right to choose— "But if serving the Lord is undesirable to you, then choose this day whom you will serve" (Joshua 24:15).

God will never come to you and demand that you serve Him—this is a choice everyone must make for themselves. But it is always

God's will that we choose Him because giving up ourselves for Him is how we discover who we are and live the fruitfulness He has promised us. When a parent tells their child not to mix themselves in a certain environment, the parent may not force the child to listen, but the child's obedience to the parent earns the child a reward, but their disobedience reaps a consequence.

Yes, God knew us before He created us. Yes, He knows our every step before we move, but He also gives us the freedom to walk toward our right or left. Eve had a choice to resist the lies and temptations of the enemy. Adam had a choice to resist the luring temptation of Eve. Indulging in any form of sin is a choice that is up to us. When the devil comes to us with fruit, we are to prove just how firm our foot is planted on the foundation of God. The enemy's reason for tempting us is to prove our weaknesses and disloyalty to God and get us to disobey Him, but through Christ, we can prove that we are firmly planted.

When God asked why they ate the fruit, Adam said, "The woman you put here with me gave me some fruit from the tree, and I ate it" (Genesis 3:12). When we indulge in anything that we know is detestable to God, we are as guilty as the one who introduced us to it. The enemy comes as a friend, a sister, a brother, a familiar and trusted face, but his voice is the same—deceptive and persuasive. The Bible says, "We are each responsible for our own conduct" (Galatians 6:5 NLT). The Holy Spirit helps us realize when we are indulging in things we're not supposed to. Submitting to any form of sin is below the standard of a child of God. We must understand that God allowing certain things to happen in our lives does not mean He is setting us up for a downfall. His will and preference for us are always good, and He wants us to realize that for ourselves and make good choices for ourselves.

How do we believe in Jesus yet live a lifestyle that contradicts His teachings? Jesus loves everyone—it is not in His nature to hate. But He hates the sinful lifestyle we choose to entangle ourselves in. He does not accept our wrongdoings. But He will always accept us when we turn away from our sinful ways and turn to Him in total repentance. He makes His instructions or commandments known; we must listen to or choose to disregard them. Choosing and striving to live by His teachings will lead to an eternal life of abundance. Adam and Eve had to lose their promised paradise because of their choices (Genesis 3:1–24). Sodom and Gomorrah were destroyed because of the choices people in the city made (Genesis 19:1–29).

Having the free will to choose does not mean there is another way to live. Christ is the way, the truth, and the life; no one can go to the Father except through Him (John 14:6). The Spirit of God guides us into making the best decisions in life, bringing honor to God's name. A person's downfall comes into play when he or she disobeys the words of God and refuses to realize His power within them to help resist temptation.

God continually chooses you over and over. He wants you to accept His Son, Jesus Christ, as your Lord and personal Savior. God giving us the free will to choose does not change His sovereignty over humans and the universe because only He knows the secrets to life. The nature of God is not meant for man to understand. He is God over all the earth, and He chooses to reveal to us what He pleases. He is God, yet He came down as a man and dwelled among us, showing us how to live. He is triune, three natures that are uncompromised with one another. Why God allows certain things to happen is a mystery that is meant for Him to know and for us to trust. God being an all-knowing God does not mean the journey to the top will be smooth. It means He knows everything; we don't know everything and must trust Him with our blind spots—this will be a problem for people with trust issues who tend to want to control everything in their lives. God wants you to trust Him in the unknown.

The book of Ecclesiastes puts it this way: "I realized that no one can discover everything God is doing under the sun. Not even the wisest people discover everything, no matter what they claim"

Ecclesiastes 8:17 NLT). The more we try to understand the ways of God or question them, the more we set ourselves up for mental exhaustion. I believe He gives us the freedom to make our own choices even though He is all-powerful because He is faithful, gracious, and merciful in all His ways, and He is God by Himself. Someone who is that powerful will be assumed to be controlling and bossy, but that is far from who God is —This should tell us how selfless, lovely, humble, and patient He is.

God tells us that His thoughts are nothing like our thoughts and that His ways are far beyond anything we could imagine (See Isaiah 55:8). There are so many things hidden from the sight of man. We will never understand some of the challenges we pass through in life; we must trust that God knows and has everything under control. How often has something drastic happened in your life without understanding what is going on, only to realize later that what you thought was the end for you was the beginning of something amazing? We may complain about the bumps on the road and blame God for why He allowed them our way, but we must realize that without those bumps to grip on, we can never climb to the top of the mountain. Instead of blaming God for the terrible things in your life and wondering why He allowed them to happen, praise and thank Him for His many blessings. Because what we may see as bumps are God's blessings in disguise and a way of helping us to the top— this is part of His giving us free will, realizing when to trust Him and not to give up.

Spiritual Procrastination

We constantly battle with the flesh as children of God. Though it's one thing to fight the enemy, it is another thing to battle the flesh. The Word of God tells us in the book of Psalms that "our flesh and heart may fail, but God is the strength of our heart" (Psalm

73:26). Google translates procrastination as "the action of delaying or postponing something."

Spiritual procrastination, as I call it, is a challenge in the Christian walk, but we may not realize it at times. This form of spiritual attack limits us from harvesting more. We would choose to keep procrastinating for many reasons, and sometimes, some are more spiritual than we think. We may see things as ordinary during these times, but when we realize what we're experiencing is more than the ordinary, we can better know how to approach it moving forward.

Some time ago, I procrastinated through the most important things in my life. I would do everything else but get tired and put things on hold for later when it came to spiritual activities. I knew something had to be done, and God was counting on me to do the work. My spirit yearned to dive into the Word of God. But the more I desired, the more I drifted far from it. My Spirit longed to finish the work God counted on me to accomplish, such as this book, but the more I yearned, the more my flesh battled my spirit. I seemed wide awake, scrolling through social media. But when I opened my Bible app, I suddenly felt exhausted and sluggish, and sometimes, battled headaches and even had to fight off sleep. These attacks resulted in my having to put off what mattered—over and over.

As this continued, I started feeling wasteful in not accomplishing more than I had planned. Each time I tried, the same feeling occurred. I would read a line in my Bible plans and drift off into deep sleep while reading the text, or I would read a line and find myself drifting off into deep thoughts about the matters of life. So, I decided to put off projects for later dates.

A few mornings later, no progress had been made. I stopped writing and paused, feeling like God was far away. I had no words to link together because the storms of life were hovering over me like a tight blanket. The more I strived to break free, the more I faced even greater battles. Sometimes, I would sit in front of the computer, and the words would rush into my mind like a waterfall flowing from the fountains of grace. I realize that these are times when I am in tune with God. I blocked out all the noise around me and fought off the attacks waging against me.

This sluggish feeling took over, introducing me to the unwanted weights of life. I was burdened and distracted. Worries caved in— the coronavirus case, the limitations I was projecting on myself, the doubts, and the army of attacks waging against me. How was I going to break free from this spiritual attack? How was I going to find my way back to God's wisdom and strength?

As soon as I realized I was in a battle, one to keep me from my harvest and far from the voice of God, I said to myself, *No, this is not normal. My flesh is weak, but I refuse to gratify it. If I want to manifest what God has revealed through dreams and visions, I must fight this off and get to work! If I want to fulfill my purpose, I must rise above this.* I knew this was the enemy's way of keeping me stagnant. Our race in life constantly threatens the enemy, and the closer we get to the finish line, the harder he strikes. I knew it was time I rose and fought back in prayer.

Many people God had singly pointed out as my audience were counting on me to rise —this required self-discipline and intentionality. As I meditated on who I was and my purpose, I asked God why I felt such a way. He replied, "What's your battle plan?" and pointed me to the scripture, "In order that Satan might not outwit us. For we are not unaware of his schemes." (2 Corinthians 2:11). *What is my battle plan?* All I knew to do was pray, wait, and trust.

As children of God, we always need to have a battle plan. The enemy uses tactics, traps, and schemes. We must be steps ahead through prayer and meditation of the word and get in good standing with God by bearing the fruit of the spirit. Go to God in prayer, asking Him for strength, self-discipline, and motivation. Through prayer, God gave me the strength to get back up and fight off this feeling that has clouded my space of clarity. When we seem to have the time and energy for activities like watching our favorite television shows or movies but have no zeal for the things God is counting on us to accomplish—the problem needs to be addressed when we find ourselves putting off spending intimate time with God. The Word of God tells us, "The flesh desires what is contrary to the spirit, and the spirit what is contrary to the flesh" (Galatians 5:17).

Our flesh will always get us to do what the Spirit of God is against, to lean toward what feels satisfying now—but because we have the Spirit of God living in us, we have the power to fight off and untangle the bondage of the flesh. Jesus tells us in Matthew not to "live on bread alone but on every word that comes from the mouth of God" (Matthew 4:4). It is not by our strength, it is not by our might—but by the power of the living God that enables us to push through and stand tall in times of trouble. Living by the Word of God gives fulfillment and makes us whole. *Procrastination* may be a mere word we use here and there, and the word is not mentioned in the Bible, but the word *laziness* is, and sometimes procrastination derives from the feeling of laziness.

Paul tells us that whatever we do, whether in word or deed, we are to do it all in the name of the Lord Jesus (See Colossians 3:17). Many successful people we see today did not make it by being lazy or procrastinating. They made it because they kept going despite difficulties and never gave up. Though some people do not procrastinate due to laziness, others do not have a solid reason for postponing, giving excuses upon excuses. When laziness, sluggishness, and procrastination persist, we must take it seriously and seek God's help rather than allow it to hold us back. King Solomon reminds us of this in the book of Proverbs: "Lazy people want much but get little, but those who work hard will prosper" (Proverbs 13:4 NLT). When we realize that the Spirit living in us is more powerful than our flesh, we will keep moving in authority and put in the work, which then results in yielding good fruits.

Does the enemy ever want us to harvest good things? No! He will do all he can and cut corners to ensure that. One way is by weakening us through the flesh—anything to keep us from winning, to keep us lacking, to keep us holding off what needs to be done! That is his strategy of keeping us stagnant.

The enemy aims to keep us from moving forward. But when God says it's time to move, that means it's time to move. Realizing God's truth will keep you pushing in times when all you see is gray skies—no holding off until tomorrow. Spiritual procrastination causes many tomorrows to pass by with no progress. God is steadfast. His strength takes over when we are weak. His mercies are new every morning. God wants you to march on. He wants you to be steadfast and immovable (1 Corinthians 15:58). God is counting on you to keep pushing. Many are counting on you to do your part. The flesh will continually fail us, but God has given us a spirit to endure.

Sometimes, we procrastinate due to fear, lack of confidence, or courage to get up and move. In his letter to the Romans, Paul talks about his struggles with the flesh as he narrates the difference between the carnal Christian's inner struggles between the spirit's desire to obey the laws of Christ and the fleshly desire to do the opposite. He brings us to an understanding that even though we are free through what Jesus did on the cross for us, which as a result helps us strive toward obeying the laws of God, we constantly battle our flesh, always with the danger of being enslaved to it due to our sinful nature (Romans 7:21–25). But Paul also encourages us in the book of Philippians that we can do all things through Christ, who gives us strength (See Philippians 4:13).

No matter what form of fleshly battles you currently face, know you have what it takes to break free. You must keep depending on God's grace, which is sufficient for us all, even in weakness (2 Corinthians 12:9). Affirm His love and word over and over in your life. Continually pray for the strength needed to overcome.

5

PRAISING THROUGH THE STORMS

--------⟨✖⟩--------

My tongue will proclaim your righteousness, your praises all day long.
Psalm 35:28

When Paul and Silas were stripped and severely beaten with wooden rods, then thrown into prison and ordered into the inner cell with their feet fastened in stocks (Acts 16:22–24), you would think that being in this situation would cause them to panic and cry out to God in anguish. But instead, they prayed and sang songs of hymns to God (Acts 16:25), praising Him through their predicament. They focused on the fact that they had a big God whom they believed would rescue them. With no fear at all, praising Him was what made sense to them at that moment. And as always, as the Word of God says, "Everyone who calls on the name of the Lord will be saved" (Romans 10:13).

God was pleased with Paul and Silas and rescued them by causing an enormous earthquake that shook up the foundation of the prison, and all the doors immediately flew open. This miraculous act of God caused the jailer to wonder about this kind of God, leading him to believe in the God who had saved Paul and Silas from prison (Acts 16:26–34). When God answers, He comes through in a way that leaves even our enemies wondering. Amidst the storm, we may panic, cry, worry, stress, feel defeated, and even attempt to give up, but we will find God's peace settled within us when we find the secret (worship) to surviving the storm.

Nothing upsets Satan more than worshiping God amidst our most tremendous storms. When we seek God during the storms, we begin seeing more clearly, helping us see our circumstances from a better perspective. Endure, fight, and lean on God through your praise and worship. Our reliance on God and trust in Him give us peace and hope amidst the storms. No matter how big or small your storms are, you must keep your focus and thoughts on the positive things—the things above! Focus on the promises of God and how He's proven His faithfulness to you in the past. You are alive! That means God is not done with you; you must keep pushing through in the tunnels.

The promises of God are there to help us survive the deepest of oceans. The psalmist said, "He will cover you with his feathers. He will cover you with his wings. His faithful promises are your armor and protection" (Psalm 91:4 NLT). Whatever storms you may be going through, whatever they may look like, and no matter what they may be doing to you, know that you have what it takes to overcome. Regardless of the weapons that are formed against us, the Word of God reminds us that those weapons will not prevail (Isaiah 54:17). As children of God, we know that it is never what we go through that matters but the attitude we carry through what we go through makes the difference.

A positive attitude through life's storms speaks of our faith and trust in God. James wants us to find joy in our circumstances. He tells us that our endurance grows when our faith is tested through trials. When we grow in our endurance, we become perfect, needing nothing but receiving the crown of life at the end if we still hang on and endure (James 1:2–4). The storms we face help us practice perseverance and exercise our trust in God. It makes us realize that only God can calm or bring us out of our storms.

Are you trusting God through your circumstances? Are you fearless through the scariest times in your life? Are you praising God through all the difficulties, knowing He is still working and arranging everything to work for you? All the storms you face never change the fact that you are blessed. They can never change the future God has planned for you. They can never change His love for you. Your circumstances have no power over you. You have every authority over the things you face in life. When you fail to realize your power as a child of God, your circumstances become loud enough to break you.

Absence of Difficulty

In my short time in ministry, I have come across many people who believe the Christian walk is supposed to be struggle-free. However, that is far from reality. Being a Christian doesn't mean we are exempt from hardship or difficulties. It doesn't give us a problem-free life but allows us to view what we go through in faith. Our major blessing as Christians is that the blood of Jesus has purchased us. Because we are made new in Christ and death could not hold Him captive, we can have hope and assurance that all things will work for our good in our challenging times.

We've all been through situations in which we've had doubts. We are not wrong for feeling like this; we are human and respond mainly through the flesh. God knows our weaknesses; however, we need to understand that being disciples of Jesus means we strive to cling to the spiritual understanding and way of doing things. Being a Christ follower does not mean that our lives will be smooth sailing and that we will not experience hurt, damage, loss, pain, disappointments, and so on. All those things will come. We will hit rock bottom. We will find ourselves lost in the middle of this journey. But we are blessed to have God's Holy Spirit with us, leading us through it all and giving us the power and ability to overcome all obstacles. As children of God, we are stars. We are the "light of the world," a town built on a hill that cannot be hidden (Matthew 5:14). Stars shine the most brightly in the darkness, so we must push ourselves to go through our dark times with grace because they birth the star hidden within us.

We must be different; we can't accept and deal with our storms like the unbelievers. We must stand out and be different. Even though God did not promise us a problem-free life, He promised to be with us through the challenging times in our lives every step of the way. God desires to exchange our pain and troubles for His peace. "He is our present help in times of trouble" (Psalm 46:1). His promises give us hope to persevere through hardship. He assures us through His Word that He will never leave or forsake us (Deuteronomy 31:6). He can do for us immediately what our earthly family or friends can never do for us in a lifetime.

We serve a faithful God. He's proven this time after time. Most of the time, we remember only our problems and ask God why He allowed them. But the truth is that without our problems, we will not discover our strengths or realize that we need God to maintain that strength. Our circumstances cause us to draw closer to God. Our faith is tested during the most challenging times in our lives. How long can you hold on to the promises of God through the storms? How well can you prove your faith in God? Is that faith there only when things are good? Is it there only when God blesses you the way you want Him to?

Let's take the story of Job, for instance. Job was a great man of God, honorable, and loved God very much, but did that excuse Him from going through the unimaginable? No! Satan could not be happier than to see us abandon God in times of hardship—because he knows that God can never and will never leave His children. We always feel as if God is the one who is far away from us, who has forsaken us during life's greatest storms, but the truth is that we are the ones who sometimes abandon Him when we go through tough times. We allow the enemy to get into our minds, worrying and stressing over and over about things God has already taken care of.

The Word of God tells us Satan toiled with Job to prove to God that Job would abandon Him and that he was worshiping God only because of all the blessings God had given to him. Job lost everything—his wealth, friends, and family. He grieved, going through great pain. Satan thought he had finally gotten Job mad at God, but instead, Job said, "The Lord gave me what I had, and the Lord has taken it away. Praise the name of the Lord!" (Job 1:21 NLT).

Job still held on to God through the biggest storms of his life, and when Satan's manipulations did not work, he made Job fall sick, inflicting sores all over his body. Through all this chaos in his life, Job still did not sin. He lost all the people around him. But Satan's plans did not work. And for Job's faithfulness, God blessed him with more than he had lost (Job 2:7).

Can you go through what Job went through and still stand firm in your faith? Nothing upsets Satan more than a believer who trusts God through their storms. Nothing makes him madder than standing tall in times when you're supposed to be broken. Trust God and believe that victory is already ours through Christ. To acquire God's priceless gifts, we must deny ourselves for His glory (Matthew 16:24–25). Regardless of how challenging life can be, we must be strong in our faith and hold dearly to the promises of God.

The Future Glory

In his letter to the Romans, Paul stood as a voice of hope and encouraged us by saying, "Yet what we suffer now is nothing compared to the glory he will reveal to us later" (Romans 8:18 NLT). Most of us live life without realizing the great inheritance we have waiting for us in heaven. Scripture describes it as a pregnant nation waiting for birth, and the difficult times we pass through in this world are birth pangs. The Spirit of God living in us helps our suffering bodies; that is why waiting for our future inheritance does not break us any more than waiting for birth breaks a pregnant mother (Romans 8:22–26). Though we do not see how God is working through and in us ahead of time, when we persevere and endure the troubles we face, the more we look forward to and enjoy what is to come.

There is more to life than what we see and our problems. We do not see the whole picture—which will be revealed at the appointed time. We must endure, persevere, and wait for that day to come. While on earth, Jesus Christ suffered through embarrassment because He knew the future glory ahead. Even though we may get tired of the storms we pass through, we are blessed to have the Holy Spirit to help us along the way. "He knows us better than we know ourselves, knows our pregnant condition, and keeps us present before God" (Romans 8:27 MSG). He speaks for us when we are weak; we must find hope in knowing that God will overrule and work for us to accomplish His will in us.

God knew what He was doing when He sent His Son to die for us (John 3:16) when He decided to adopt us as His own—this makes us siblings to Christ. He calls us by name and will always be on our side. Why put yourself in a position to worry about the things around you? You are a chosen people, and thanks to Jesus Christ our Lord, an inheritance is held in place for all God's children—a place and position we never have to fight for, a place given to us as an act of love, a place that can never be taken away from us no matter how far we may wander. What a future glory!

The love of God drives out the fear inflicted on us by this world of sin. The glory is hidden in our mess. It is hidden in the pain and hurt of our pregnant state. When we go through the uncomfortable pain to get to the glory season, we'll appreciate and treat the season with a higher value than if it were given to us without us having to feel the weight of our cross. Jesus came to earth to go through humiliation and pain for us, so we must live for Him and proclaim the good news as believers. He genuinely paid a cost He did not owe so that we may have freedom and be worthy enough to experience the future glory God promised us.

So endure, persevere, and grow through the storms of life because what you face right now is nothing compared to what is set for you ahead. God loves you and has embraced you. Glory to the name of the one who gives us undeserved glory and inheritance. May the Spirit of the Lord be with you as you endure life's challenges and, most importantly, as you grow through the storms of life.

O God, My Vindicator

David was the enemy's target at a point in his life and pleaded for God to vindicate him against his enemies. Accused of misconduct, he turned to God. In desperation and anguish, he called out to God to contend with those who contend with him (Psalm 35:1). He looked only to God to vindicate him and never took matters into his own hands because he believed God would hear him and come to his aid.

Through his predicament, David gave us one of our favorite psalms today, which begins with "The Lord is my shepherd" (Psalm 23:1). David never allowed his problems to draw him away from God but grew closer, trusting Him with all his heart and wanting his vindication to come only from God. As with David, we may go through situations in which we are wrongly accused or misunderstood. The Word of God tells us in Proverbs 3:5–6 not to lean on our own understanding but in all our ways, submit to God, and He will make our paths straight.

How many of us can proudly say that through our problems, our first instinct has been to leave matters to God and trust Him to handle our issues in the heat of the moment? I can admit I have faltered several times. I felt the need to race and defend myself from being accused or misunderstood by others, especially when given no chance to clarify or speak. It can be an unfair situation; in those moments, we can forget that we have a Father who can vindicate and fight for us better than we can for ourselves. The Bible tells us not to lean on our understanding because God knows our thoughts. He knows our flesh will always fail us and that depending on ourselves will result in self-destruction. He knows we do not think as He does. We are not nearly as perfect as He is; most importantly, He knows and sees what we can't and can better vouch for us.

We often go by how we feel and then make decisions based on that. But we can easily be deceived by our feelings. Through my experience, I have learned to look and depend only on God for vindication. As hard as it was, I gave total control to God. I knew that anyone who surrenders and looks to God for their well-being would never fall because the Lord upholds them. We may stumble, but we will never fall (Psalm 37:24).

Why take matters into your own hands when you have a Father whose hands can do more than you ask? The storms in life are meant to draw us closer to God, and our greatest mistakes come about when we choose to do the opposite. Our emotions can make us act out of character, but placing our trust in God can prevent us from making a fool of ourselves. When we cry out to God in desperation, He hears the righteous cry of His children and never turns His face away from them (Psalm 34:17). He knows our hearts, our deepest thoughts, and our motives. He knows things even before they happen. Most importantly, He sees the big picture, whereas we see only from our point of view and what is being played out now.

Trust your battles into the hands of God, and you will never lose. Whether it is being accused, misunderstood, or wrongly judged, no matter your situation, place your battles in the hands of the one who knows you better than you know yourself—the one who is never surprised by the storms you face. Nothing is ever what it seems. The path we walk on can suddenly grow bushes and thorns along the way, forcing detours and turns we never expected. But as Christ-followers, we are to remember God's goodness, believing He will give us victory in the presence of our enemies and turn our problems around to bring glory to His name.

God has your best interests at heart. Surrender to Him and watch what happens. He is who we ought to present our issues to. Even though He already knows the storms we pass through, He loves it when we come to Him and genuinely seek His help. He loves it when we draw near Him through our storms and speak to Him as we would with our parents or close friends. Remember: you never have to take on life's battles alone. God has given you the Holy Spirit to be a friend, help you through life's difficulties, and direct you to the right path.

Pastor Steven Furtick of Elevation Church said, "When you understand that God is positioning you, you don't have to fear what people might do to you because there's not a situation that they can put you in that God will not show up in the midst of." I needed to hear this word when I needed it the most. When no one cares to listen and understand, when no one is left standing with you, and those you once knew as close friends or family turn their backs on you, know that God knows and sees you. He stands with you till the end—this alone should give you peace amidst whatever storms you find yourself in. Yours is to walk in your authenticity no matter what, loving everyone, apologizing for your faults, and leaving the rest for God to handle. Sometimes, it's not about fixing our focus on waiting on God to vindicate us, though He will in His own time. The focus should always be on "Why am I going through this?" and "What is the message God is giving me through it?" and not burdening ourselves with questions such as "When will it pass?" We need to be focused on what God wants us to learn and how He uses what we're going through to do His work in us and through us—focusing on the lesson more than seeking so hard for an escape route.

When we surrender, God gives us peace and the strength to continue. The enemy will always try to use our storms to distract us and use our situations to define us. However, remember that no one can redefine what God has defined. No one can rewrite your destiny. Sometimes, we recall only the negative aspects of things, but God always remembers us for who we are in Him, even during the storms of life. In our storms, God never lets go. It doesn't change His mind or plans for us. Our faults and weaknesses do not change

God's love toward us; instead, when we turn to Him, He changes us through His love and compassion!

If we allow the enemy to have his way, the hurt we experience from the storms of life will dwell in our hearts and minds, keeping us from experiencing the joy of the Lord. Stay blessed and encouraged, and always remember to *let go and let God*. Celebrate every growth milestone, and strive to be a better version of yourself daily despite the challenges. Be thankful for where you are now and where God is taking you, and never hold on to things of the past, but choose to allow God to step in for you as you enjoy His love, compassion, and peace. You've come a long way; you are doing great!

6

GROWING THROUGH
THE EMOTIONS

*The action taken at the end should produce
the righteousness God desires.*

Life comprises a series of daily choices, and every decision has consequences. Sometimes, we make these decisions based on our emotions or understanding. But even in our wrong choices, we have a God who still works for us when we turn to Him. Our feelings may cause us to want to do one thing one minute and another a few minutes later. As humans, that is normal, and that is also why we should never disconnect from God but look to Him for guidance so He can show us the proper way to navigate those feelings.

How often do you change your mind about certain decisions based on your understanding or other people's perceptions and opinions? Why do you think God wants us to lean on Him instead of our own way of thinking? – because our way of thinking can easily deceive us. Our emotions and reasoning are developed momentarily. God can see everything and knows us better than we know ourselves. We sometimes can't even decide what to wear, let alone depend on ourselves to navigate this life. One minute, we may love someone; the next, that love changes based on our emotions or how offended we may feel. We act conditionally, and God is the total opposite of that. He is powerful. We are powerless! But through Him, we attain the ability to have control. He is pure; we are easily tinted. He is limitless; we are limited. But because of the blood of Jesus, He sees and deals with us through grace. God knows our innermost being, our deepest wants and needs. God is interested not in *what* you do but in the *motive* behind what you do, and sometimes, our emotions can lead us to make bad decisions.

Sometimes, when life's storms hit hard, we may feel all types of ways. We may feel like quitting, like holding on longer or going left or right. We may feel so many mixed emotions. No matter how you feel during life's challenges, nothing makes the enemy madder than when you depend on God, acknowledge Him, and keep hanging on to Him for guidance—especially when it's easier for you to give up.

The Word of God tells us to give all our worries and cares to God, for He cares about us (1 Peter 5:7). Going by our understanding leads to a crooked path—causing us to act out of character and make disappointing moves. The wisdom of God helps us navigate our emotions. Ask God for wisdom to help you in decision-making before emotions fly out of control.

When Anger Sets In

"Human anger does not produce the righteousness God desires"(James 1:20). Being angry is not terrible; it is a way of expressing your emotion toward something, but where it gets challenging is what you choose to do with that anger. The apostle Paul shines a light on this topic in his letter to the people in Ephesus. He said, "Do not let the sun go down while you are still angry" (Ephesians 4:26).

We have all been at a point when we've been furious at someone for wrongful and unfair treatment and, worse, allowed our anger to get the best of us. Yes, to be dealt with wrongly is not a great feeling, but what is even worse is responding to it by being harsh on yourself by putting yourself in an uncomfortable situation. When you allow anger to control you, you make way for the enemy to take over; this is what Paul meant when he said, "Do not give the devil a foothold" (Ephesians 4:27).

The enemy will never hesitate to get you exactly where he wants you. Usually, we hold on to anger and act on it because we want others to see that they hurt us and somehow believe that holding onto the pain will also cause them pain. But the person you end up hurting the most is yourself, which saddens God. Paul said, "Do not grieve the Holy Spirit of God, with whom you were sealed for the day of redemption" (Ephesians 4:30). We belong to God. How we react must reflect who He is to us, not what we go through or how angry someone has made us. In all situations, you must know how to conduct yourself in a way that represents who you are as a child of God. James warns us to be quick to listen, slow to speak, and slow to get angry as Human anger does not produce the righteousness God desires (James 1:19-20).

Though it may be hard to get over your anger, your response in such times will determine your way of moving forward. Stay silent, turn to God, and allow Him to speak to you in those moments. Allow the Spirit of God to permeate your heart more loudly than the desire to retaliate. When the feeling of anger is not dealt with constructively, it will certainly control your actions and behavior, and that is precisely what the enemy aims at—for you to make a fool out of yourself and miss what matters now. When you let your anger control you, you only regret your actions later. Worse, you feel bad about acting outside of God's righteousness.

The ramification of allowing anger to control your actions is a chain of more problems. Soon, that anger becomes bitterness, then follows all types of evil acts. In times like these, it's best to remember who you are and what God has shown you in His Word concerning the emotions you may be feeling. Allow God to mend your hurting heart. He is more than faithful to see you through whatever hurt you're passing through. Paul further advises us to "Be kind and compassionate to one another, forgiving each other, just as in Christ God forgave you" (Ephesians 4:32). When you allow your anger to have the best part of you, you disobey this word. In your anger, the enemy will step in with his voice—recognize his voice and reject it quickly. His voice is deceptive and luring. His voice makes people do the opposite of what God wants; his voice tells lies, brings fear and shame, and keeps you wandering with revenge plans. His voice offers a moment of satisfaction and a lifetime of suffering; it brings accusations and guilt. It tells you there is no way to freedom unless you avenge your pain. His voice brings torture and dissatisfaction. Resting in God's love creates a stance that will help you recognize and refuse the enemy's voice. Resting in God's presence allows us to control ourselves and helps us settle.

The voice of God brings on a sense of freedom. It is loving, calm, and protective. God's voice is true; it is humble, graceful, merciful, powerful, forgiving, and saves all those crushed in spirit. God wants to speak to you, especially when you feel vulnerable, but to hear Him speak, you must seek Him through your emotions and be transparent about how you feel. Being conscious of what you allow inside your heart can save you from going through unnecessary pain.

King Solomon said, "There is a way that appears to be right, but in the end, it leads to death" (Proverbs 14:12). In the heat of the moment, we may feel that how we respond is right, but when we pause and think biblically; we will better make the decision that speaks of the righteousness of God. Not heeding the voice of God in our vulnerable moments can be fatal. God wants you to focus on Him regardless of your unfair situations. Why? Because keeping your eyes fixed on God will help you to make the right choices. God wants you to seek Him and allow Him to be that bed of rest you desire in times of trouble.

When Pain Sets In

"The Lord is close to the broken-hearted; He rescues those whose spirits are crushed" (Psalm 34:18 NLT). Pain is not something that we all look forward to in life, but we are bound to experience it in our lives one way or another. No matter what pain you are going through, whether from a breakup, rejection, being misunderstood, or something from the past, always remember that it comes to serve a purpose, and to find out its purpose, you must walk confidently through it. This means surrendering, letting go—stop gripping too tightly to what is causing or what caused that pain. In the silence of your pain, allow yourself to feel and heal.

David said, "God heals the brokenhearted and binds up their wounds" (Psalm 147:3). Learn to give your pains to God and ask Him to bind them for you. Ask Him to take any resentments, anger, bitterness, and ill feelings that may have developed due to your pain. There will never be a breakthrough without you surrendering to God and intentionally walking through your pain. The anxiety, the heartaches, the knotty feeling in your stomach, and the sense of brokenness accompanied by pain are not fun to experience but are necessary for growth and strengthening. Don't just look at your painful moments as what they are; look at them through the spiritual lens—because we serve a God who turns our ashes into beauty.

God is close to the brokenhearted, so trust Him with your pain and heart. Don't run to human beings to convince them of your feelings because they might not understand your emotions, at least not how you need to be understood. Do not put such a burden on another person. Don't let God be your plan B—the one you run to when your first choice fails. Seek the Lord in Spirit. Run to the Father from the very beginning. He understands.

Sometimes, the enemy might even bring up past pain to distract you from moving toward the glory set before you. So, if your past tries to poke itself into your present, remind it of the doors God has set before you. They are doors that not even your past pain can shut. Remember your past, not camp there, repeat its mistakes, or live in the bondage of its infections, but remember it as the key to gaining the resources for elevating your future.

How do you move on from the past pains when things or people around you keep taking you back or doing something that reminds you of the pain and disappointment you've worked hard to heal from? The enemy will repeatedly replay scenarios in your mind, making you believe things to despise the people who have inflicted pain in your life. Satan will cause you to feel that the only way out is by distancing yourself from anyone and anything that brings you pain and will make you fear the future because of past hurts. That's what he does. His presentation is always alluring and enticing as if he is on your side and wants to release you from your pain. He always forgets one thing: that we are god over him. The same Spirit who raised Christ from death lives in us. We are the sons and daughters of the most high God! Therefore, we are overcomers.

It is never about distancing yourself from things, people, or incidents that remind you of past pains that will bring healing—but being able to stand amidst those things—the things that break and scare you and stare you in the face each day is where true healing begins. Saying to yourself, "I am more than a conqueror in Christ Jesus." Waking up daily and asking God to help deal with your pain will keep your mind at ease.

Your strength and efforts alone cannot give you permanent freedom, but allowing God in and being transparent with Him about every pain will help you gain clarity on how to heal. "It is not by our might, nor by power, but by the Spirit of God" (Zechariah 4:6).

7

MANY ARE THE PLANS OF MEN

*Many are the plans in a person's heart, but it
is the Lord's purpose that prevails.*
—Proverbs 19:21

I have gotten to know and understand that in life, we may make
many plans and, most times, have no idea how they will turn out,
but we plan them anyway in hopes of things turning out as we had
planned. As believers of Christ, we take steps forward because we
believe God will see us through, so we depend on Him and keep
moving. Making plans without the involvement of God will crumble
because "in him, we live and move and have our being" (Acts 17:28).
Where people see failures, God sees victory. Family members may
talk you out of a dream you have worked hard for. Friends may
discourage you and make fun of your plans and dreams. Still, the
reality is that when we acknowledge God's plans for us instead of
living out the will of man, the people who doubted your dreams
will soon see how powerful God is and that with Him, all things
are possible.

Where man doubts, God proves Himself faithful. God sees
a winner when everyone else sees a joke. None of us knows what
tomorrow holds, but I know God has each day in His hands. We
can make all the plans we want in the world, but God's purpose
prevails, and we must have an open mind in our planning, knowing
that He controls our lives. Whatever your plans, goals, or dreams,
never doubt your capabilities, and never give up or give in to the

naysayers. Instead, keep pushing hard. Put God in the front row and allow Him to take the wheel.

His plans for our lives are far better than what we have planned for ourselves. His plans require your participation and partnership with Him. You will never live God's abundance if your plans hold you captive. Ask God to help you see His plans for your life so that you are not forcing yourself to make plans that contradict His for you.

Where God Leads He Provides

When God asked Moses to free His people, the Israelites, from Pharaoh, Moses did not know how he could do so. He said, "Who am I to appear before Pharaoh? Who am I to lead the people of Israel out of Egypt?" (Exodus 3:11 NLT). But God told him, "I will be with you" (v. 12). Just like Moses, many of us may be scared of what is next for us, afraid to take a step because of the lack of confidence in completing the task entrusted to us. But throughout the Bible, we see God keeping His promises to His people. When God instructs, He gives guidelines and provides the necessities to face all afflictions along the way. God may lead us on a different route than we usually are used to, but rest assured that when God reveals His vision for your life, He will also equip you for it and be there with you through it.

One of my biggest fears is missing God's voice due to life's distractions. We all want to come out of our storms shining as pure as gold. But most times, we are unwilling to go through the challenges and the refining process and unwilling to pick our cross and start walking. We become afraid of what we may bump into, so fearful of what we may lose, and we start questioning whether we have what it takes to get to where God is taking us—but this is when our faith in God must rise. It may feel scary, but we must remember that we are never in anything alone and that if God leads us to a particular thing, it is because He trusts us to get on with it.

Whatever God's vision or plans concerning your life, He will never leave you to accomplish them alone. God gave Moses all the necessities needed for the safe delivery of His people and made way for them where there seemed to be none. That is the way God works! God will never take you to a place where His grace will not see you through. He will never take you to a place where His arms will not embrace you, or His riches will not provide for all your needs. For God to guide you, you must put aside your will and seek His. You must be willing to commit to Him in total surrender. You must stop and ask Him to reveal His word concerning your life. You must ask Him to help you see beyond the normal.

Sometimes, we focus too much on what we do in our daily activities, so much so that it keeps us from pursuing the right things. You must learn to pause to hear God's voice and direction for your life. Without the guidance of God, you are like a blind man walking with no sense of direction. But with God, you can journey through even in your blindness because He becomes your eyes, holds your hands through every turn, and never lets go. That is the kind of God we serve; He is beautiful in every way and never leads us to a dead end. If He has gotten you to where you are today, He will take you to where you must be tomorrow.

Under the Sun

Whether or not we believe God enabled what we go through, we must understand that everything in life happens for a reason, a reason that only God knows. King Solomon tells us to "accept the way God does things, for who can straighten what he has made crooked? Enjoy prosperity while we can, but when hard times strike, we must realize that both come from God and remember that nothing is certain in this life" (Ecclesiastes 7:13–14 NLT). If

God has allowed something in your life, He has done so for a reason. Mistakes can be made when you try so hard to straighten the paths God has made crooked—frustrations, doubts, and pointing fingers at God come into play.

As a child of God, you must know and recognize what God has allowed in your life to accomplish a more significant purpose. These things He allows may be problematic, but for the right reasons. Throughout the Bible, we learn of many incidents in which what seemed like a bad situation in the lives of God's people turned around for their good, for God's glory, from Joseph being betrayed by His brothers (Genesis 37:12–32), Job's predicaments (Job 2:7–10), to the death of Jesus (Matthew 27:32–56). Even in your most painful and darkest moments, God still reigns and has a plan for you. All these incidents in the Bible help us know that everything under the sun happens for a reason. It is a reason that only God knows, and we are to trust Him through the unknown until He reveals them to us at the appointed time.

The Word of God tells us in Ecclesiastes that everything is made for its time. When Saul's father's donkeys strayed, he sent Saul and one of the servants to search for them. During the search, the servant suggested they see a prophet of God in the nearby town. As they journeyed there, they met Samuel. Bear in mind that God had already told Samuel a day prior that He would send a man his way whom He had chosen to be the king of Israel. Samuel turned out to be the man of God whom Saul and the servant were seeking in the first place. And though Samuel knew who Saul was, Saul had no idea who Samuel was. As the story continued, Samuel told Saul what the Lord had said concerning his life. He was to be the leader of Israel (God's special possession). Samuel anointed Saul with oil, the Spirit of the Lord came upon him, and he became a different person with a refined heart and prepared to take on the task God had entrusted to him —the king who delivered the Israelites from the Philistines.

God loves you very much and has an excellent plan for your life. But for this plan to manifest, you will have to be renewed with a brand-new heart, and this refinement and pruning process may come in the form of pain, hurt, and rejection. You may be in a season of your life, feeling left out, rejected, and misunderstood by people you once trusted or the world around you. You may feel lost and as if life has no meaning without what it once was. Although this can be a normal emotion through the storms, it can be ongoing if we lose sight of who we are and our true life purpose. This can contradict God's plans for you, especially when you allow yourself to stay in that state.

I am sure Saul never thought of becoming the king of Israel. No matter where you are in life, feeling stagnant, feeling as though God cannot use you because of how you see yourself or how the world sees you. I want to encourage you with this story today to take heart and believe that your destiny does not lie in the hands of men or in the limitations you put on yourself. Your future lies in the hands of God. As Samuel referred to the Israelites as God's special possession (1 Samuel 10:1), that's the same way God feels toward you. You are that important to Him. And even though you may not know what His plan for your life is, you must trust that it is a great plan, and for it to manifest in your life, you must get closer and closer to Him. What may seem like an unpleasant situation, like your donkeys running off and your having to go after them, might be God's way of leading you toward something great.

God led Saul to where he was supposed to be through what looked like a predicament —this can also be your story. Through the storms in our lives, God's sovereignty is shown. "And we know that in all things God works for the good of those who love him and are called according to his purpose" (Romans 8:28). So, whether your problems are from your own mistakes or the enemy orchestrated them. Whether they are there as a test of your faith, when you lean on God to take you through them, you will come out victorious. Everything works together for your good. When the appointed time comes for His plans to be fulfilled in your life, He will reveal them to you.

God never takes us on the road of discovery without giving us a heads-up, but most times, we never realize the shifting until we've been repositioned—this is because the ways of God are too big for our minds to catch on to. It usually all makes sense when we get to our destination. Through all the changes, His voice and directions become evident as we trust and stay close to Him, mute all the distractions around us, and zoom in on Him alone. He has a vision for you. He sees something in you that you do not see in yourself. Trusting Him is the answer to making those visions a reality. When the time is right, He will send the right people your way to help you through the process.

So, never let the storms of life make you feel as if your existence on this earth is unnecessary. You were created for a reason and have a specific task entrusted to you to complete. Stay faithful as the Lord is always faithful to you, and believe that "it's all good." Rejoice in Him today!

The Power of a Faithful Circle

"Finally, they entered the region of Zuph, and Saul said to his servant, 'Let's go home. My father will be more worried about us than about the donkeys!' But the servant said, 'I've just thought of something! There is a man of God who lives here in this town. He is held in high honor by all the people because everything he says comes true. Let's find him. Perhaps he can tell us which way to go.'" (1 Samuel 9:5–6 NLT).

The people in our circle can hinder or push us further toward our destiny. There are certain people in life when we're around them; we remain stagnant—no progress, demotion, promotion, contribution, nothing! Just stagnant. God wants us to keep walking. He wants us to reach our full potential; sometimes, being around the wrong people blocks us from moving. We encircle our life decisions around loved ones, and because of that, we are often left in one place, afraid of what they may think of the steps we want to take. Their approval becomes so important to us, and we forget the primary purpose of why God created us. Our relationship may be okay with God, but because we are surrounded by people whose opinion means the world, we lack the confidence to move in a direction God wants us to. We start living in fear of change.

We need people in our lives who will help pull us up when we're tired and broken, people who will see our full potential and are willing to help us fulfill our calling, and people who will see the gold in us even when we're in a mess—those who will never give up on us, even when we feel like giving up on ourselves. When Saul gave up on looking for his father's donkeys, he said to the servant, "Come, let's go back, or my father will stop thinking about the donkeys and start worrying about us" (1 Samuel 9:5 NLT). He gave up on the search because he did not know he was walking toward His destiny. Fortunately for him, he had the right person with him who kept them going when he (Saul) wanted to give up. The servant told Saul that they should see a prophet of God in the town who could show them the direction of the donkeys.

Saul said they couldn't go because he had no gift to offer the prophet. But the servant said he had a quarter of a shekel of silver they could offer the prophet (See 1 Samuel 9:8–10). Saul would have gone home without the servant, missing a life-changing moment.

Know that whatever vision God has concerning your life, He will also provide destiny helpers. He will give you the people, the opportunities, the resources, and the road map to guide you. All God does in our lives is so that we live the abundance promised to us and bring glory to His name. Roadblocks in this story were such that Saul would have missed meeting Samuel if He had given up and gone back home. Additionally, His will for noting any gifts for the prophet would have kept him from going farther if not for the servant with him. Things like these can keep us from moving on toward our destination.

Life is filled with many roadblocks; sometimes, these come our way by surprise, while at other times, we create them ourselves through excuses and fear. But God says, "Where you are weak, I am your strength" (See 2 Corinthians 12:10 NLT). God's strength is the only thing that can keep us going. May we stay rooted in Him so that we never miss or give up on our journey before reaching our destination. I pray that God refines you. I pray that He separates you from every relationship that stands as an obstacle and connects you with people who will pull you up when you want to give up.

When God Opens a Door

The Lord said in His Word, "I have placed before you an open door that no one can shut" (Revelation 3:8). God promises you an open door that no man can shut. Still, through life's journey, you may be tempted to try opening these doors by your own will and efforts. You will fail in the process because they are doors not meant for you to open except in God's appropriate time. They are doors beyond human abilities to open, and even if you succeed in opening a door, you will later find out it was the wrong one for you. Too often, we want something so badly that we will contort and conform to get what we want. But, the doors God has opened for us do not require us to compromise our faith or who we are to fit into it.

The doors that God has placed in front of His children are permanent. They are doors that no human effort can shut. God goes before you and is with you to break down every hindrance in your way of entering those doors. So why should you allow yourself to struggle in vain through your efforts when you have a Father who can do it for you? You must let God do His work in your life. Trying to do it alone only interferes with what He wants to do in your life.

Have you ever wondered why you might feel so drained and stressed over the issues in your lives? The feelings of stress and frustration come from the fact that you are trying to do everything yourself, with your faint strength and limited abilities. You carry so many burdens that are too heavy, trying to open doors too tight. The Egyptians came to a roadblock known as the Red Sea when they were after the Israelites. But God did the impossible through Moses by making way for His people. He opened the Red Sea for His people and closed it so the enemy could not use that same way to get to God's people (See Exodus 14:1–29). When God opens a door for you, it is only for you. It will not be accessible to anyone else but you.

The enemy can't hinder it. He will try in several ways, but he will not prosper. Sometimes, our trials are used as a doorway to God's blessings for us. That is why you must be thankful in all circumstances and embrace every bit of what goes on in your life. You must trust that God will never lead you toward danger. He will never lead you to a roadblock without intending to deliver you from it. Trust that His grace will be enough to see you through wherever He leads you. Stand still, surrender, and allow Him to act. What God gives, no man can provide. You never have to live a life of fear and worry about the enemy closing a door God has opened. Nothing can derail you from God's plans except your doubts and the limitations you place on yourself.

God went beyond for us when He sent His Son to free us from all our iniquities (John 3:16). Now He wants you to live a life of freedom, trusting that He can do the impossible. He wants you to live your life trusting that He will make a way where there seems to be none. He will open that door for you. Trust Him! God does not want you to live in fear, worry, or doubt. He wants you to live in assurance and confidence because of who He is to you—knowing that no one can nullify what He has prepared for you, no one can open what He has closed and close what He has opened. He is the only one with such access to your life. Find rest in this truth today.

The Solution Before the Problem

"Your eyes saw my unformed body; all the days ordained for me were written in your book before one of them came to be" (Psalm 139:16). Often in life, amid our problems, the first reaction is to wonder how and when those problems will cease—how we can free ourselves and what we can do to fix our situation. We then start spinning in circles with confusion, looking to the wrong places and turning to people to help us solve our problems. God invites us to come to Him, and He will exchange our weary and burdened hearts with His rest (Matthew 11:28). You can view your storms as an invitation from God to draw nearer to Him. As you grow in deep connection with God, you will start seeing Him in your situations instead of seeing them for merely what they are.

We dwell on our conditions through fear and allow them to steal our joy. God is never deaf to our cries or blind to what is happening to us. He is the solution. He is the only place we can find the answers to the questions of life. We can't find what we're looking for if we're looking for it in the wrong places. David acknowledged that his help does not come from the mountain but from the one who created those mountains — the God who created the heaven and earth (Psalm 121:1-2). The mountains represent the places we feel we can run to for help. The places in our life, or the people in our life, we know for sure will be able to extend a helping hand. David knew that his help could not come from those places because nobody can do what God can for you. The president can never do for you what God alone can. It is through God that even those reliable places can help. We often search for answers from secondary sources —loved ones, from ungodly resources such as tarot cards, palm readings, fortune telling, and so on, and then wonder why we are not making any progress, why life is still not at its peak.

The answers to all life's questions are found in God's presence. Run to Him. He sees you and knows your future. Spinning in despair will not give you the help you're seeking. Leaning on a loved one will not bring fulfillment as he or she is as limited as you. When it comes to running to those around you for advice, you need to be careful that you are not following what they merely do or say but instead ask the Holy Spirit to help you identify His voice through their words—else you can be misled by the voice of the enemy without even knowing it. Depending on secondary resources always makes things worse than they initially were.

There is no problem in this world that God cannot help us with. He gave us His Word to help and guide us through life. The outcome of our circumstances will be determined by how we apply God's Word in our lives. The problems you face in life are not a surprise to God. God will never forget nor fail you, as a mother who can never forget her nursing child (Isaiah 49:15).

A child of God always stands tall and is never shaken by the storms of life because they know that God is by their side. I have never known a problem to last forever or known God to disappoint those who diligently seek Him. You win over every situation by default. The victory was given to us through the blood of Jesus. Trust God for your calm and guidance in seasons of detours, bumpy roads, and turbulence. Through faith, you are more than a conqueror.

8

THE FULL ARMOUR OF GOD

------- ⟨∞⟩ -------

You can't win the battle of life without
putting on the whole armor of God.

In my tender years, whenever I heard a preacher say to put on the whole armor of God, my mind immediately took me to a person wearing a heavy steel costume with a helmet, like a knight. As funny as that may sound, I may not be the only one who thought like this as a kid. Now that I am a full-grown adult and I've gotten to know God on a deeper level of intimacy, I understand what Paul meant by "put on the whole armor of God" "Be alert and of sober mind. Your enemy, the devil, prowls around like a roaring lion looking for someone to devour" (1 Peter 5:8). Know your enemy, be sober, trust the Holy Spirit, and stay alert to win the battle against the enemy. How? By putting on the whole armor of God. What is the armor of God? His armor is the spiritual weapon you need to clothe yourself daily to stand against the enemy and win your spiritual battles. Your weapons are to be worn daily as protection against any opposition. The Christian walk comes with challenges. It is one we must endure, even if it means suffering as Christ did for us (1 Peter 4:1; 2:21). As the word of God says, the enemy is constantly seeking someone to devour, so in preparation to help us stand against him, Paul advises us to equip ourselves by putting on the whole armor of God (Ephesians 6:10–17).

Put on the belt of truth and keep the truth in your heart; this will help distinguish God's truth from the enemy's lies.

Keep the breastplate of righteousness in place.

Put on the shoes of peace, that peace that transcends all understanding. This peace can come only by dwelling on God's promises.

Always hold up your shield of faith. Faith can move mountains. It is the top tier, the icing on the cake. No evidence is needed through faith because you already know victory is yours through Christ. Through faith, you can stand against the fiery arrows of the devil.

Put Salvation on as your helmet.

Take the sword of the Spirit, which is the Word of God. In the end, Paul tells us to be persistent in prayer—always pray in the Spirit on every occasion and about all that concerns you, never giving up hope (Ephesians 6:18). Prayer is the key that unlocks all doors, especially the impossible ones. *You must learn to use God's armor.* You must always clothe yourself fully and be ready to battle. The biggest mistake believers make when it comes to the battles of life is not knowing their weapons and, worse, not clothing themselves with their armor. We can't go to war without the weapons of our warfare.

Never Cease to Pray

Some time ago, I prayed to God about a desire in my heart and felt His presence. In my moments of silence, He led me to the verse, "Weeping may stay for the night, but rejoicing comes in the morning." (Psalm 30:5), and for some reason, I was drawn to YouTube to listen to one of my favorite preachers, Pastor Steven Furtick of Elevation Church, which I usually did at the time. The message was what I needed to hear. I sat there and listened to God speak to me through this man of God, providing me with the answers to my prayers—this gave me assurance and fullness that only God can provide.

I do not know what you are currently seeking God for, but I do know that God hears us, and not only that, but He also delivers. He is a prayer-answering God. He speaks to us in our stillness. The

Word of God tells us to be still and know He is God (Psalm 46:10). In our stillness, we see His power displayed in our lives. Sometimes, the answer to our prayers may come immediately; other times, God reveals them later.

God answers at the right time—this is a guarantee. How do you hear from God? You must seek Him in the right places. You don't lose your car keys and search for them in the neighbor's dumpster. You look where you believe you will find them. In the same way, you cannot expect to hear your answers from God while you lean on other sources for an answer. Life can be chaotic, and sometimes, we may be staring at the solutions right in the face, but we lose sight of the signs because we are consumed with so much.

God wants you to seek Him in prayer and be encouraged in hope. Do not be discouraged when your prayers seem as if they're never going to be answered because the Word of God assures us that "Everyone who calls on the name of the Lord will be saved" (Romans 10:13). God is the answer to it all, and He's in your corner. Prayer is an essential part of a believer's life.

One of the most essential tools for a healthy relationship is communication. Lack of it can dim any relationship. Communication between you and God should be the most important part of your daily routine. Going days, weeks, months, and even years without communicating with God can keep you dried up, lacking, and fruitless. This means no daily bread and no living water are consumed. When this happens, you start feeling disconnected, not only from reality but also from yourself. Your mind starts playing games on you, and you might sometimes find yourself slipping into depressive moods—because you are now disconnected from the source of life.

God loves it when you come to Him. Speaking with God can be as simple as expressing what is on your mind, as you would with your parents or a friend, and doing so in all authenticity. Jesus said, "When you pray, don't babble on and on as the Gentiles do. They think their prayers are answered merely by repeating their words repeatedly. Don't be like them, for your Father knows what you need even before you ask him!" (Matthew 6:7–8 NLT). We serve a God who is all-knowing, searches our hearts, and knows what troubles us even before we present it to Him. David was aware of this when he said, "You know what I am going to say even before I say it, Lord" (Psalm 139:4 NLT). God answers the desires of our hearts and not merely what comes out of our mouths. One may ask themselves, "Why do we need to pray if God knows what we need?" Should this keep us from communicating with Him? No! Prayer is more than just asking for what we need. It brings us closer to God. It speaks of our dependence on Him. When we pray, we engage in intimate conversation with God.

God loves you so much, and even though He knows what you need and has already granted it, He still loves for you to come to Him. He pursues you, yearns for you, and values your company. So, never think you need to twist and bend your prayers for them to be heard or answered. No matter what is on your mind, God wants to listen to it. This tells Him you are acknowledging that you need Him.

Remember: your purpose for praying is to give glory to God as He already takes care of all that concerns you. Yes, you may ask Him anything, but that should never be your primary purpose for praying. Give Him all the glory in your storms, celebrations, pains, and uncertainties. This means that even though you have a long list of things you would want God to do for you, you choose to appreciate Him with praise and worship to glorify His name for what He is doing in your life.

Communicating with God through prayer is the key to unlocking the impossibilities of life. When you pray to God, you must also yield to His response. It is not always about asking, but listening is the most important part of communication. When you pray and pray and never yield to God's answers, it prompts you to create your own answers, leaving no room for God to respond. Often, we worry too much about our needs amid challenging times.

The Word of God tells us not to worry about anything but instead to tell God what we need and to thank Him for all He has done (Philippians 4:6).

Thanking God in advance for the things we pray for shows the strength of our faith in Him. It shows that we trust His answer for us, no matter what. Through faith, we ask, and through faith we receive. God, in His faithfulness, grants our request according to His will for us. "I will answer them before they even call to me. While they are still talking about their needs, I will go ahead and answer their prayers!" (Isaiah 65:24 NLT).

Prayer is powerful. Prayer unlocks solutions, solves all things, and is the master key. When King Ahab prayed to Baal, his idol, to send down rain, and rain did not fall, Elijah told him it was because he was calling on a statue instead of the one true God. Elijah wanted to prove that God was the only true God. He challenged the Baal prophets to build an altar to their god and would do the same for his God. They placed an offering on each altar. The worshipers of Baal prayed and cried out to their god to send down fire. They shouted and danced around the altar, and nothing happened. Elijah dug a trench around his altar and poured water over everything; he prayed, and suddenly, fire came down from heaven and burned up everything on the altar. When the people saw this, they bowed and worshiped the one true God.

God also caused rain to fall when Elijah called on Him (1 King 18:1–40). This is the power of our God—He is our altar. The God whom our prayers reach and never come back void. We pray to a God who answers and does so by fire! The power of God displayed causes those who do not know Him to want to know Him and those who see His handiwork bow down in worship.

When prayers go up, God works. Prayer cures, and breaks bondages, chains, and generational curses. It heals, gives freedom to the oppressed, and moves mountains – this is why Paul urges us never to stop praying (1 Thessalonians 5:17). In the bible, we read of a man who brought His demon-possessed son to the disciples of

Jesus. They couldn't drive the spirit out of the boy (Mark 9:14–29). The man asked Jesus if He would have mercy on them and help his son. Jesus replied by saying, "Anything is possible if a person believes" (Mark 9:23). After Jesus commanded the spirit to come out of the boy, His disciples wondered and asked Him why they couldn't drive out the spirit, and Jesus said, "This kind can come out only by prayer" (Mark 9:29). Prayer is the master key! It is a powerful armor.

God wants you to carry a heart of gratitude and joy in all circumstances. The overall secret is that you must never stop praying, whether rainy or sunny, facing hardship, or living in luxury.

The Power of Being Persistent

In the gospel of Luke, Jesus told His disciples the parable of the persistent widow as an example to always pray and never give up. The parable was about a judge who neither feared God nor cared about what people thought. A widow kept coming to the judge, begging him to grant her justice against her enemy. The judge refused for some time but finally gave up and granted her request to stop the widow from bothering him. Jesus told this story to His disciples as a reminder that if an unjust judge can grant that woman justice, wouldn't God do the same for His people? The widow had no one to intervene for her. She was helpless, seeking help against her enemy. What saved her was her persistence. She never gave up, no matter how many times the judge refused her (Luke 18:1–8).

God wants us to persist in seeking Him for what He alone can provide. How often have you asked God for something, and when it seemed slow in coming, you gave up trying? James puts it this way: "You do not have because you do not ask God" (James 4:2). This widow in the story could have turned to other means; she could have wallowed in distress or found different ways to get justice, resulting in sin. But she knew of only one way and place to get help, which is what she did despite how long it took to fulfill her plea. Sometimes, it is not about whether God will do it for us but rather about the heart we carry. When we ask, a portal of trust is opened—this alone moves God to work on our behalf.

How persistent are we in our prayers? Do we give up when the answers to our prayers are far from coming, or do we keep praying until our situation changes? Are we the "ask today and expect it tomorrow" type or the "ask and keep asking until you see a change" type? We must have faith in God and be persistent in seeking Him. As David said, "Look to the Lord and His strength; seek His face always" (1 Chronicles 16:11). Jesus told this story about the widow and judge to advise us to keep praying for God's justice.

I can confidently and shamefully confess to being one of those who used to pray for God's justice today and expect to see the world shake the next day. In the Sermon on the Mount, Jesus taught His disciples an effective way of praying—never giving up in asking, seeking, and knocking (Matthew 7:7). Consistency is the key to results. Jesus asked, "Which of you, if your son asks for bread, will give him a stone?" (Matthew 7:9). I must admit that sometimes this verse can be pushed to the back burner, especially when you have been in the waiting season for so long. It can be discouraging when the light at the end of the tunnel seems distant, and hope seems far. But as a believer who has been through the toughest of storms and stood tall in the midst of it, I can attest to the goodness and faithfulness of God. I can say that giving up is not and should never be an option in the life of a believer. I've learned to lean on God and His faithfulness through the storms. He has always been there. He has always made a way. He has always done more and better than I ever ask. By realizing all this, I developed patience and trusted Him to lead.

Never give up if you do not see an answer soon or the skies are not as clear as you hoped. In the story above, Jesus wants us to focus on the fact that He is never deaf to the persistent cries of His people. Even what we may perceive as "no" is an answer—a powerful answer. God is loving; He does not turn His face away from His people. Even if what you ask for is not aligned with His will, He gives an answer that will situate you on the right path. He always gives better and more. A lot of things must be taken into consideration when you ask. Is your heart pure toward what you are asking God for? What are the motives behind your asking? No matter when the answers to your prayers will manifest, you must never fail to recognize God's goodness in your life. You must keep pressing on and remain steadfast.

Changing the Narratives

Yes, God has called us to ask, seek, and knock. At times, we lean more toward asking because of life's challenges. However, seeking and pursuing God is the answer to the manifestation of His glory in our lives. Going through the storms of life can cause us to ask and ask, which is not bad because Jesus tells us to ask, and it shall be given to us (Matthew 7:7).

But when do we stop asking and start praising? Is it after our requests are fulfilled? When do our prayers change from asking to rendering thanksgiving? Changing the narrative pushes out praise, no matter how long your "wants" list is. Changing the narrative focuses on God and who He is, not what He can do for you. It focuses on being grateful even in the unknown.

At a point in my life, I found myself stuck during prayers, in my alone time, with my family, or even during church service, not because I had nothing to say or that I had nothing to ask God. Oh, how I had a long list of wants and desires—complaints, concerns, and numerous whys, whats, and hows. I had a lot on my heart and wanted God to show Himself strong in certain aspects of my life.

But my prayers shifted from my expectations to simply pouring out gratitude in His presence. I realized this was because my trust in Him had heightened. I believed He was working for me even without my having to stress myself. I knew He had already taken care of all that concerned me before I asked (Isaiah 65:24). My faith in God automatically brought me to a place of praise—and this is all I needed Him to know, that no matter what I was going through, I acknowledged Him still as the God of the impossible.

He is the God who sees our hearts and attends to us before we utter a word. I understood that God does not answer our prayers based on our long list. No matter what is on our list, His will always prevail. I understood that His will for my life was more significant than anything I could ever ask, so all I knew to do in those moments was *praise*—this changed how I approached Him. It was no longer about me and what He could do for me. It was more about Him and what He has done—the good and the bad things in my life. God turns around even bad things for our benefit and, ultimately, wants the best for us more than we could want for ourselves. I had the assurance that whatever circumstance I was facing in my life could not be compared to what God had planned for me. He knew everything that flowed from my heart, and though it was hard to pin my words together, He knew what was on my heart. As David said, "The Lord will perfect that which concerns me" (Psalm138:8 NKJV). David believed in God's love for Him and was convinced that God would never forsake the work of His hands—these were words I adopted into my spirit and moved on.

God gifted us with the Holy Spirit, who continually intercedes on our behalf. The apostle Paul reminds us that "the Holy Spirit prays for us with groanings that cannot be expressed in words" (Romans 8:26 NLT). God hears the silent cries of your heart when the storms of life get hard to bear, and you don't have the strength to utter a word or push through. God speaks to our hearts constantly; He hears our silent screams for help, and saying thank you is what makes sense. All the things God has ever done for me and still does for me outweigh everything else, so I was simply in awe of Him in His presence. He has given me everything I need and more.

A heart of praise and worship to God helps us focus on His goodness even amidst the storms. It helps us appreciate what we have while waiting for His plans to manifest. It changes the way we act and responds to our situations. There is more power in showing gratitude than expecting because a heart that shows appreciation receives more.

What is your prayer life looking like currently? Do you find yourself constantly expecting? Don't miss out on what God is doing around you because you are too busy focused on what He can offer you.

9

FAITH ASSURED

⸻ ⟨❦⟩ ⸻

*Your faith in the written word of God plays a vital role
in the manifestation of His glory in your life.*

Faith shows us the reality of what we hope for and the evidence of
things we cannot see" (Hebrews 11:1 NLT). I once read a story about
a house that was caught on fire and a young boy was forced to go up
onto the roof of the house for his dad to save him. His father was on
the ground with his hands stretched out to his son, telling him to
jump, and he would catch him, but the boy could hardly see a thing
due to the smoke—this made him even more afraid to jump. But
his father kept on yelling for him to jump! The boy said he couldn't
see his father, but the father assured him that he could see him and
that this was all that mattered.

This story spoke deeply to me as it gives an accurate picture of
what having faith in God should look like—proceeding even if we
do not see what's ahead and that the only thing that matters is the
fact that the Father's eyes are on us, and He says to trust Him. This is
enough reason for us to take a step into the unknown. Faith in God
means trusting His vision for you, even if you are blind to what's
next. It is natural to hesitate as humans when we do not see what's
on the other side. Still, God wants you to surrender because He has
already seen the other side and knows what you are heading toward.

You will not be able to achieve many things in your life if your
decision to proceed is always based on your current circumstances
or on what you do not see. Faith tells us to move, to do our part,
and trust God to do His. Lack of faith in Him makes us refrain due

to fear of what might happen to us if we proceed; it makes us doubt God's power. God wants you to depend on Him, so you must let go of anything that holds you back, let yourself go, and fall into His arms, believing that He will catch you. Your confidence should not depend on how sturdy you are when walking but on knowing that when you trip, you have a God behind you who will catch you from falling.

When you ask God for things, and He seems to delay, discouragement is the first emotion that kicks in. You wait and wait, and nothing happens. This is the period in our lives when we start pacing, wondering whether there is a God who sees us. But the good news is that He does, and having that faith in Him means depending on His strength through the tough times; otherwise, you will never be able to take the first step when the road is steep and your vision is hazy. The only way you will see a possibility is by waiting for a clear path before taking a step, which may never come because faith works only through the unknown, through believing, not by seeing. It is within our season of lack that God can change our story. This season serves a purpose: it reveals our mustard seed of faith and manifests God's glory.

Through faith, we can have assurance and encouragement in the Word of God. Faith comes by knowing God through His Word (Romans 10:17). Sometimes, we find it hard to stand in faith because we do not know God's Word. We hear it, toss it aside, and allow the teachings to fade. The knowledge of God has not been abiding in us. The faith hall of fame found in the book of Hebrews shows us how God's people navigated through life as they depended on their faith in Him. It was by faith Abraham listened to God and went to another land given to him as his inheritance and continued living there by faith (Hebrews 11: 8–9). Abraham could have doubted, refused, and stayed back because packing up and leaving one's place of comfort to go to another place is a bit tough to do. Still, He went knowing God, who led him there, would also provide for his every need. Through his faith in God, Abraham offered Isaac as a sacrifice

(Hebrews 11:17). James reminded us of this when he said that we are shown to be right with God by what we do, not by faith alone (James 2:24).

Faith in God means nothing if we do not prove it through our works. James instructs us that our faith and actions must work together, reminding us of the story of Abraham giving Isaac as a sacrifice, insisting that faith without work is useless (James 2:17). Faith in God should not be based only on what we say and proclaim with our mouths but also on what we do. By faith, Sarah was able to have a child even in her old age (Hebrews 11:11). It was by faith that Moses's parents hid him for three months when he was born. Through his faith, he did not want to be identified as the pharaoh's son when he grew up (Hebrews 11:23–24). The Israelites crossed the Red Sea by faith as if they were on dry land (Hebrews 11:29). Throughout the book of Hebrews, we see people of God acting based on their faith in God, and none of them were ever disappointed by Him.

Like these people, you must also have faith and believe that no matter what you go through, no matter what concerns you, God has already taken care of it before you face it. He always has our best interests at heart. Your faith shouldn't be based on what God can do for you in a moment but on who He is and what He did for you on the cross. If you trust God to come through for you, reflecting on His Son, Jesus Christ will keep you going. The results are often better than expected.

The Word of God tells us that without faith, it is impossible to please God (Hebrews 11:6). You cannot go to God without believing that He exists and sent His Son to die for your sins. You cannot go to God without believing that He will reward you for sincerely seeking Him. It is impossible to get close to God without having faith in Him. Faith in God drives out our fears. Faith drives out worry, stress, discontentment, and so on. Faith turns our "what ifs" into "whens." Faith tells us that God has already been there and figured it out, telling us to move. God knows what He is doing in your life.

He is not finished writing your story. James tells us to "count it all as joy when we face trials of all kinds" (James 1:2 NLT). As you go through life and face trials of all kinds, your faith in Christ will help you stand still amid any storm. As time passes, your endurance skill will develop to great heights, whereby when you face storms, you can have control no matter how hard the wind blows. The funny thing about putting your faith in someone is that you make moves blindly, trusting the person to be your eyes, and in the case of believers, we are to trust God as our eyes and ears. Having sets of eyes doesn't mean we can see through the unknown or hear everything said about us. It doesn't mean that we can easily see past the ordinary. That is where God comes in. Suppose we can trust our loved ones, a bus driver, a pilot, a taxi driver, or an Uber driver, to get us to our destination safely; why can't we trust the one who gave His Son as a sacrifice for us? I can guarantee you that He is the one who can get you to your destination safely, even with the bumps and storms.

The only way through life is by continuously taking leaps of faith. So when you find yourself faltering in your faith, the only way to keep sturdy is by keeping your focus on the cross and what it represents. After we've been tested and tried and never given up, just like Job, we will come out as pure as gold (Job 23:20).

One of my favorite miracles performed by Jesus was the woman with blood issues who had been bleeding for twelve years (Luke 8:43–48). I love this miracle because it proves God's power and demonstrates what having faith in Him can do. It is through your mustard seed of faith that your mountains move. I can relate with this woman in so many ways, as sometimes all I have is my faith in the one and only true God, convinced that no matter what I'm facing, no matter what storms are in my way, through my faith in Him those storms will be calmed. Her story tells us that no matter how long it takes for a promise to be fulfilled, we can hold on to hope, trusting that there will come a day when we get to hold on to the hem of His garment. When our faith is tested, we grow through it if we endure and never give up. We practice endurance when we have fully mastered the act of bearing through the worst; afterward, we will be perfect, needing nothing (James 1:4). You may be tired, discouraged, and frustrated. But I encourage you to stand tall and keep pushing ahead in faith.

Facing Your Giants

In the story of David defeating Goliath, the Word of God says, "David ran quickly toward the battle line to meet him" (1 Samuel 17:48). Scripture tells us that for forty days, Goliath placed fear in the hearts of the Israelites, so much so that when the Israelites heard that the Philistines wanted to fight them, they were consumed with fear. As soon as they saw him, they began to run in fright. They said, "Have you seen the giant? He comes out daily to defy Israel" (1 Samuel 17: 25 NLT).

The storms of life will threaten us, make us feel fear, and make us anxious about facing situations alone. But as a believer in Christ, I realize that none of those feelings are valid. Our problems are not greater than the power that lives inside us. The Spirit of God resides inside us, meaning He is always with us. You are walking in power, and if you lack this knowledge, it makes sense that you will shake in fear, giving that power right into the hands of the enemy. And as the enemy realizes that you are not aware of the power you carry, he will easily make a move and lie to you, manipulating you to believe so many things that are not true. When you do not know the power you possess as a child of God, it tells the enemy that you don't know who you are.

Have you ever heard of identity theft, how people steal the identity of others and use their names and information to commit fraud? As a child of God, His Spirit lives inside you; because this is so, *you are power.* Now, the enemy we all know comes to steal, so if you don't know your power, the enemy will steal it and destroy you.

But glory be to God for the mercy He shows us day and night. Because of His compassion and faithfulness, the enemy can never steal the one thing that will always give us victory: our identity as children of God. When we lack the understanding of the power we carry, the Spirit of God is constantly around to bring to our remembrance the power He has given us to fight, command, rebuke, overturn, and declare. The Word of God tells us that upon hearing about the battle, David said to King Saul, "Don't worry about this Philistine . . . I'll go fight him!" and Saul told him, "Don't be ridiculous! There's no way you can fight this Philistine and possibly win! You're only a boy, and he's been a man of war since his youth" (See 1 Samuel 17:32–33 NLT).

This is precisely what we hear when facing problems: what Saul said to David: How can you *win?*—you know, that voice of deception that tells us that we are weak, powerless, and that there is no way we can face our giants. That hopeless voice makes us feel there is no hope for us.

But I want to encourage you today that all the power required to stand against your giants is within you. You have all it takes to overcome and are more than a conqueror. God wants us to react to our issues as David did. He wants us to be fearless and face our problems boldly, knowing He is never far from us. David was not afraid. He knew that God was the one who would give him the strength to fight. The Word of God tells us that on the day of the battle, David "quickly ran out to meet him" (1 Samuel 17:48 NLT). With no fear at all, he ran. He took down the problem that had haunted the Israelites for forty days.

God has not called us to live in fear. He has not given us that spirit. Instead, He has filled us with a power that defeated death, a power that set the captives free, a power that causes the lame to walk and the blind to see—this is the power that walks with you. God has not called us to hold back. He has not called us to fear the giants who stare us right in the face. We've been called to live purposefully through the resurrection power!

The enemy will always manipulate you. He will always make you think your giants are too huge to defeat. He will always deceive you into running away from the things that can bring you breakthroughs and victory. David won the battle with what he had had with him all his life —a stone and slingshot. As a Christian, you cannot utilize what you do not know you have. You can't face your battles under the mighty power of God if you do not see that you have access to it. The Spirit of God that is made perfect in you gives you the strength to go on, and David knew this secret. God had given him the power and authority over the enemy. David said to Goliath, "You come to me with sword, spear, and javelin, but I come to you in the name of the Lord of Heaven's Armies—the God of the armies of Israel, whom you have defied" (1 Samuel 17:45 NLT). This means the Lord's name is a weapon right at your fingertip. The enemy comes with his many arrows; all you must do is lift your voice and speak in the name of the Lord. Remember that you are in authority here. Don't beg the enemy to leave you—you *command* him to leave.

"This is the word of the Lord to Zerubbabel: 'Not by might nor by power, but by my Spirit,' says the Lord Almighty" Zechariah 4:6). What giants are you currently facing today? What problem is standing in the way of your breakthrough? I encourage you to break through, run through it, and take on your victory. I have always imagined storms in my life as a dark room, and on the other side of the room, there is a bright light—and the only way for me to get to the light is by walking through that dark room. Many of us are camped outside that dark room, afraid to walk through it because of what we may encounter. We miss a lot in life because we have allowed fear to hold us back. But I want you to know that the only way to a breakthrough is to face the things you allow to limit you. God walks with you, so walk boldly and face your giants with the courage to get to that place of light.

John wrote, "But you belong to God, my dear children. You have already won a victory over those people because the Spirit who lives in you is greater than the spirit who lives in the world" (1 John

4:4 NLT). When John said "those people," he was referring to the enemy (the antichrist). Your problems either push you toward God to realize His power in you or push you away from God, lacking the knowledge of that power. God wants us to draw near Him, especially during our most challenging times. Stand firm in the position given to you through the blood of Jesus. God can use any battle you face for your good. God has given you everything you need to face your giants with boldness and faith. Walking in faith is vital in facing the giants in front of us.

When faced with battles, another secret to victory is for you to realize the power within you and to have faith in that power. Faith believes in the mighty power of God. When you don't see how situations will turn around or how things will work out, faith reminds you of it. Learn to walk in victory because it already belongs to you. Jesus died, fought your greatest battle, and was resurrected with your victory—your freedom. Decide whether you want to be a David when you face the battles of life or to be the Israelites who ran away in fear when they saw the Philistine giant. Whatever giants haunt you from your past, whatever giants you face in the present, know that your victory is determined not by the magnitude of your giants but by the magnitude of our God.

Rise and Shine

In preparation for delivering the Israelites from Egypt, God showed Moses the signs to use so that the Egyptians would believe that God had indeed sent him (Exodus 4:5). Moses pleaded with the Lord, questioning his ability to complete the task. He told the Lord he was not good with words. "Then the Lord asked Moses, 'Who makes a person's mouth? Who decides whether people speak or do not speak, hear or do not hear, see or do not see? Is it not I, the Lord?'" (Exodus 4:11 NLT). And when he kept pleading, the Lord sent Aaron, his brother, to be his spokesperson and assure their safety. We will face situations in which we doubt ourselves and our abilities. But bear in mind that the Lord knows us better than we know ourselves, and when He places a task in front of us, He believes we can handle and complete that task.

Never underestimate yourself and what God can do through you. We will never face a challenge that God has not prepared us for. Where we are blind, He will be our eyes. Where we can't speak or express ourselves as we ought to, He will be our voice and ears. Our insecurities sometimes make us step back from what God is counting on us to accomplish as we worry about the failures we could face, about who would approve and who would not. We sabotage our calling and dreams, all in the name of fear!

Believe in the Lord. He will never lead you on a route that He knows is dangerous for you. He gives you the strength to rise beyond defeat. When there comes a moment in life where your fears draw you back, God will always appoint the help you need in moving forward, help to remind you of who you are and the power you possess as His child. Our God is a God who never puts tasks before us and leaves us to figure it all out ourselves.

In Moses's case, the Lord appointed Aaron as a helper—not a replacement. We each have a destiny that can never be replaced unless we willingly walk away and take our path. Just like Aaron, we may also be used by God as an instrument of help in another person's journey to fulfill their calling. Whatever your calling may be, whatever task God trusts in your hands to accomplish, rise confidently, start walking, and get it done. No matter where you are in life, feeling as if you are stuck because you do not have the potential or the resources to move forward, know that God has you covered. He will provide for you, your Aaron.

Going in a different direction will destroy you, as Jesus is the only way to true fulfillment. God is patient in our self-discovery, but do not take His patience for granted. Rise to the occasion and do your part, knowing He is with you all the way through. Arise and let your light shine!

10

FIX YOUR EYES ON JESUS

‹❈›

*One thing will always remain—we are
blessed, even in the worst of storms.*

"Immediately Jesus reached out his hand and caught Him. 'You of little faith,' he said, 'why did you doubt?'" (Matthew 14:31). One of the greatest lessons we must learn in life is what to do when going through life's greatest storms. The Word of God teaches us to fix our eyes on Jesus, who is the author and the perfecter of our faith (Hebrews 12:2). The story of Peter walking on water, narrated in Matthew 14:22–33, is a fitting example of what happens when we turn our eyes away from God during the storms of life. The Word of God tells us that as Peter saw Jesus walking on water, he got out of his boat and stepped on the water toward Jesus, but when he saw the wind and waves, he got distracted. He was afraid and took his eyes off Jesus, and this caused him to sink. Then he cried out to God for help. Immediately, Jesus reached out, caught him, and said, "You of little faith, why did you doubt?" (Matthew 14:31).

I want to highlight the word *immediately*. Notice how the Word of God says that Jesus immediately reached out to Peter and caught him. In this story, we were not told how close Jesus was to him, but as Peter cried out to Him, Jesus immediately caught him. The story does not state that Jesus rushed from where He was to come to Peter's aide but says *immediately* He reached out to him. This assures us that no matter how distant we may feel God is in times of storms, He is always next to us.

When you find yourself sinking, and you feel as if no one is around to pull you back up from falling, remember that Jesus was right there and immediately reached out to Peter. He is right there, ready to reach and pull you out.

In Matthew 14:29, notice how the Word of God says that Peter got out of the boat, walked on the water, and walked toward Jesus. This means Peter was walking on water perfectly fine until He got distracted and afraid by the wind. See—just like Peter, it's easy for us to be strong in our faith when nothing terrible is happening around us. But faith in God means you keep going no matter the obstacles, even through the storms. It means you will not allow yourself to sink but keep your eyes solely on God, graced and rested in Him. It means to be unbothered by what is in front of you. You believe God can make it all better when you call on Him for help.

He is never far away and will always be there to catch you. When we focus on God, all other things align perfectly in place. Taking your eyes off Him will lead you only to waiver in your faith. Getting wrapped up in the giant in front of you will place fear and anxiety in you. You must know that the God we serve —the God of Abraham, Isaac, and Jacob, the one who is always on your side and in your boat, can do more than calm the storms in your life—if only you remember to invite and acknowledge Him in all aspects of your life. Challenge yourself today to look forward directly at Him amidst your storms. Block out all the distractions around you and look directly at God as He reaches for your hand through the storms.

Take Courage. Don't Be Afraid!

When you read the three versions of "Jesus walks on water" told in the gospels of Matthew, Mark, and John (Matthew:14:22–36; Mark 6:45–56; John 6:16–24), one thing you will find that is constant and also stands out in each of their stories is Jesus words "Take courage. It is I. Don't be afraid." This life can offer us problems we never see coming. Yes, we may go through different predicaments in life. Though we may have a different narrative in life, we all have something in common—a friend in Jesus, a friend we can always depend on no matter the season.

In the storms of life, the Word of God is meant to give us the courage and boldness required to stand still. God's Word assures us that He is with us no matter what we go through. David referenced it so well in Psalm 121 when he said the Lord who watches over His children, the one who neither sleeps nor slumbers, who will never allow your foot to slip, because He watches over you and will not allow any harm to come to you. You are God's number-one priority—always remember that. He calls you by name, and safety is a guarantee where you are concerned. God will satisfy your deepest thirst when you pass through the dry land. You will not be overwhelmed with more than you can handle when you go through the rivers. The fires of life will not consume you. God promises to be with you as you go through flames (Isaiah 43:1–2). You will go through many storms in life, but rest assured God will go through them with you. Your faith in Him should not depend on Him taking all your problems away but on knowing that even in the storms, your safety is assured and the strength to endure is promised (2 Corinthians 12:10).

Your circumstances may cause you to feel worn out and alone. But bear in mind that no one knows you as well as God does, and no one loves you as much as He does. God knows your heart and will never abandon the work of His hands. People may remember you through the lens of negativity and cast stones at you; your problems may leave you questioning your strength and capabilities—but the presence of God is there to uplift you, giving you the answers and the fulfillment you need.

God never uttered words about us having to go through the fires of life alone. He never promised we would not hit rock bottom, but as He promised Paul, His grace is sufficient (2 Corinthians 12:9). The same promise stands for you, and that is all you need—the grace to pull through. There is nothing to worry about, as God is a refuge to all who seek safety in Him. No matter how hard the wind blows, never let go of God's hands; never take your eyes off Him. We serve a God who takes the worst things in life and turns them around in our favor (Romans 8:28). Everything in your life passes by Him first.

Trust that He has your best interests at heart. God has your back, no matter how low you may feel. He is an ever-present help in times of trouble (Psalm 46:1). Never forget all the good things He has done for you. Take courage! Don't be afraid. You are not alone!

The Vine and the Branches

To say that you can live without Jesus Christ is like saying that you can live without air. Jesus makes it clear in His Word to remain in Him so He can remain in us. The blood of Jesus has cleansed us, and to maintain purity and be fruitful in life, we must remain in Him. We cannot live this life without Christ. We cannot be fruitful without Him. He is the vine, God is the gardener, and we are the branches.

You cannot bear fruit in your own will and strength (John 15:1–17); you would wither away. Jesus Christ made it clear that we can do nothing apart from Him (John 15:5). The only way for God's people to live a life of light and acquire all the things God has prepared for them is to dwell in Him and stay connected to Him. Life can sometimes shift us, but remaining in Christ means standing on a firm foundation. It means having access to a supernatural strength when our strength fails us.

The Spirit of God gives us the strength to endure life's hardships and the motivation to wake up each morning with zeal. God is the source of life; He created us in His image, then breathed life into us (Genesis 2:7), meaning our mortal bodies can not survive outside Him. Disconnecting from Him will cut off the oxygen He breathed in you, and you may feel suffocated by the affairs of life, alive but not living. Life has no meaning without God. Life has no form without God. There is only one true God, and His name is Yahweh! No other one can do what He does; no one or nothing else can give us security. He is the air we breathe, the bread of life. In Him, we live, move, and exist (Acts 17:28). Our story can never be written without the author of life.

Without God, we have no peace amidst the storm; without Him, there will be no hope for tomorrow. Think of a woman's body and how it can carry a child for nine months—the labor process and all that is made possible through God's Holy Spirit. No mind can fathom the ways of God or what He can do. All that exists comes from Him and survives through Him for His glory. Only by His power are all things made possible (Romans 11:34–36).

Remaining in Christ opens us up to experience the love of God —the love that carries us through life, both in our happy times and especially when we go through the storms of life. Because of His love for us, we can endure through perseverance. Cling to the fact that you are breathing today only because you have the breath of God flowing through your veins, filling you with new life each day. Your life and your sanity depend on your staying rooted in Him. We can be here today and gone tomorrow, but by the grace of God, you are here today reading this book—this means God is not through with you. This means He has so many things in store for you; the only way to discover that is to walk in partnership with Him, abiding in Him. You may have questions right now and wondering where the answers will come from—Jesus Christ is inviting you today to draw near to Him and rest in Him. What matters is how you allow Him to soak your life with His unconditional love and presence. You must abide in Him, trusting Him with every aspect of your being. You must depend on Him as a child depends on their parents and allow Him to have His way in your life.

The God Who Always Intervenes

One Sunday during service, my pastor, Phil Kniesel, said something that struck a chord: "When we get to heaven, our biggest miracle stories will be the incidents that were prevented from ever happening." We often see and recognize only the obvious things, but no one considers what God does for us in the background. It is easy for us to be grateful for the things visible to the eyes, like family, food, life, job, business, friends, and so on—but what about the things no one sees? What about the accident the enemy planned for you, but God caused a delay that prevented that accident from happening?

It's easy for us to go about our daily lives and not be grateful for certain things because we do not see the details. For example, in some cases, it's easier to say thank you to someone who hands over a gift to you than to say thank you to the person who provided the money to purchase that gift—because all you see is the person who gave you the gift and not the one who toiled to provide the funds for buying that gift.

God does so much for us, and we have much to be thankful for. Never once in life think that God does not come to your rescue. There has never been a day that He has not fought for you. At the right time, He sent His son to redeem you from your sins (Galatians 4:4-5). This is something you never worked for or did not deserve—but He did it anyway. Though your circumstances may sometimes make you think that you are alone and doing hardship by your strength, God is always proven faithful in the lives of His children. He has proven to be the Father we can always turn to and count on. He always sends us the necessary help at the right time.

We never see what He does for us daily, but there are so many dangers He has prevented us from. Because we never witnessed them, we go about our lives as if nothing happened. These are just some of the little blessings we overlook each day. The number of things He has done for us unknowingly can never be compared to the obvious ones we witness daily.

Be grateful always in every circumstance. Faith in Him doesn't mean we need to see to believe; instead, it means we need to believe *before* we see (Hebrews 11:1). No matter how difficult your current situation is, never for a minute doubt God, His endless love for you, and whether He has your back. Our God never sleeps or slumbers (Psalm 121:4). He never loses track of those who trust Him. We must never forget that the best times in life are not permanent, nor are our worst times. When Job's wife suggested that he curse God and be free, he said she was foolish and that hardship is also a blessing from God. We must be ready to accept them as they come (Job 2:10). We must realize that God uses even the bad times to pivot us into new dimensions. I encourage you never to question Him when the wind blows you off the edge of the cliff because God will never watch you fall to ruin. His goal is to advertise your life for the world to see how we all need the hope found in Christ.

I challenge you today to count your blessings and be grateful to God for everything He has done for you, knowingly and unknowingly. Be thankful even when life gives you no reason to keep going. Rest assured that God will always bring honor and glory to His name through your storms. You are protected and loved. God's works and love shown in the lives of His people throughout the Bible long ago can also be shown in your life if you trust Him.

11

PLANTING ON FERTILE LAND

━━━━━━━━━━━━━━ ⚬⚭⚬ ━━━━━━━━━━━━━━

Understanding and knowledge are given to those
who listen to the teachings of God.

In the gospel, according to Matthew, Jesus told many stories in parables. I want us to focus on the Parable of the Sower (Matthew 13:1–58). He said, "A farmer went out to plant some seeds, and as he scattered them across the field, some fell on a *footpath,* and the birds came and ate them" (Matthew 13:3–4). Some fell on *rocky* places where it did not have much soil. It sprang up quickly because the soil was shallow. But the plants were scorched when the sun rose and withered because they had no root (Matthew 13:5–6). "Other seed fell among *thorns,* which grew up and choked the plants" (Matthew 13:7). Last, other seeds fell on *fertile soil,* where it produced a crop that was hundred, sixty, or thirty times what was sown. Jesus then concluded the story by saying, "Whoever has ears, let him hear" (Matthew 13:8–9).

He explains that the seeds that fell on a footpath are like people who hear the Word of God and do not understand it; the enemy comes and snatches away what was sown in their hearts. The seeds that fell on rocky places are like people who hear the Word of God and immediately receive it with joy, but because they don't have deep roots, God's Word does not last within their hearts. It fades when trouble arises or they are persecuted for believing the Word of God. The seeds that fell among the thorns are like people who hear the Word of God, but no fruit is produced because the message is crowded by the worries of life and the lure of wealth. The seeds that fell on the good soil represents people who truly hear and understand the Word of God and produce a harvest of even a hundred times as much as has been planted (Matthew 13:19–23) —These people are those who reach out to many other people to make a difference in their lives from the crops they harvest through the Word of God.

Which of these seeds are you? Are you one to hear the Word of God and forget its contents the minute life gets out of control? Or one who practices what is preached regardless of hardship? God wants us to plant on fertile land. He wants us to be both hearers and doers of His word, to live our lives free of what the world offers, and to engage ourselves in what He offers. Stress kicks in when we try so hard to make happen the things only God can. Though it is human nature to always try to fix things, we must learn to let go and remember God's promises in the storms of life—because His promises help us to look ahead with hope.

Our lives are the only daily bread many will consume, exposing them to the source of life through how we live and apply the Word. What example are we setting for those who have not tasted the goodness and love of Christ? Those who are lost and need a push in the right direction? What are we telling the world about Christ through how we handle our storms? As believers, we should have a different attitude through life's tough times because of whom we represent. Sometimes, we allow the worries of life to get in the way of our positive impact on others. Strive each day to live out the Word of God and be a blessing to those who look up to you along the way. I trained myself to do this during life's storms, to get to a point where it's no longer about how I was feeling but what was required of me even in my downtime. God pulled me so close and reminded me of who I was, especially amidst the storms of life.

I don't know if it's a plan from God, but whenever I am emotionally down, I am approached by many going through similar issues as they seek my help. I realized that the more I allow God to speak through me to these people, the more I uncover the solution to my own problem. This is why we can't let the Word of God die out in us but must cultivate it and pass it on to others. In the past, when life's boat rocked and the wind became heavy, I usually looked to the wrong foundation. I looked to people to offer me a heaven's gate—a way out of my predicaments, sowing on the wrong foundation. It may take many trials, disappointments, and betrayals to get our heads straight in the right direction —the direction to seek and yearn more for who God is and allow His Word to take root in our lives.

I was one of those who planted their seeds on a rocky path. As soon as life got a bit chaotic, I forgot I had a mighty God behind me, beside me, and in front of me. I ignored His promises and started playing the "what-if" scenarios in my mind. When we take in the Word of God and allow it to penetrate our being, it takes root in our lives, becoming a saving grace for ourselves, those around us, and those we meet. We not only have rich soil in our yard, but we also bear rich fruit, putting us in a position to bless others —This is real wealth; this is what success looks like—not that we have so much money to give, but instead, we become so rich in Christ that we begin sharing His love and speaking about His promises with others.

We can begin to sow in rich soil only when we've identified life's solid foundation—a foundation that cannot be shaken. May God help you be attentive to His Word, and may He give you the strength to withstand and not be distracted by the worries of life. May His Word become the only firm and concrete foundation you stand on amidst the greatest battles in your life.

He Calls Not the Righteous

Throughout the Bible are many stories of God using ordinary people to accomplish His work —people the world shames as sinners or not worthy of being in the presence of God or in the presence of those who consider themselves more righteous. The Word of God tells us that God chooses the foolish things of the world to confound the wise and the weak things of the world to confound the things which are mighty (1 Corinthians 1:27).

Take Zacchaeus, for instance. Of all people, God chose him, a tax collector, to stay at his house. People were displeased and pointed at the fact that Jesus chose to be a guest at a notorious sinner's home (Luke 19:1–10). My favorite part was when Jesus said to him, "Today salvation has come to this house, because this man, too, is a son of Abraham. For the Son of Man came to seek and to save the lost" (Luke 19:9–10). Saul was not so great either; he was one of the most awful persons ever to rule the kingdom of Israel. He did terrible things; he pursued and tried to kill David (1 Samuel 19:1–24). Peter denied Jesus three times, and Jesus knew that from the very beginning before He called him to be one of His disciples, but he was the one God appointed to preach on the day of Pentecost (Luke 22:54–62; Acts 2:14–17). You see, God sees you through the blood of Jesus. He sees you through His plans and purpose for you—the plans He had mapped out before He formed you in your mother's womb. When He looks at you, He sees the vessel He has created, not what the world has inflicted on you or made you out to be. You are a child of the King of kings (Galatians 3:26). You are a new creation through Christ (2 Corinthians 5:17). You are a friend of God (John 15:15). You are God's workmanship made in His image (Ephesians 2:10). The Spirit of God who raised Jesus from the dead lives in you (1 Corinthians 6:19). You are forgiven (1 John 1:9). You are the salt of the earth (Matthew 5:13). And last but not least, you are loved (Romans 5:8).

While people, including you, point and dwell on your flaws, God makes plans based on who He has called you to be. No one can nullify the plans of God in your life, but the greatest mistake is to walk away from His plans—this means you're choosing to give up on yourself. The Word of God tells us that if we claim to be without sin, we only deceive ourselves, and the truth is not in us. If we confess our sins, He will forgive us and purify us from all unrighteousness (1 John 1:8–9). God wants you to come to Him, even in your vulnerability. Being perfect in your own eyes means you do not need God, who is perfect. It refutes the actions Jesus took on the cross for you. The whole reason Jesus Christ came down to earth was that we are not perfect. God knows this about each one of us. Christ came for you and me. Remember that your imperfections do not keep you from God's grace because everything God does for us, to us, and through us is never based on our perfect performances but simply on who He is as God!

Never think you are disqualified from being called and used by God because of your sins and past mistakes. When the Pharisees saw Jesus eating with tax collectors and sinners at Levi's house, they wondered why Jesus ate with sinners, but Jesus said, "It is not the healthy who need a doctor, but the sick. I have not come to call the righteous, but sinners" (Mark 2:17). Seeing ourselves as perfect and of no sin prevents God from perfecting us for His glory. It prevents Him from working on us and through us. He did not come to call Himself. He came to call us to Himself; all of us have fallen short of the glory of God (Romans 3:23).

Never think or utter words such as "I am undeserving of God's love." The truth is that Christ, knowing that, accepted you still and made you worthy. Do not think that you are undeserving of His call. He wants you and is most interested in you, as broken and vulnerable as you may be. Remember what Christ did for you in the past? He did it so you can be pure and whole in His sight. Start living your life by acknowledging His unconditional act of love for you. Open your heart and arms to His calling. You are chosen and called, and I want to encourage you today to accept that and live your life based on that. Mentally prepare yourself for whatever God has planned for you. Never deny your calling or who you are in Christ. Let go of the things holding you back and live through the hope that God is faithful and that His love for you is eternal.

Gaining an Increase through the Everlasting Love of God

When you think of an increase, what comes to mind? I am sure your mind takes you to material gains. The first increase we gained as children of God was when Jesus came to die for us. We were nothing, but He made us something. Scripture says, "When we were utterly helpless, Christ came at just the right time and died for us sinners" (Romans 5:6 NLT). The New International Version says, "when we were still powerless," and the English Standard Version says, "while we were still weak."

The death of Christ gained us an increase. We were "weak," "powerless," and "helpless." We were sinful and had nothing, but God gave us an increase by sending His only Son in exchange for our weakness. We gained strength, forgiveness, redemption, and a relationship with God, and He wants us to achieve more in the land of the living; that is why Paul advises us to seek God first, and He will give us everything else that we need (Matthew 6:33) because the real increase comes from dwelling in the presence of God first! The real increase comes from accepting His ultimate act of love to you through the blood of Jesus.

Today, God wants to remind you that He loves you with everlasting love. But the thing is, it's not about how much He loves us because He has proven His love for us countless times, and as Paul said, "Neither death nor life, neither angels nor demons, neither the present nor the future, nor any powers, neither height nor depth nor anything else in all creation, will be able to separate us from the love of God that is in Christ Jesus our Lord" (Romans 8:38–39).

The thing is, how does that look on our part? How are we also proving our love for God? Are we drifting from Him by the day, or are we drawing near? Living a life of increase is not only about having a massive mansion with cars parked in front of it. I mean, that is a beautiful vision—a luxurious life. But living a life of increase as a believer is also about gaining the wisdom of God, about living in the fulness of what God has called you to do, about making an impact in the lives of people, and proclaiming the love of God throughout nations—these are also considered as a life of increase. I believe this is far from what we see when we think about gaining an increase in our lives.

Being close to God is the increase He wants for you because you will gain all other things through it. Scripture tells us that Hagar fled to the desert after being treated harshly by Sarah. The Word of God says, "Hagar used another name to refer to the Lord, who had spoken to her. She said, "You are the God who sees me." She also said, "Have I truly seen the One who sees me?" (Genesis 16:13 NLT).

Have you also asked yourself if the God who appears to you and pursues you day and night, the God who fights for you daily through the blood of Jesus, if you've truly seen Him? Have you wondered if you are taking every measure to see Him, dwell in Him, and camp in His presence? Have you tried to know the one who sees and watches over you? The love of God is certain, but human love wavers, so even when things are not going well for you, do you still make it a point to be in His presence, to seek Him, to speak to Him? Or, because of the distractions of life, are you unaware of even times when He has revealed Himself to you? Have you seen the one who sees you?

Do you know the secret of seeing the one who sees you? The key is to seek Him in solitude by stepping away from the world and zooming in on His voice. Hagar did not see the one who sees her in a busy place but in the desert—an abandoned and neglected place without distractions. This is where you can see and hear the one who sees and watches over you—in the wilderness, in solitude. How can we see the love of God displayed in our lives if we're too busy and too consumed by the movements of life? The love of God is so powerful that even in busy places and in the mess of life when you call on Him, He hears. But because we are so limited as humans, we have to get to a quiet place to see and hear the one who sees us, and this is the part we have to play. We must make it a point to get to the quiet place to be with God. What steps are you taking to prove your love for God?

My phone was in my hand some time ago, and the battery was at four percent. A friend messaged me, and I realized the battery was on low percentage and needed to be charged. I was lazy about getting the charger, so I sat still using the phone and waited until it was one percent, then decided to run upstairs to get it. I ran to get my charger because I'm not too fond of it when my phone dies, and I must wait for it to restart—it's like starting all over again.

The moral of the story is that some of us wait until our batteries run out before we run to God. We wait until life has knocked us down and out; then, we suddenly know who God is and then run to Him for a recharge. If that is how God displays His love for us, would we be where we are today? God desires that we draw near to him no matter our state. His desire is for us to overflow, to be overcharged, and not to sit there and do nothing; then, when life leaves us dry, we either blame Him for our problems or suddenly know who He is. As Paul said, "Since he did not spare even his own Son but gave him up for us all, won't he also give us everything else?" (Romans 8:32 NLT).

Why wait until the worst happens before you know to run to God? He loves you, and nothing can separate you from Him. He wants you to seek Him first above anything else in this world, pursue Him, and He promises to give you everything else you need.

God never gives up on us, and He pursues us when we stray until we return to Him, but can we say the same for ourselves when things are going backward for us? Can we stay faithful? Can we stick by Him and trust that He will never fail us, no matter the circumstances? Do you know why most people are lost in the world, and some even commit suicide? Though many battles with ailments beyond their control, many are lost because they never got to experience this love of God. They never had the opportunity to be told about this everlasting love. When they can't get it in the world or the material things, the enemy gets in and causes them to believe they will only be free if they end their lives before their time.

But for you today, God wants you to know of His love. He wants to remind you of this love that should stand as a pillar in your life so that you can also evangelize that love to the world. He reminds you of His love every day, and if you could get to that place of silence, you would see His presence around you. What increase are you chasing after—an increase in what the world offers or an increase in the kingdom of God? One of our mistakes in life is our drive to chase after temporary love when we have God, who gives us love unconditionally at no cost. He instead paid the cost for you through His Son, Christ Jesus. His desire for you is to walk hand in hand with Him as He sparks up the light within you.

Why are you rejecting Him and choosing to carry all the burdens of life on your shoulders? Why are you choosing to figure out everything on your own? Why are you trying so hard to gain the love and acknowledgment of others? Sometimes, we put all our hopes in empty places, chasing after what only God can offer us, forgetting that we hold a prominent position in the kingdom of God. The Word of God says you are a chosen people. You are royal priests. You are a holy nation. You are God's possession (1 Peter 2: 9). Because of this goodness and love shown to us, we can also pass it on to others—not so that people will recognize us but so they will recognize the goodness and love of God through us. He called you out of the darkness into His light, a light meant to illuminate God's love in us. God's love—

- Keeps us going in times when we feel stuck.
- Gives us warmth and comfort.
- Assures us that we do not have to fear uncertainties.
- Give us a sense of self-worth and confidence.
- Counts us in, not out.
- Saves us and picks us up when we fall.
- Separates us from the world and makes us stand out from the crowd.
- Liberates us and gives us hope to push through.

Sometimes, we may find ourselves in deep thoughts and weariness during tough times, but this should push us even closer to God. The choice to allow our problems to move us closer and closer to God's love is determined by our acceptance of Christ and what He did for us on the cross.

The Everlasting Love of God

"When the Lord began speaking through the prophet Hosea, he said to him, "Go and marry a prostitute, so that some of her children will be conceived in prostitution. This will illustrate how Israel has acted like a prostitute by turning against the Lord and worshiping other gods." (Hosea 1:2 NLT). Throughout the Old Testament, God loved to illustrate His messages through His prophets. God told Hosea to marry a prostitute to demonstrate how His people, the Israelites, had turned against Him and worshipped other gods, and Hosea did just that. The beauty of God is displayed in chapter three of the same book. God told Hosea to go and love his wife again, and this was to illustrate that God still loves His people, even though they turned their backs on Him (Hosea 3:1). We serve a merciful God. No matter how disappointed and furious He was, He fought for His people and said, I want to purify and beautify them back to myself. This is a glimpse of the love God has for His people.

I have understood God's love by getting to know Him more deeply. It feels safe, secure, and warm. It is a place I never want to depart from or lose sight of. It is a place where I find peace, hope, and worth. God's love gives us hope and joy in a cold world. I would be nothing without the embrace of His love. It is one thing I have come to depend on and dwell on, one thing I feared to lose but am now certain I will never lose. Not even His moment of anger can cause Him to turn His face away from us (Psalm 30:5; Romans 8:31–39). The Lord hates it when we turn away from Him; it makes Him incredibly sad, but even that can never change His love and compassion toward us because He is merciful and gives us a chance to return to Him.

What more can we ask for? God thinks highly of all His children, and His arms are wide open, always ready to receive us. You are so dear to Him that in your wanderings, He makes it a priority to pursue you until you're found. What divine love! What mind can comprehend such deep love? Why drown in sorrow when we have a heavenly Father who gives love unconditionally and joy unspeakable with no cost? Why worry? Why put down your worth to gain the love and acknowledgment of others? Sometimes, we forget that we hold a prominent position in our Father's house. We are royalty in the kingdom of God (1 Peter 2:9).

God's unconditional love keeps us going when we feel stuck. In His love, we find comfort when we're sad. We may be weary during rough patches, but this should push us closer to God. The choice to allow it to move you closer and closer to God is determined by your acceptance of Him and what He did for you on the cross.

There is a significant difference between God's love and the love we receive from our loved ones. When I started seeking God's will for my life, He showed me what real love should feel like. The warmth, the peace, and the inner joy it brings are unexplainable, especially in times of storms. Imagine facing the most giant storm and dancing through it joyfully. Not even my husband or children can give me that kind of joy. Nothing comes close to the love of God. His love for us is deep, pure, endless, and perfect. You can trust yourself with God, tell Him all your deepest concerns and secrets, and trust Him with every part of you. You can endure the storms just by dwelling on the love of God—nothing more, nothing less, just that pure, deep love! Every blessing in your life flows from the love God has for you. To wake up each morning and go to bed each night in good health is by His love and grace.

The nature of God's love for His children is everlasting, enduring throughout time. The Word of God tells us, "No one is abandoned by the Lord forever. Though he brings grief, he also shows compassion because of the greatness of his unfailing love. He does not enjoy hurting or causing his children sorrow" (Lamentation 3:31–33 NLT), and this was proven in the lives of the Israelites. We often act out of control toward life's unwanted situations because we become blind to God's amazing love for us. Within that moment, all we see is chaos and dead ends. In many of the decisions we make, the worries, the stress, wanting to do it all on our own—if we knew how much we are loved, we would never allow any of these time-wasters to drain us.

Those who know about God's goodness, love, and mercy never worry about what is to come because they trust God with all that concerns them. Our heavenly Father is for us; nothing in this world can change that. He said, "I am the Lord, your God, the Holy One of Israel, your Savior. I gave Egypt as a ransom for your freedom; I gave Ethiopia and Seba in your place. Others were given in exchange for you. I traded their lives for yours because you are precious to me. You are honored, and I love you" (Isaiah 43:3–4 NLT). There is nothing God will not do for His people; time after time, He proves this to us. Oh, how He loves us!

One of my greatest wishes is for everyone to know and accept just how deeply God loves them and that they do not have to try so hard to seek love elsewhere. When I see loved ones worried about things that I know God can fix and put everything under control, it makes me sad. This is where I once found myself, lingering, forgetting for a moment that God is always there for those who love and seek Him. What a deep love!

Can you think of one person in this world who would not hesitate to lay down his or her life for yours, to go through pain and humiliation for you, to forgive you and love you when you're so hard to love? God's love for you can never be compared, and the comforting part is that nothing can separate you from His love (Romans 8:38–39). The unfortunate situations do not consume us because of God's love and compassion. It is a love that never fails or withers and extends to all with no favoritism, a love that knows no bounds.

One may frequently ask, what have I done to deserve this love? The answer is absolutely *nothing*! His love is not earned—it is given. The story of the prodigal son (Luke 15:11–32) reminds us that when we go astray, realize our mistakes, and come back home to our Father, He is always ready to receive and never turns away from us. He will embrace us and rejoice in finding our way back to Him. Jesus said, "There will be more rejoicing in heaven over one sinner who repents than over ninety-nine righteous persons who do not need to repent." (Luke 15:7). Heaven is always ready for our return. In God's presence, we find that all our needs are met. And just like the prodigal son, we may lose sight of that truth and think there is more out there for us, but God is patient. He doesn't rush us to get it right. He waits for us to realize our faults and that we need Him and can't make this life journey without Him. His love assures us that we never have to feel that there is more for us outside His presence. We never have to wander around again searching for more—because His presence quenches our thirst and brings us endless satisfaction. He constantly watches over us and has a shield of protection, commanding His angels to watch over us wherever we go (Psalm 91:11). Even when we stray, His protection never ceases. We are indeed blessed and favored beyond our wildest imagination. Remember His deep unconditional love when you go through the storms of life— to help keep you away from wandering in empty places trying to figure it all on your own.

Revealing Love

In our relationships with those around us, we might not always like each other, but Jesus Christ calls us to love each other. Love and liking are two separate things. We may not like others for whatever reason best known to us, but we must love them with the love of

Christ. Jesus did the same for you and me; the least we can do as His followers is to live our lives in reflection of His and pay it forward. He claimed us as His own.

It is pretty flattering to know that God loves us and is still kind to us despite our negative actions toward one another and, worse, toward Him. The Bible teaches us to love one another and to do so the way God loves. Jesus makes it clear in the gospels of Mark and Matthew that the most important commandment is love: "You must love the Lord your God with all your heart, soul, mind, and strength." The second is equally important: "Love your neighbor as yourself." No other commandment is greater than these (Mark 12:30–31; Matthew 22:36–40).

First, God wants us to love Him with our whole being, and second, He wants us to love others as ourselves. When one loves God, loving others comes naturally. As God has loved us and continues doing so regardless of our flaws and mistakes, He wants us to pay it forward to others. His love is an example of how we are to show love. Mimicking God's love means extending forgiveness. It means being your neighbor's keeper. God's love is unconditional, meaning that nothing you do will ever change the depth of His love for you. Hate is not a trait of His. Everything about God remains the same no matter what. People may love you, but once you no longer meet their requirements, their love for you ceases, but God's steadfast love for His children never ceases (Lamentation 3:22).

God wants you to live a life that illustrates His love, light, and Word. He is love, and that is what we are to represent, loving others regardless of their flaws, with a love that gives chances and sees the good in others even when they're at their worst. If God can look past our annoyances and worst behaviors and still claim us as His own, who are we to decide whether another person deserves our love and affection? God wants us to love others even when it's hard for us to because we live not based on our human reasonings but on God's. His love binds us in this broken world.

Through some of the worst storms in my life, when I wondered what love was, God taught me that loving others has nothing to do with our feelings toward them but what we feel toward God. Whatever we think about God should radiate through our actions toward others. Love is never about feelings but about what we do. Jesus Christ demonstrated this for us on the cross. He proved His love for us by laying down His life (2 Corinthians 5:21). A believer's real test comes from the ability to love those we find unlovable. Jesus did this for us and continues to do it for us daily. We are unlovable, yet He loves us in a way no one ever can.

There is no reward in loving when it is easy. What good is it to love those who love you, to be kind to those who are kind to you, and to give to those who can give you more in return? (Luke 6:32–36). Love should be given outside our comfort zone. We must do it even when loving and showing kindness toward others is hard. Anyone who genuinely loves is born of God and experiences a relationship with Him. The person who refuses to love doesn't know the first thing about God—because He is love! (1 John 4:7–8). God made man in His likeness, and then He said you couldn't love Him, whom you have not seen if you have no love for your brother or sister, whom you have seen (Genesis 1:27; 1 John 4:20).

In the book of Matthew, we also read the words of Jesus about what will happen on the day of final judgment: "I was hungry, and you fed me. I was thirsty, and you gave me a drink. I was a stranger, and you invited me into your home" (Matthew 25:35–36 NLT). Then He goes on to say that the righteous will ask Him when they met Him to feed Him when He was hungry, give Him a drink, and invite Him into their homes, and the King will say, "When you did it to one of the least of these my brothers and sisters, you were doing it to me!" (Matthew 25:40 NLT). We may not see God in the flesh face to face, but of all His creations, it was man He made in His likeness, so to see man is to glimpse God's most unique and special handwork.

Love is not just a commandment but also the very essence of God. To love man is to love God; to see man is to be in awe of Him for giving you the privilege of seeing what He has created with His hands— in His image! When you glance at yourself in the mirror, see God's amazing and excellent work—this should make you fear Him in humility. Love is a weapon against the enemy. It is incredible how you can defeat the enemy by simply showing love to someone. He wants you to hate. The battle is never against another human being but against the forces of darkness (Ephesians 6:12). Love is the solution to a lot of the confusion in the world. To be like Jesus carries one secret: to embody His very essence—love—and to do this is to love the Lord your God with all your heart and soul and love your neighbor as you love yourself (Mark 12:30–31).

12

A SEASON IN THE WILDERNESS

The wilderness is a lonely place —a place of
opportunity to encounter God face to face.

Webster's dictionary defines *wilderness* as "an area essentially undisturbed by human activity and its naturally developed life community." Being transformed for His kingdom has been one of the most exhilarating and liberating experiences I have ever gone through. In 2018, I decided to seek the will of God for my life, as the pull of God was strong on my life—too strong to avoid. I chose to allow God to direct my path toward the purpose by which He has called me. God took me in a season of wilderness. During this season, I was tested, tried, challenged, and left to stare at my flaws in the mirror and say to myself, *Here I am, Lord. Transform me, prune me into the vessel worthy of accomplishing your task. Do with me all you desire so that I may be all you want and represent you as I am supposed to.*

The wilderness is a place of uncertainty. See it as being in the middle of nowhere and having no escape route. The only way out is to run into the arms of God. The wilderness is where God wants you all to Himself, to teach, equip, and prune you into the gold He knows you to be. You will be faced with many tests and trials, many challenges beyond your human strength, and you will need to realize in those moments that only God's strength will get you through. The enemy will come at you with full force in diverse ways. You will feel lonely, lost, confused, tired, discouraged, and abandoned. But know this—when you start recognizing what God is doing in you, around you, and through you, the way you view this season changes from feeling alone to where you get to encounter God in the most fulfilling ways. When rooted in Christ, you're protected and surrounded by God's mighty angels in the wilderness, and clarity becomes the bigger picture.

It may feel like you are in a dead zone where nothing is happening. You may feel stuck, but that is exactly how a seed feels before germinating. You are planted this season, and loneliness and abandonment are expected. When you're buried, you are hidden – but in this case, in God's presence, growing and renewed for His glory.

God was restoring me in those dark moments. His purpose was for me to evolve into who He has destined me to be. The life of Jesus was a great reminder to me that the road to fulfilling purpose is not easy. But we can rest assured that God runs with us and understands our challenges and attacks. Jesus reminds us in the gospel of Matthew that our reward is the kingdom of God if we endure persecution for the sake of righteousness (Matthew 5:10).

The transformation season in my life, I believe, is not over, as there is much more to learn and much more to uncover about myself and the woman I'm becoming for God. I can boldly and gladly say that I am not where I was when I decided to answer His call. I leaned on the verse, "I can do all things through Him who gives me strength" (Philippians 4:13). This verse gets me going. It reminds me that though my strength may fail me and my efforts may limit me, God's strength will keep me going, and I can accomplish more than my strength would allow me to. God also gave me Romans 8:28 to lean on: "And we know that in all things God works for the good of those who love him, who have been called according to his purpose (Romans 8:28). He said, "Lean on this verse when things don't make sense. When all odds seem to be working against you." God has given us power over our enemies (Luke 10:19) and assures us that we can conquer every battle through Christ. This planting season taught me the importance of enjoying quiet time alone in the presence of God and taking in the peace and freedom it brings.

If you are in this season and wondering what is happening, know God is setting you apart from the crowd. He is re-positioning you, pruning you for greatness. Today, I want to assure you that you are not going through a death sentence if you are currently in this season. You are journeying through the best experience of your life. The process is essential for growth. Do not be discouraged in this season. God wants your attention to capacitate you. He wants strict one-on-one time with you without any outside disturbance. Yes, it may feel as if nothing is happening for you, though this is the season when the most is going on in your life. The experiences you go through in this season are what God will use to propel you toward greatness. The enemy will constantly push you to the edge. You will sometimes question your worth, capabilities, and existence and wonder if you have what it takes to pull through. Rest in knowing that the wilderness is where you hear God's voice the loudest, drawing you closer to Him. You will go through the fires, but the Word of God tells us, "When you walk through the fire, you will not be burned; the flames will not set you ablaze" (Isaiah 43:2).

When you fight the battle right, you will not be defeated. The adversary (Satan) throws trials and circumstances our way to distract us from getting to where God wants us. Deciding to walk and work with God opens the doors for opposition—both from Satan and his army and sometimes from those around you. This season, God raises you to develop a thick skin. He raises you to be a warrior to stand against the enemy. At a point, you may feel as if the world had shut you out, as if you've lost all the people around you, when in reality, God separated you for much more. The enemy aims to attack the area where God has called you; if you allow him, he will triumph over you. Recognizing his tactics and meditating on God's truth and what He says about you and your current season is essential because that is where you will gain the strength to keep enduring.

Going through this season in my life has not been easy for me. In the beginning, I was so lost that my mind could not understand most of the things happening to me and around me—so many tests along the way. One of the most challenging was being tempted to respond to false gossip from those I once knew as "sisters in Christ." This resulted in not only me being rejected but my family as well by those we were around. Through it all, God made me understand that it was all part of His plans for me. There are specific battles; the more we try to fight with our strength, the more we look bad.

Some battles are meant to be fought in the Spirit. It bothered me initially to know that negative words were being passed around, and I couldn't do anything about it. I couldn't vindicate myself.

What if gossip and people's negative opinions about us are God's way of teaching us that only His voice matters? Would that change the way we react to them? If yes, we must seek the lesson in every uncomfortable situation, not the problem. Remember—it is what God says that prevails in your life. What if all the terrible things you face pave the way for the most significant things that could ever happen to you? I surrendered to God, and with the advice of loved ones, I began to see the situation for what it was—a test! My reaction to this test will determine whether God will allow it to repeat until I get it right and learn to let go and let God. How convenient that all this was around the same time God asked me to leave my past, including my previous church, and pursue Him more deeply—to chase His will for my life. I knew right then that the pruning season had begun.

God wastes no time. He is all for us and wants to see us grow by teaching, equipping, and strengthening us for what is ahead. Through the storms, I heard God's voice tell me to write every emotion and question I had concerning what I was facing. God wanted me to write, so I went to my computer and started writing as the Holy Spirit directed. If you are reading this book today, realize that I decided to obey the voice of God and start writing. What seemed like the most horrible time in my life is what God used to catapult me into pursuing my purpose. He used what I faced to establish His plan in my life. He urged me to start my ministry, gave me the name for that ministry, and told me to share His Word and spread hope to His people.

It was clear that all I was going through was more than what meets the eye, so I stopped seeking to understand what I was going through and followed God's voice. It was beyond my control. We can never control what others do to us or think of us, but we can control how we respond and how we allow those things to affect us. I was alone this season but knew God was up to something. He directed my every move and ensured I was not hit with more than I could bear. He gave me all the comfort I needed. As everyone walked out of my life, God held me close. I felt as if my existence had no meaning in this season until I heard God's voice, and He pulled me out of that dark pit and showed me what I was missing all along.

The wilderness experience is not meant to keep us stranded, though it may feel that way; it's to prepare us and show us what the love of God is all about. Jesus was in isolation for a long time before He was announced. If you're in this season, may you be reminded that God is not punishing you. He loves you, and when you go through things beyond your understanding and control, the right thing to do is to seek the face of God and surrender to Him—this will help you identify the source of your problem. Look at your wilderness season this way—an opportunity to get one-on-one with God and know Him intimately. He wants you and is calling you to Himself. This season is an opportunity to experience Him in a way you never have before. Allow Him in.

Imagine being alone in a place without human interactions for weeks, months, and sometimes even years! It can be draining and mind-wrenching, but you must understand that when God chooses you, you are set apart before you were conceived. Trust the voice of God above any other. As humans, when we go through misfortunes, we will always see things on the surface, but when we dwell in Christ and develop a relationship with the Holy Spirit. He opens our eyes, and we no longer see things for what they are but rather see them through the lens of God.

Our circumstances will always come and go, but God remains constant. You are in this season of your life because God trusts you and wants to do more in you, through you, and with you. Embrace every aspect of this season —self-reflection, strengthening exercises, lessons, growth, discipline, and spiritual maturity. God teaches us and gets rid of all the branches that bear no fruit, and the ones that bear fruit He prunes (John 15:2). When you come out of this season successfully, you come out as pure as gold (Job 23:10) to be a blessing to the nations. "Yes, there will be an abundance of flowers and singing and joy! The deserts will become as green as the mountains of Lebanon, as lovely as Mount Carmel or the plain of Sharon. There the Lord will display his glory, the splendor of our God" (Isaiah 35:2 NLT).

Suppose your time in the wilderness is utilized correctly. In that case, you may find it exhilarating and be glad to see, feel, and encounter God. We may not like the wilderness experience, but it births greatness through endurance. Allow this season to pass gracefully without attempting to manipulate things because doing so will negate the purpose and jeopardize what God is trying to do in you and through you. In Matthew 4:1–11, the Spirit of God led Jesus into the wilderness. While there, the devil tempted Jesus. He had fasted for forty days and forty nights, so He was hungry. The devil approached Him and said, "If you are the Son of God, tell these stones to become bread" (Matthew 4:3). Jesus refused and defended Himself through the Scriptures. But the devil never rested; he tried to test Jesus, and at a point, he even quoted scriptures. Jesus then defeated the devil by asking him to leave. After that, the angels of the Lord came and took care of Jesus (Matthew 4:10–11).

The enemy does this to test us; you are no exception to his tricks. The Bible tells us to be faithful when we're tempted, even to the point of death. God will give us life as a victor's crown (Revelation 2:10). The devil will always tempt you where you are most vulnerable. Still, you are more than a conqueror through Christ and can overcome anything—through God's Word, prayer, and faith as the foundation.

Meditate on the Word of God this season and lock it up in your heart so that you can stand against the temptations that come your way. Every attack must be fought, not physically but spiritually. Stay encouraged in the Lord, and never give up on Him through the tests and trials. Hold on with firm faith and obedience through the uncertainties. God has His fence of protection around you, and when the time is right, He will make a way where you will receive your crown of glory. But for now, embrace your learning and pruning season, your intimate time with God, and enjoy the bumpy ride.

He Restores My Soul

We often pray to God to change our situation when we go through afflictions. But what if those afflictions are there to change us and prepare us for what is ahead? The psalmist said, "He renews my strength. He guides me along right paths, bringing honor to his name" (Psalm 23:3 NLT). When God renews our strength, it calls for testing and trials. It calls for emotions that are out of our comfort zone. Our strength cannot be restored to its full capacity without going through storms. These storms are not to penalize you for your sins but to break open what is stored. You will birth the strength within through the challenging times in your life. When your strength is renewed, you're automatically healed in places of weakness.

The New King James Version says, "He restores my soul." Google defines *restore* as "bring back," to "reinstate." God restores in us the reusable things and prunes them. He brings life to a dead soul and awakens a still spirit in us. He gives rest to the weary and provides a new song and vision. Through the storms of life, we get broken by many things, leaving us dry, but David reminds us that we serve a God who restores and brings us back to Himself. When God renews us, we no longer remain the same. We start losing things of the old—people, places, jobs, unhealthy habits, and so on.

In this season of restoration, you must allow God to bring to life what has been dead in you. Allow Him to restore your soul and lead you on a straight path. You may be a diamond in the rough, but He sees the diamond, which is where He focuses. Everything you are facing is for a reason. When God restores, He makes new; you must stay in Him to maintain this newness. This means that anyone who remains in Christ is a new person. "The old life is gone; a new life has begun!" (2 Corinthians 5:17 NLT). After God renews our strength through what may come like a storm, He then guides us onto the right path, bringing honor to His name. Sometimes, things happen in our lives that make us think we are headed in the wrong direction because it does not fall into our category of what a blessing should look like. It does not appear to be the comfort we pray for or crave. It is challenging, so we automatically think we are headed to destruction. Though God leading us to the right path will not be smooth, we can be sure that the destination is worth it. Sometimes, what we may see as the end for us is the beginning of what God promised us long ago. Something new is breaking! Sometimes, the best thing that can happen to any of us is our problems. Now that we are made fresh in our strength, we are back on the right path, ready to face our giants.

You can't be stuck in your old ways and bring honor and glory to God's name. You can't keep putting one leg in and the other out. You must allow God to restore, lead, and work through you. Do you know why we go through the unimaginable in this world and still can face each troubled day as it comes? It's because God renews our strength every day, which is why we can endure; that is why we are not broken even after the worst! (2 Corinthians 4:16–18). I pray that God restores anything fruitful in you that has been put to sleep for some time now.

Mercies

"For He has rescued us from the kingdom of darkness and transferred us into the Kingdom of his dear Son, who purchased our freedom and forgave our sins" (Colossians 3:14 NLT). Life can be draining at times. We do so much day in and day out without realizing the changes that are taking place in our lives. You might have repeatedly faced regrettable moments, replaying a terrible situation, wishing you had handled it differently. Being faced with choices we regret can be a hard pill to swallow, and because the enemy is aware of that, he will take those things and use them against you. Paul tells us that God has rescued us from the kingdom of darkness and transferred us into the realm of Jesus Christ, who purchased our freedom (Colossians 1:13).

Maybe you carry around a regret that no one knows about, and because of this, you are stopping yourself from doing so many things for God. You don't see yourself as worthy enough. You place limitations on your life due to the shame you carry around. You dwell on your past mistakes, allowing them to stop you from moving forward. Whatever your regrettable moments may be, you are not alone. We've all been there, but God is faithful. "The faithful love of the Lord never ends! His mercies never cease. They begin afresh each morning" (Lamentation 3:22–23 NLT). Through Christ, you are released from the weight of past mistakes. His mercies for you are new each morning. Today's mercies are not from yesterday, but God's compassion and mercies on your life restart in full each day. No matter your regrets, know they are a vital part of your story. If you allow yourself, God can use those moments to shape you for His glory, giving the enemy no chance to guilt-trip you.

God's love and mercies assure us of the hope to face each day without being consumed by yesterday's burdens and today's worries. God does not want you to live a life of regrets and fear of what may come. He does not want you dwelling on yesterday, and He certainly does not want you to live in fear of your past. Because what that does is hold you hostage. What matters now is how you choose to move forward, understanding that those moments in your past that you wish would be a blur are moments God has woven into your story to help you grow and become the best version of yourself. These moments are eye-opening moments that awaken our sleeping minds. They are the moments that contribute to the renewal of our minds.

You may be thinking, *Is it too late for me to get back on the right track?* The key to life is leaning on God and knowing that we live, make mistakes, learn from them, and move on better and wiser. Today is a new day, and God is counting on you to embody His mercies and look ahead with peace in your heart. Never allow the enemy to lie to you that you are still living in the kingdom of darkness. Resist his lies. In the kingdom of God, there is freedom and light! Dwelling on the should haves, could haves, and would haves is not the answer to moving forward, and it's not the life God intends for us. Today, let go of what was, allow yourself to grasp the freedom God has given you through Jesus Christ, and lean toward what's to come.

Seeking Him through the Loneliness

"The Lord will not abandon his people, because that would dishonor his great name. For it has pleased the Lord to make you his very own people" (1 Samuel 12:22 NLT). It is so common to experience abandonment from the people we love. It can make one shift into a lonely state—this is a season we will all face at a point in our life, but sometimes, we do not need to go through abandonment issues to feel lonely. Sometimes, we may go through loneliness or a void, and no matter how financially or socially stable we are, we still find ourselves in deep distress. It is a void that no luxury or a big company of people can fix because it is a form of loneliness that only the presence of God can quench.

David, a man after God's own heart, struggled with fear, loneliness, and depression; he can relate to our seasons of loneliness. David sought God through his loneliness and used that time to pursue God because he knew that only God could satisfy his thirst. Through all he went through, David still set an example and reminded us to call on God in our times of distress. As he wondered with a lonely heart when God would remember him and come to his aid, when he felt the most abandoned by God, he chose to rejoice in the Lord and recalled God's goodness in his life (Psalm 13:1–6).

Loneliness can bring on the idea that no one understands, that you have no one to lean on, that everyone around you, including God, has abandoned you, and the feeling of worthlessness kicks in. The good news is God can never leave His children; it is out of His character. You are never alone; God has always been and will be there until the end. The void you feel within you is a reminder to run to the Father, saturate yourself in His presence, and allow Him to fill and cause you to overflow.

When you try to replace the everlasting joy that can only come from seeking God's presence with the things of this world that give temporary happiness, you may start feeling as if something is missing. No amount of material pleasure can bring fulfillment. Jesus Christ invites you to draw near Him, as He is the only one who can quench that thirst called loneliness (John 4:14). He understands exactly how it feels to be alone. On the cross, "at about three o'clock, Jesus called out with a loud voice, 'Eli, Eli, lama Sabathani?' which means 'My God, my God, why have you abandoned me?'" (Matthew 27:46 NLT). This was a moment where He felt alone and rejected, not only by people but also by His Father. He experienced the ultimate betrayal, rejection, and loneliness anyone can ever experience, and all that was so you and I could be close to God.

Know that He certainly understands you when it feels like no one understands. Only Jesus can fill up that emptiness. Only He can give you complete rest. Loneliness can put us in total isolation, but as a good friend once told me, loneliness means God wants you all to

Himself—this statement has impacted my life positively and helped me seek God through my time in the wilderness seasons. Have you ever woken up in the middle of the night and tried to put yourself back to sleep, only to find yourself struggling to fall back asleep? Well, you are not alone. This can feel very unpleasant, especially when you have a few hours to wake up. I see these moments as an opportunity you can use to talk to God. When you can't fall back to sleep in the middle of the night, *pray!* Just as when you feel lonely, see it as an opportunity to speak to God about what's on your mind and grow closer to Him.

Loneliness means you are disconnected from the source of life—Jesus Christ—because there is permanent joy and freedom in the presence of God (Psalm 16:11). There is so much power in silence. In our silence, God speaks volumes. The feeling of loneliness is one of the most challenging storms to pass through. If not dealt with properly, the dangerous side of feeling alone can cause us to slip into episodes of depression.

In your loneliness, allow God to Isolate you from the crowd. When God chooses you, the world will spit you out. You can't be chosen by God and be accepted by the world. A season of loneliness is not a dead end. It's just God pulling you to Himself. Allow Him to prepare you in this season. You are His veiled bride. Your unveiling season is around the corner, and it will be glorious. But until then, be okay with being shunned by the world around you. Be okay with being alone. Take pleasure in God's presence and enjoy that intimacy with Him.

God is always with and ahead of you, even when you don't feel He is. Ask Him to renew your mind into seeing your season of loneliness in a positive light, an opportunity to get close to Him, seek Him, and spend quality time with Him through His Word. Know that God loves you immensely and is always there waiting with arms wide open. It's time to turn a new leaf. It's time to shift your focus, and it's time to stop looking at what is wrong and look up ahead.

No matter what happens in your life or where you find yourself stranded, one thing to be sure about is that you will never camp outside God's grandest plan if you seek Him. Everything you are going through right now, the feeling of distance and abandonment —know that it is all mapped up in His plan for you. Nothing you go through is a coincidence. He knew it would happen before He created you. Rejoice in the Lord always because His plans for your life defeat all your struggles. Allow God to meet you right there in your loneliness. Allow Him to embrace you. Paul tells us, "All God's promises concerning your life have been fulfilled in Christ with a resounding Yes! And through him, our yes ascends to God for His glory" (2 Corinthians 1:20 NLT).

Never mind the thoughts of doubt that pass through your mind; the truth is, God's promises offer hope amid the storm. He is constantly knocking on the door of your heart. Now, dim the noise around you, look away from the distractions that tell you demeaning things about yourself, saturate yourself in His Word, tune into His voice, and open the door for Him to come into your heart and quench all your deepest thirst.

None of the things you go through change who you are in Him. Trust Him with your nothing, and He will give you everything. God's Word tells us, "No eyes have seen, and no mind can ever imagine what God has prepared for those who love him" (1 Corinthians 2:9 NLT). There is no limit to His goodness.

Many things can make us happy—buying that beautiful dress, booking that amazing vacation trip, buying those gorgeous shoes, or moving into that beautiful house. All that can make a person happy, but to have endless joy in our hearts is to have God in our lives, a joy that we never lose despite the storms.

Father to the Fatherless

"Even if my father and mother abandoned me, the Lord would hold me close" (Psalm 27:10 NLT). I remember the goosebumps I had the first time I read the above verse. "Even if my parents abandon me, God will hold me close." My dear friends, you may have grown up without a mother, a father, or both. Whether one or both parents have passed or are absent by choice, having an absent parent or a horrible upbringing is not what we all hope for. You may have had sad moments while growing up, but there is good news for you today: no matter how bad you had it growing up or how bad you have it now, you never were and never are alone. There is a perfect Father who loves unconditionally and wants an unbreakable and intimate relationship with you. God is more than what we can ever expect in an earthly parent. David wrote that God is the "Father to the fatherless, defender of widows" (Psalm 68:5 NLT). This is who God is. He has and will never abandon the works of His hands. We can find hope in Him, compassion, a friend, love, unspeakable joy, and peace that transcends all understanding and rest in Him.

You don't have to feel abandoned when there is greater companionship in Christ. We all need to be loved and valued by the ones we love and hold dear in our hearts, but the sad truth is that not all of us are privileged with that kind of love in this world. We can't depend on people to love us without condition; only God can fully love us with all our baggage, weaknesses, and flaws. A caring Father whose forgiveness, companionship, and unconditional love for us exceed those of our earthly parents. Our earthly parents may get mad at us if we go against their plans. You can rest in knowing that no matter how much you yearn for closeness with your parents, you can find that in God beyond your expectations—only if you will draw near to Him and call on Him.

I got to a point in my life when I started seeing myself as an orphan because as I answered God's call for my life, many close relationships detached naturally from me, including my parent, not because they were against me walking in my truth, but I got to a place where I saw the world beyond the natural. I gravitated more toward those whom I knew could guide me on a path I was uncertain about. I knew that I had a solid father and mother in God.

In this season, God reminded me of the time in Abraham's life when God instructed Him to leave His family and his native land and go where He would direct him. A land where the Lord would make him a great nation and be a blessing to others (Genesis 12:1–4). I understood that certain assignments for the Lord cause natural separation from the people we are used to. So, it was not something I dwelled on or felt bad about. Did I sometimes wish I could have the attention of an earthly mother or a father? Yes, but knowing and feeling God's warmth always helped me push through, and I knew I was never alone.

I want to encourage someone today. I want you to know that God can never abandon you because doing so is out of His character. Dwell on the good news that God will hold you close even if your earthly mother and father leave you. Solomon speaks of God as a friend when he writes, "There are 'friends' who destroy each other, but a real friend sticks closer than a brother" (Proverbs 18:24 NLT). He is our everything.

God Understands

When we go through the unimaginable, most of the time, our first move is to rely on the people closest to us, not only for comfort but also for understanding. Life has taught me that our biggest mistakes come when we expect what only God can provide from the people around us. We seek understanding, unconditional love, and freedom from places we're familiar with. But through life's experiences, I have learned that living in such a way could be what breaks us. Yes, we have loved ones to confide in through our difficulties, but only God can offer us the divine comfort and understanding we seek through the storms. Our emotions are always safe with God. We can trust ourselves, our worries, our thoughts, and our deepest hurts in His hands.

God is the only one who can turn things around for us. When you depend on people, you might be judged where you need understanding and abandoned where you need comfort the most. These are things that God freely offers. But unfortunately, we find ourselves searching, climbing, and running to those around us and other sources for what only God has the answers to. We can't turn to others for what God has already put on the table. God does not just offer us absolute comfort, love, and understanding—He is the *essence* of those things. He loves not as we love. He comforts us, not as we comfort. He understands, not as we understand. You can learn how to unconditionally love and offer these things only by getting close to and mimicking the ways of Christ.

God is in the business of healing and restoring all that is broken in the lives of His children. If you expect others to be what God is to you, you will live a life of disappointment and regret. David understood this when he acknowledged God during the emotional hiccups in his life. He said, "When anxiety was great within me, your consolation brought me joy" (Psalm 94:19).

God is always ready to meet you in your pain and vulnerability at no cost. Seeking someone else for what God freely offers may cost you. No one understands you more than God. No one understands the pain you go through more than He does. Bring God in on your pain. Overlooking God and looking elsewhere might bring unnecessary drama.

The storms of life will come, which is a guarantee, but it is up to you to decide whether you will allow those storms to make or break you. Every season serves a great purpose, and it is our responsibility to find out what that is and what God is communicating to us each season. Have you ever shared a problem with someone, and in the end, he or she had you feeling even worse than you were initially? I'm sure we've all been there at some point. That is because we present and trust our problems in the hands of the wrong source. We are alive today because of God's power and grace, so what makes us think we can handle our problems without Him? What makes us believe that another as limited as we are is the best and first choice in our quest to seek sanctuary?

Going through storms makes us great warriors. Storms shape us into the best version of ourselves, and most importantly, they make us realize that we need God to survive this life. Our storms push us closer to God. We belong to Him; without Him, we can't function and make it through this life with a sound mind. Growth is acquired through the storms. Wisdom is gained when we seek God through the storms. Endurance is practiced through the storms. Strength is developed through the storms, and patience, perseverance, and determination are practiced through the storms. Most importantly, you become aware of who you are through the storms.

You will go through the pain and tough times regardless of whether you are prepared for them. It is part of life, but know that God understands, and seeking Him will give you a better outcome. Leaning on your strength, understanding, and efforts will only cause more damage, and trying to block the pain or ignoring your storms will certainly not help either. We must face and embrace our problems and allow God to meet us in our mess. He is always ready to take it all on His shoulders for us.

Pastor Steven Furtick of Elevation Church said, "Your greatest life messages and most effective ministry will come out of your deepest hurt." My life is a testimony to this statement. This book I am writing to you was birthed out of deep hurt. Please, do not sit in your pain and milk it. Allow the strength of God to help you stand firm and His voice to guide you to see the messages in what you go through. Seek God through your storms and help another with the wisdom you acquire by seeking Him. There is always a profound message in our pain that many people are counting on. How you deal with and heal from your hurts will determine how you impact others positively.

13

FORGIVENESS

❧

Pivotal life-changing stories are determined by
how we handle life's painful moments.

The psalmist asks, "Lord, if you kept a record of our sins, who, O Lord, could ever survive?" (Psalm 130:3-4 NLT) It is troubling and heart-throbbing to go through the pain of other people's poor choices, but we must also understand that allowing ourselves to go through pain is a choice! When someone does something against us, we become disappointed and hurt; sometimes, we allow this pain to take root in our hearts. When we face offense from others, we must pause, search within our hearts, let go, and allow God to step in; this is when we must practice forgiveness. Forgiveness is the antidote for our pain. Forgiveness is intentional; forgiveness is healing; forgiveness is freedom; forgiveness is love! When you forgive someone or yourself, you consciously decide to let go of any anger, resentment, and bitterness and accept freedom.

God first demonstrated His love for us by forgiving us of our sins. Forgiving one another as God forgave us is one of the true essences of a faithful Christian. This tells others we belong to God and frees us from the emotional bondage of pain. Staying angry at those who hurt us does not fix the matter or help them realize what they did. If we allow that anger to take root in our hearts, it will change us into something far worse than what they did to us. Yes, you've been hurt by someone you loved and trusted at some point in your life, but while the past cannot be changed, it doesn't have to control you from moving forward. The most important part of going through the storms of life is how you move on from the damage it causes. We become vulnerable when we hold on to resentment and anger; worse, we become slaves to those things — a position where it's quite easy for the enemy to tempt us.

Unforgiveness is a place of discomfort, a place of damage, a place where prayers are hindered. How long will you wallow up in your hurts through unforgiveness before you realize that the one you are hurting the most is yourself? Having a forgiving heart toward those who wrong us, no matter the offense drives the enemy away and shows the offender the love of Christ. Nothing makes the enemy happier than to see us burdening our hearts with offenses, and nothing makes him madder than to see us united with those who wronged us. Being offended is a choice, and letting go and forgiving others is the ultimate gift we give ourselves after we've been wronged.

Forgiveness is a choice, one that can be made only once. The minute you decide to forgive, you must try hard to forget the offense and the feeling of resentment attached to it. You cannot forgive someone and take it back when you remember the hurt; if that is the case, the enemy will keep playing with your mind repeatedly. We have offended God more than anyone has ever offended us.

Many struggle with forgiveness because they believe they gain the upper hand over their offender by not forgiving. None of us are perfect. We've all fallen short. We were all once sinners who have been saved by grace. No one is above the other, and whether we see ourselves in a higher class than another, we hold the same worth in the eyes of God. Remembering the times God had forgiven us when we did not deserve it will help us forgive those who wronged us.

From time to time, the enemy will take you back to the offense, making you relive the painful moments and wonder if forgiveness can happen. This is his job: to mess with your mind, hold your mind captive, keep you dwelling on the unnecessary, and keep you from moving toward what matters. Choosing to forgive someone does not mean you forget how they treated you, but rather, you free yourself from whatever toxic attachment there is so that you can move on with a clean heart toward that person.

You take matters into your own hands when you hold on to the pain inflicted by others, which makes it hard for God to bring justice into your situation. It is not God's desire for you to hold a grudge against another. Maintain the freedom Christ gave you, and do not lock yourself up in darkness by doing what is contrary to the Word of God. Think about the greatest act of love shown to you through Christ; if God can do that for you, why can't you do the least for yourself and others? We are to mimic the ways of Christ, and holding on to hurt and pain is not what Christ would do.

Our flesh may fail us, but we are powerful and conquerors through Christ. Through the storms of my life, I learned that one secret to forgiveness is to pray for those who offend me. Pray for each one of them. Whenever they pop into your head, it makes sense that you will remember the pain inflicted on you, and in those moments, do what God would want —pray for them! Doing this helps you and allows you to see what God is doing in you through what was done to you.

One may ask, "How can I pray for those who hurt me?" Praying for those who hurt you makes it hard for you to have any form of ill feelings toward them and hard for you to speak negatively about them. It gradually becomes a habit once you take the first step in praying for them. It's a waste of energy to stay angry at someone or be offended by them. But it takes strength to let go and pray for them. The Word of God tells us, "If you forgive those who sin against you, your heavenly Father will forgive you" (Matthew 6:14 NLT). Forgiveness is self-love, a route to experience peace and clarity.

Jesus tells us that before we offer anything to God, we must leave them at the altar and reconcile with our brother or sister, then come and offer our gifts to God (Matthew 5:24)—this is because we must go to God in all honesty. God is love. We sadden Him with our disobedience in more ways than we've felt hurt. But He is always faithful to forgive us. We must also do the same. The bad things that happen to us are not a secret to God. Joseph forgave his brothers for selling him to the Egyptians because he knew what happened to him was all part of God's great plan for his life. Though they meant to harm him, God meant it for good (Genesis 50:20). I have realized that everything we go through, whether orchestrated by the enemy or God, works out in favor of those who trust God through it. God will never watch His children go through the valleys of death and not save them. God can take our pain, betrayals, offenses, humiliations, and anything the enemy plans against us and make something beautiful. God has the habit of turning our ashes into beauty. He habitually uses whatever we face to bring out the light in us.

You must trust and obey in surrender. Always ask yourself, *Why should my peace be disturbed by anything or what another can do to me? Has God not promised to turn things around for the good of those who love Him? Why should I sit and wallow in my offenses?* When Peter asked Jesus how often we should forgive someone who sins against us, he wondered if it was perhaps seven times, but Jesus replied by saying, "No, not seven times, but seventy times seven." Jesus then told a story about a servant who owed a king millions of dollars, and he didn't have the money to repay his debt. His master pitied him, forgave him, and canceled his debt. Then that same servant went to his fellow man who owed him a few thousand dollars. He grabbed him by the throat and demanded payment, even after the man begged for more time to pay him back. He refused and had the man thrown into prison. The other servants who witnessed this went to the king and told him everything. The king then called the man and threw him in prison for not showing the same mercy he (the king) had shown to him (Matthew 18:21–35). Then Jesus said, "This is how my heavenly Father will treat each of you unless you forgive your brother or sister from your heart" (Matthew 18:35).

Don't let the enemy keep you captive in your hurts. Today, choose not to be offended. Forgive, let go, and let God choose freedom, choose love, choose you, choose God!

Pride X Humility

"When Jesus noticed that all who had come to the dinner were trying to sit in the seats of honor near the head of the table, he gave them this advice: 'When you are invited to a wedding feast, don't sit in the seat of honor. What if someone more distinguished than you has also been invited? The host will say, "Give this person your seat." Then you will be embarrassed and have to take whatever seat is left at the foot of the table!

'Instead, take the lowest place at the foot of the table. Then, when your host sees you, he will say, "Friend, we have a better place for you!" Then, you will be honored in front of all the other guests. Those who exalt themselves will be humbled, and those who humble themselves will be exalted.' Then, he turned to his host. 'When you put on a luncheon or a banquet,' he said, 'don't invite your friends, brothers, relatives, and rich neighbors. They will invite you back, which will be your only reward. Instead, invite the poor, the crippled, the lame, and the blind. Then at the resurrection of the righteous, God will reward you for inviting those who could not repay you" (Luke 14:7–14 NLT).

Humility—what is it? Humility has often been sometimes associated with being a quiet person. However, the fact is, you can be outspoken and still possess the quality of a humble person. To me, humility realizes that nothing is in the scope of one's strength. It is the concentration of God's strength and not our own. A humble person does not overthink things out of their control. They accept situations for what they are without making it about themselves and finding ways to make things fit into their puzzle. Humility: "Let go and let God."

A humble person knows that the height of his or her life is not by human efforts but by the hand of God in their life. Jesus said, "Those who exalt themselves will be humbled, and those who humble themselves will be exalted" (Luke 14:11 NLT). A person with the spirit of pride magnifies their strength, giving credit to themselves and disregarding that things are made possible by God's grace, faithfulness, and power. As children of God, we show humility by not worrying because Christ orders our steps.

James said, "God opposes the proud but gives grace to the humble" (James 4:6 NLT). This does not mean He does not give grace to the proud because the grace of God is what is constantly sustaining us all in this dark world. James says God provides *more* grace to those who humble themselves before Him. Grace is already eminent, but to the humble, He adds more. He lifts them in honor.

Pride causes us to ignore or take for granted vital Revelation from God. It makes us believe we know it all. It makes us make statements such as: "Who do they think they are to tell me this or that? I am also capable of knowing what they know." Pride is a thief. Pride is deceptive - it makes you believe what is invalid, making you adopt the "false" as the reality. It gets you to a dead end and leaves you feeling worthless. It is the downfall of those who fall victim to its allure.

Paul said to the Romans, "Those who are led by the Spirit of God are the children of God" (Romans 8:14). A humble person is led by the Spirit of God, by the decrees of God, but a person who possesses a prideful spirit is led by his or her own way of thinking.

We may not be aware of this, but when our worries easily control us or we get angry at other people's opinions about us, we display the spirit of pride. The fight is never for us to handle but for God. We may think that pride is bragging about the things we have or our qualities, but pride believes we are too important to be wronged. We are not immune to the criticism of others, we are not exempt from hardship, and we are not invisible to persecution. Getting angry and complaining about such things brings us pride—because a humble spirit knows and accepts that it is expected to face such things in life, as Christ Himself went through worse. When it happens, we must surrender peacefully to the one who fights for us.

Pride is unforgiveness! Pride and humility can never collaborate. Yes! Some people will offend you over and over, and out of love for

God and them, you will choose to forgive and move on, but those same people can lack the capacity to do the same for someone else or you in return, just as we read in the parable of the unmerciful servant (Matthew 18:21–35).

A humble person knows they are not resistant to the pain others throw at them. When it happens, they are always ready to let go and forgive because that is what is expected from a believer in Christ. Pride is throwing stones at people and being angry when it's done to you in return. Humility is showing love even when it's hard to do.

Let me ask you this: If the roles were to be reversed and you had to lay down your life for someone else, would you? Without hesitation, would you? But in His humility, Jesus did that for you and me.

I have always been a woman of action. Words do not mean much to me, so love is action, especially in the uncomfortable. This makes me give people more chances than they deserve, and though it may make me look less than smart, I do not dwell on the rewards of man, but on what I know I gain spiritually. Jesus said, "If you love those who love you, what credit is that to you?" (Luke 6:32). If I love someone only when it falls in my comfort zone, what is the point of that love? Is it even genuine? A true act of love is forgiving when it hurts, letting go, and hugging when you want to knock that person down. In reality, many of us are too proud, and we say, "Who do they think they are to wrong me?" My question is, "Why not?" Does love exempt us from pain? We can't control what is done to us in this world, but we can control how we compose ourselves through it.

You know someone is filled with the Holy Spirit when placed in a position where he or she is tempted to react but instead chooses to halt. Humility knows that we must always compose ourselves as followers of Christ, no matter what life throws at us. The actions of others should not dictate our path. Humility knows not to take things to heart.

Pride is envy—envying the achievements of others, saying to yourself, "Why do you have this and that, and I don't?" But humility is being happy for someone, knowing God has a table specially prepared for you.

Retaliation

The apostle Paul instructs us never to take revenge but rather to leave it to the righteous anger of God (Romans 12:19). The best decision you can make as a believer when someone wrongs you is to draw back and allow God to speak to you about what to do next. When you retaliate, you get in the way of God's work. When you are in Christ, you never need to try so hard to do things independently because God sees and knows all that concerns you. He can better solve your problems in a way you can never, and retaliating only makes it hard for Him to help you.

Never internalize the negative words spoken about you, and never allow them to control your actions. Take notice of this—at any point in your life, when you go on your knees and pray your guts out to God about something and suddenly you start experiencing random changes in your life, things beyond your control, and, at the same time hard to understand—take a step back and refrain from retaliating too quickly. Even if what is going on causes you to look bad in the eyes of men, allow the process to flow naturally. Look to God because what is happening might very well be the answer to your prayers, and it doesn't mean it's terrible because it did not come as you expected.

Through the storms, I have learned that sometimes the answers to our prayers do not come wrapped up in a pretty box with a pink bow on top but come as what we may see as an obstruction. God knows you on a much deeper level, and when you focus solely on Him, you will feel His love so strongly through the worst times in your life. It is quite easy to retaliate when you're mistreated, and the world around you has a certain perception far from who you are. It is hard to grasp hope when you go through storms. Bear in mind that the human mind and eyes do not know what God knows or see what He sees, so in times like these, God teaches us the power of restraint. He teaches us how to develop a thick skin against the things we cannot change or control. He teaches us humility, strength, patience, discipline, and dependence on Him. You never have to feel that you must prove yourself to people to be worthy. You are not responsible for the way people treat you. But it is your responsibility to see and treat others as God does.

Sometimes, to get to your promised land, you must go through the uncomfortable, the humiliation, the rejection, and the storms. If it is a situation in which you are tempted to retaliate or avenge, remember what Paul said in the book of Romans: "Do not take revenge, my dear friends, but leave room for God's wrath, for it is written: 'It is mine to avenge; I will repay,' says the Lord" (Romans 12:19). Never forget the importance of being a child of God. Sometimes, our problems make us forget who we are and who we represent in this world. When someone wrongs us, the first thing we may think of is retaliating without stopping to think about why the person did what they did in the first place. We are too quick to attack and judge without asking ourselves, *What did I do to contribute to this person's actions?* Then, we allow our pain to influence how we treat or handle the matter and those who wronged us.

Be careful who or what you allow to influence your life's decisions. The Word of God tells us not to repay evil with evil or insult with insult but to repay evil with blessing so that we may inherit a blessing (1 Peter 3:9). I have grown to understand that the way we respond to those who wrong us is always between God and us and never between the person and us. How we treat and answer people is a service to God. The Holy Spirit told me this. We must never allow how others wronged us to determine how we treat them in return.

Yes, it makes sense; you would feel like defending yourself when people are saying all kinds of wrong things about you, but the Word of God tells us that it is God's will for us to do good and silence the ignorant talk of foolish people (1 Peter 2:15). Why do you think that is? You see, not only does God know you very well, but He also knows every step you will take before you take them. He knows your future. Your days are recorded in His book.

As hard as it can be to ignore the wrong done to us, we practice the wisdom of God when we ignore it and trust Him to handle it for us. Imagine if Joseph fought back against his brothers and did everything he could to save himself. It would be a lost and wasted battle, as God fights for us better than we can ever fight for ourselves. Retaliating ungodly is not a great representation of God, and the enemy loves to get us to the point of making a fool out of ourselves. I have been there, and it took the grace of God to pull me out. I allowed my hurt to cause me to retaliate in the name of trying to defend myself, forgetting that God is in a better position to do that for me. I have wanted to fight for myself whenever I was wrongly accused or misunderstood. The Holy Spirit helped me realize that I belong to God, which means I do not need to try so hard to defend myself, especially after placing everything in the hands of God.

We can't take back what we've handed over to God. Once you give it all to Him, leave it at His feet and walk away. I learned to allow God's calm to saturate my mind, and it was no longer about my pain or anyone else but my relationship with God. When we surrender, we give God control, and even when it seems that our cries for help are not being heard, when it appears that nothing is happening, be encouraged that in the silence, something is indeed happening, and He is still working. "Don't be misled—you cannot mock the justice of God. You will always harvest what you plant" (Galatians 6:7 NLT). May these words give you the satisfaction that God looks out for His children. Nothing is hidden from Him. We all reap the results of our actions.

You may not like your circumstances, but you must embrace them and ask God for help. Instead of dwelling on what's happening, the pain it's causing, and how unfair it seems, ask *God, what are you trying to teach me this season in this storm?* The most important thing to remember is that everything you place in the hands of God is better taken care of, and for that fact, find comfort in Him in letting go. We may not understand some things we face, but God does. As the Word of God says, those who hope in the Lord will not be disappointed (Isaiah 49:23). Even if you have an army against you, even if you're walking through the darkest path or the heaviest storm, it does not matter because God is on your team, which is far greater than any opposition. Never give the enemy a foothold. Better days are ahead—not behind!

14

GENEROSITY ENCOURAGED

---

*After the verb "to love," "to help" is the most
beautiful verb in the world.*
—Bertha Von Suttner

Jesus sat opposite the temple where the offering was placed and watched as people put their money into the offering box. Many rich people put in large amounts, but a poor widow came and dropped in two small coins. Jesus called His disciples and said, "Truly, I tell you, this poor widow has put more into the treasury than all the others. They all gave out of their wealth, but she, out of her poverty, put in everything she had to live on" (Mark 12:43–44).

Everyone who knows me well knows I love to give. It is my love language and part of my ministry. I start feeling bad about it when I cannot give. I always wish I had enough to keep giving, buying my loved ones more gifts, or offering to ministries doing the genuine work of God. But as with the widow in the story, the real test is giving when we do not have enough, genuinely giving out of the little we have left in faith. That is the type of selfless act God is looking for. In offering your good deeds, God wants you to do so privately and not with the intention of public praise. God, who sees all things, will reward you. Our charitable deeds should not be about us but about our relationship with God. Everything you do should flow from your love for God, including how you help others. When we make giving about ourselves, we lose every good gift we stand to gain from God. Giving is expressing your gratitude to God by extending your hand and time to others so they will praise God for what you have done for them. Giving is a choice we make.

The Word of God helps us understand that giving is better than receiving (Acts 20:35). When you give from your heart, God fills you up in every way. Showing gratitude for what the Lord has done for you by giving is a natural response, but what about giving when you're waiting on God to make way for you? What about when you're financially drained? God is our ultimate supplier. Everything we have comes from Him. So we must trust that as we give from the little we have, He will surprise us with more. But that should never be our reason for giving. We give because it is the right thing to do; it's a loving and godly thing to do. God loves a cheerful giver.

Giving can be done in many ways: tithing (ten percent of our earnings), offering ourselves to God in service, providing our time, resources, and finances, being there for someone, and so on. We must learn to give and do so generously, especially in our time of need. Sowing a tiny seed can turn into a bountiful harvest. Giving in times when you're most drained financially shows the strength of your faith and trust in God.

The motives behind our giving should be authentic. It should come from a pure heart and must be done freely and with an open mindset. Everybody gives, but not all people give generously. God wants us to be generous in giving—giving more than we "ought to" and doing so without motives. Where is the reward if there is a motive behind your giving? Some people give their time to be noticed. What reward is there to gain in that? The Word of God tells us that such people will always earn rewards on earth, not heaven. And the praise and love they seek from people will be all they receive (Matthew 6:1–4).

Another thing to watch out for when giving is to have the mindset that you are doing it for God and not man. As followers of Christ, you should never make others feel as if they are indebted to you because you extended a helping hand to them. Our services to others should be because of who they are to God and not because of what they can do for us in return or how we can gain control over them. We live to give God the glory in all things, not to glorify ourselves. God always wants our services to come from a place of kindness, love, pure genuineness, and nothing less.

God rewards us in so many ways. It may not be financially, but He gives us everything that money cannot buy—a complete spiritual luxury! 2 Corinthians 9:6–15 gives us all the reasons and how we should give as believers:

- Whoever gives in small quantities also reaps small quantities.
- Whoever gives generously also reaps generously.
- Give what your heart has decided, not reluctantly or under compulsion.
- God loves a cheerful giver.
- God will bless you abundantly with everything you need and in everything you do.
- God will enrich your life in every way.
- God will enlarge the harvest of your righteousness.
- Giving is not only supplying the needs of people but is also an expression of your thanksgiving to God.
- Give so others will praise God.
- People to whom you extend your generosity will remember you in their prayers.

There are so many reasons why and how a believer should extend a hand to others, and my favorite is seeing it as a service to God and not man. Let's also be advised that giving can also be in the form of surrendering all your worries to God—You give your worry; you harvest His peace.

15

KNOWING YOUR WORTH

*Walk in confidence, knowing that you are royalty! You
are chosen. You are God's special possession.*

"Are not five sparrows sold for two pennies? Yet not one of them
is forgotten by God. Indeed, the very hairs of your head are all
numbered. Don't be afraid; you are worth more than many sparrows"
(Luke 12:6–7). Have you ever gone to the supermarket for bananas
only to walk past them because they looked rough and bruised
outside? We often reach out for the beautiful ones on the outside,
which display perfectly. Few people know that a bruised banana
does not necessarily mean it is spoiled and that even though it looks
rough outside, it still makes delicious muffins and bread. A banana
is a banana in all stages. Whether beautiful on the outside or bruised
on the inside, a banana remains what it is, and its value remains the
same. Those unable to recognize the value in its bruised stage are the
ones who do not see and have the capacity to put it to use.

Only those who can spot your use and value in all seasons of
your life are the true representatives of God. Just like those who see
the value of a bruised banana, God knows and can see your worth
even though others may not. People may see your mess and bruised
self, but God sees the value beneath all the scars. In all stages of
your life, your value to God remains the same. He does not value
you based on your capabilities or excellent performances but because
He loves and sees you through the lens of grace.

The truth is that not only do other people fail to see our worth,
but at times, we also look past it. We look in the mirror, see so many

imperfections, and start pointing out everything we would change about ourselves, forgetting who we are and our true purpose on earth regardless of how we may look or feel about ourselves. We devalue ourselves based on the slightest flaw, giving ourselves a tough time, and forget how loved and cherished we are by God.

When you start seeing yourself in the light of God, you develop confidence through Him. Failing to see your value will cause you to lean on others to make you feel important, but knowing that God places so much importance on you that He gave His Son in your place should give you the confidence required to live the life He has called you to. God did this because He thought you were worth it—He wants you to know that you are not what you feel, how you look, or what happens to you, but how He feels about you, what He sees in you, and the plans He has waiting for you.

Sometimes, we wonder why the people we value do not see us in that same light. We must realize that these individuals are not for us, and at the right time, God will send those who will walk into your life and see the beauty within and a light that no one else sees. Never feel as though you must chase people to feel worthy. The only one you must never cease to pursue is God because He never stops pursuing you. There is a tribe of people for you every season or for a lifetime. Chasing others to see your worth is forgetting who you are. Walk in your authenticity, and the right people will gravitate toward you. Know your worth! You are a child of the King of kings! God's love for you is too big and should be accepted and embraced. When you realize God's love for you, you will never need to go out of your way to be noticed by those around you because you will be satisfied and made whole in Him, lacking nothing.

True Identity

"You are a chosen people, a royal priesthood, a holy nation, God's special possession, that you may declare the praises of him who called you out of darkness into his wonderful light" (1 Peter 2:9). This verse speaks so deeply to my heart as it was a verse God led me to when I struggled to find my identity in this world. It reminds me of who we are as children of God. We are *royalty*—a truth I have come to embrace. We are *chosen!* And we are God's special *possessions.* This is a truth we must take personally.

One of the most challenging things we all go through at some point in our lives is the need to know who we are. We often base that on what we do for a living, what we've failed to achieve, or other's opinions of us. You must be aware of how you accept other people's negative opinions in your heart. Believing other people's stories about you that do not align with what God has written about you can destroy you— this might redirect you on a path God has not called you to.

After years and effort of schooling, I had to sacrifice going back to work for a while to stay home and care for my kids. Does this mean my identity is known as a stay-at-home mother? Of course not, though many saw me that way. I knew who I was and realized I was made for more than my situation, so people's opinions did not matter.

Your current situation is part of the bigger picture. God has for us. Your real identity is tied to God. It is who you are in Him. It is linked to why He sent Jesus to die for you. What you do right now in your life, what you juggle day in and day out, is not who you are. God calls us His own, His beloved children. We cannot live our lives by letting the things we do, our careers, or what others think of us determine who we are. When you base your identity on these things, which are things that can easily be taken away, you will constantly feel lost and inadequate.

Before we were born, our identity had already taken form. God knows who we were before we became who we think we are now. As the Lord said to the prophet Jeremiah, "I knew you before I formed you in your mother's womb. Before you were born, I set you apart and appointed you as my prophet to the nation" (Jeremiah 1:5

NLT). When God called Jeremiah to be His prophet, his reply was, "O Sovereign Lord . . . I can't speak for you! I'm too young!" God replied, "Don't say, 'I'm too young,' for you must go wherever I send you and say whatever I tell you" (Jeremiah 1:6–7 NLT).

So, with that in mind, what would your reaction be if God were to call you today and tell you it's time to take on what you were destined to do? Would you also say you are too young, not fit for it, or not ready? You might question your capabilities and what others might think. But the thing about God is that no one can retract when He speaks. Being a deep thinker, being able to read people all my life, and always trying to find the underlying cause of things and find solutions were never wasted traits. These were the purpose of God embedded in me.

Just as God told Jeremiah, He knew and had called him before he was conceived. In the same way, He knows you and me so well and has placed in us all He wants us to be. Being around the wrong people and environment can dim your mission in life. Follow the trail God has set for you, and ignore all other routes. No one can nullify His plans for your life, not even you. He does not necessarily appoint the guy in the Porsche or the guy with the Lamborghini, but rather, He surprisingly appoints the guy at the city gate who sits in front of the rich man's house begging for his next meal.

Our destination is not determined by the circumstances we go through. It is not determined by the limitations others project on us, or we project on ourselves; neither is it by what others say or think about us. God uses our unfortunate circumstances to propel us toward our destination. Some successful people we know today have also passed through unimaginable storms. Still, they never defined themselves as what they went through. They knew what they possessed and chased after it. They used their circumstances, pain, and the stones thrown at them as stepping stones to get to where they are today. I believe that at some point in their lives, they never thought they would be where they are today, but when you are destined for greatness, there is nothing anyone can do to stop it, as God's plans for you are permanent. The well-known pastors who impact with their talents and anointing and speaking God's truth did not come from their mothers' wombs carrying Bibles or trophies in their hands—physically, no, but spiritually, yes. And that is the part of our stories we do not get to see firsthand—who we are destined to be.

To know and uncover your greatness, the Word of God says to seek first the kingdom of God and His righteousness (Matthew 6:33). Only God sees the part about us that no one does. We must trust Him and draw near to Him to manifest all we are in Him. We must realize that our lives are not measured by how many people accept us but by the story that a well-known, powerful God has already written about us. Going through what we go through in life prepares us for the grand moments. There is nothing that God cannot turn around for our good to use for His glory.

Growing up can be challenging for many. How we grow up significantly affects us. Whether we were brought up in a loving or dysfunctional home, separating our identity from the life we know and are used to can be hard. And like many out there, we may find it hard to accept the truth about who God says we are over who society paints us to be. We have blinders on and shut ourselves out of this world simply because of our many unhealed scars. The Bible tells us that we are "God's handiwork, created in Christ Jesus to do good works, which God prepared in advance for us to do" (Ephesians 2:10). Once, we were sinners and had no meaning in life. But because of God's mercy, we are who we are today, worthy to be called His own. Peter, the apostle, makes it clear who we are. He said, "Once you had no identity as a people; now you are God's people. Once you had no mercy; now you have received God's mercy" (1 Peter 2:10 NLT). This verse should give you a sense of satisfaction and pride that is hard to lose.

For me, knowing this truth makes me feel secure and important. Knowing that I belong to God and am His very own possession who is part of His royal priesthood calms my heart. In this life, we cannot please everyone—it is impossible—but we can please the one who matters: God! He is the one to whom we belong and can trust. Our God keeps choosing us, no matter where we find ourselves. Claim your rightful identity as a royal priest in the kingdom of God.

Acceptance

Paul said, "I'm not trying to win the approval of people, but of God. If pleasing people were my goal, I would not be Christ's servant" (Galatians 1:10). Pleasing man is not what makes a person, but pleasing God is. We live in a world that makes it seem that you are more likely to be accepted only if you follow and practice the norms and patterns of this world, that it's the only way to make it in life. But when we find ourselves stuck deep under the pressure of life and feeling left out of many things, we are forced to follow and not lead. In these moments, we should always ask ourselves, "Am I living for the acceptance of this world or God? Is it God I am trying to please or people?" It's never about what the world thinks versus what God thinks. It's always about the latter. When you do not know your identity, you will live for the acceptance of this world and people's approval. Through life's storms and lessons, I have learned that we can't desire to be seen as great in the sight of man and expect to be great in the sight of God. It's one or the other, but I know God's grace and favor give us both when we desire Him alone. Desiring after man means abandoning God.

The apostle Paul knew this truth and reminded us through the Word of God that it is not about being accepted by people that is important but rather knowing that our heavenly Father already chooses us. God commands us in His Word to love one another as Christ loves us so that everyone will know that we belong to Him (John 13:34–35). But when we make it a chore to try so hard to please and be accepted by others, we start replacing those people with God. Our attention now focuses on pleasing others to be in their circle because we believe that's the only way to get by. We can love others as Christ wants us to and not please them in the way we are to please only God, or we can make a mistake in idolizing them. We begin believing that we need people, which is true. We do need people, but we need God the most, and through God, we are gifted with great people, and everything else follows.

The obsession to be seen and approved by those around us can become an addiction and is a quick way to forget what God thinks of us. The acceptance of others can never fill up the void in your life. Only God can do that. When you obsess over human acceptance, your actions become the opposite of what God expects of you. For example, you refrain from certain people so that you can be accepted by another group whose acceptance you desire. This happens when you are unaware of who you are in Christ and would do anything to fit in with the crowd. I can expect such acts from unbelievers, but sadly, this also occurs among the body of Christ. Many people live in the bondage of trying to belong or be accepted by a particular group, believing it is the only way to be noticed. The question is, "Noticed by whom—God or people?"

You never have to try hard to be noticed by God. He already sees you. He already knows your name and accepts you. "God does not show favoritism. He does not choose one person over another. He is a God of equality (Romans 2:11), and He knows you personally better than anyone in this world—this should make you feel proud and confident. You are named and approved by God. You are His masterpiece, a joint heir with Christ. You are chosen. He knew you before you were born. You are His pride, and you are loved. You are free!

David knew and believed this truth when he wrote, "How precious are your thoughts about me, O God. They cannot be numbered! I can't even count them; they outnumber the grains of sand! And when I wake up, you are still with me" (Psalm 139:17–18 NLT). All the things we've been doing to look for affirmation, to feel important, and to be praised by others are meaningless! We have the answers and everything we look for in the kingdom of God.

When you know your rightful place within the kingdom of God, you will never need to rule someone out to be accepted by another. You never need to be connected to people at the top to feel important or accepted because you are already accepted and connected to the Most High. It's impossible to meet everyone else's expectations, but we can meet God's expectations of us, and through that, He will meet ours. The need to be accepted may sometimes make us pretend because we're forced to commit to a certain act to be approved and accepted.

The Son has set you free. Why place yourself in a position to live in the bondage of people-pleasing? The Bible tells us that "many people who believed in Jesus, including some of the Jewish leaders, wouldn't admit it for fear that the Pharisees would expel them from the synagogue, for they loved human praise more than the praise of God" (John 12:42–43 NLT). This is what people-pleasing does; it keeps you from dwelling on the important things in life. It prevents you from seeing what is before you because you are too focused on what is not. Pleasing to be accepted turns you into an actor or actress, and you constantly must put up an act to keep entertaining those you want attention from. You can't please two masters; You can't desire people's approval and expect God's blessings. You can't sow your seeds in someone's backyard and expect a harvest in God's kingdom. God wants all of you. He is all the things we hope for in *one*! His approval sets us free from the opinions and condemnation of this world. When everyone else excludes you, find confidence, freedom, and peace in knowing that God includes you. He chooses you!

Rejection Re-directs

One blessed evening, as I was preparing my children for bed, my oldest daughter, who was four then, looked at me and said,

"Mommy, if no one wants to be your friend, Jesus will be your friend." Her statement gave me instant chills as it was random but very much needed. I couldn't help but smile and wrap my arms around her. I was so happy that God used my daughter to deliver a message He knew I needed to hear at that moment. God knew what was on my mind and delivered it through my daughter. And for my daughter to believe those words that we still have Jesus in our corner even when the world rejects us warmed my heart. God speaks to us in many ways; sometimes, He does so through those around us.

The feeling of rejection can sometimes leave us feeling unwanted and unworthy. But that is never the truth. We live in a time when people like to be well-known and do anything to be noticed. Jesus knew His Father's voice, and because of that, He was not distracted by the rejection of man or focused on how much He was despised. He knew He was God's beloved Son and that God was pleased with Him (Matthew 3:17). He did not need people's validation to feel whole or to belong. He was the Messiah, but did everyone accept that? The Pharisees doubted, but what mattered the most was that He knew who He was and was never shaken by those who rejected or persecuted Him. He knew to whom He belonged and what He came down to accomplish.

Like Jesus, you must recognize God's voice and what He says about you so you are not distracted by secondhand words. No one can go to God and tell Him lies about you, hoping He turns His back on you or abandons you because He knows you more than anyone else. Other people's perception of you does not matter to Him and should not matter to you. Not being liked or accepted does not change God's mind about you or His plans for your life. People's inability to see your value doesn't make you less valuable.

Firsthand, Christians should not make others feel rejected. When we walk with God, we are to emulate Him, including making others feel loved and welcomed, no matter what we think about them. We must put our differences aside and ask ourselves, how would I feel if God rejected me based on what He knows about me?

God wants us to accept one another, just as He has accepted us so that the world may glorify and praise Him (Romans 15:7).

I have seen instances in which people have given up on God based on how other believers of Christ treated them. The world is watching. They depend on us, the ambassadors of Christ, to be good examples and accept them in hopes of leading them toward fulfilling lives through Jesus Christ. However, our weaknesses and behavior sometimes drive these people farther away than closer to God. Followers of Christ are supposed to be different, giving hope to those who are lost and seeking to be heard and seen.

The perfect one, Jesus Christ, accepted both Gentiles and Jews; why do we feel it's okay to reject others when they do not fall into our category of perfection? Why do we shun others when we are the only Word of God they'll ever get to read? God is unhappy with us because we accept those we value and reject those we see beneath us. Saying things like, "That person right there is too short and petite." That man right there is wearing dreadlocks and does not fit into the category of a Christian." "That woman over there has a body filled with tattoos." Those people's way of dressing does not fit into how a real Christian is supposed to dress"—and so on. We need to understand and realize how God moves and does His things. When we go through the Bible, we see that God habitually uses the rejected to do mighty work, bringing honor to His name. The people we would never think God would use are the people He uses to do extraordinary work.

God seeks the broken, rejected, wounded, and willing heart. We must never assume someone's destiny based on the level of value we have for them. We must start seeing people how God sees them. Being liked by everyone does not guarantee success in life. It does not mean we are great, and neither does it mean we are perfect. Jesus was the perfect person on earth, yet that did not change the fact that He was despised and rejected by the crowd because it was never about the people who hated Him. It was never about the people who loved Him. It was about what was destined to happen regardless of who loved Him or did not. What mattered was that He had God. Though being rejected in any situation may be part of our story, it is not the focus. The focus is on where God is taking us. We can't be upset when people reject us because we never know where God is redirecting us or protecting us from.

As a child of God, being rejected by people is not the end of your story. It's rather the beginning. Sometimes, it just means that certain people are not used to your type and can accept you only to the capacity by which they can accept themselves. The Word of God tells us that even though a mother may forget her baby at her breast and have no compassion for the baby, God will not forget us (Isaiah 49:15). It is never a loss to be rejected by the crowd. No child of God loses unless he or she denies Jesus.

You must never allow rejection from others to take root in your heart and life. Many people and companies you apply to will judge and reject you before they know your qualities. This does not mean your qualities do not exist. You must learn to see others' refusal of you as a sign that God wants the best for you and saves you from where you do not need to be. He knows you best. Jesus Christ is your road map to life. He was the stone the builders rejected, who later became the cornerstone (1 Peter 2:7). The rejection of man does not mean your life is built on a weak foundation; it just might mean you are the cornerstone that will hold many lives in place. Fix your eyes on the one who sees you, the one who truly knows you, because He is the one who picks you from where others discard you.

You must move forward in life without being crippled by the weight of rejection. Rest in the fact that God will never reject you— because His love for you is not based on your perfection. Believe that what belongs in your life will never pass you by, and always remember that if you can't handle rejection, you can't handle where God is taking you.

16

HIS WILL

───────────── ⌘ ─────────────

Obedience is a setup for an eternal harvest.

When it comes to God's will for our lives, one thing that always comes to mind is the Bible stories we read when a person's life will suddenly take a route that the person never mapped out for himself or herself—this is what happens when you are living in God's will for your life. The sudden shift from what you've known as your reality for so long will be hard to understand—for you and those around you, but in the end, it's all worth it. The Word of God commands us to obey the Lord (Deuteronomy 11:1–32; 4:30), taking His Word to heart and doing what it instructs—this shows how much we love Him.

Let's look at the story of Joseph (Genesis 37:1–36; 41:1-45). Do you think Joseph grew up knowing he would one day become the second most powerful man in Egypt, besides Pharoah? I bet that never crossed his mind or the minds of those around him, but it sure was in God's plans. God's will for your life may differ from what you have set for yourself. No matter which direction life takes you, the powerful force of God will continue pursuing you so that His will can prevail in your life.

Birthing and coming to a full realization of your calling is vital in your journey with God. You must surround yourself with people or connect to a community to help you cultivate your gifts and walk in your purpose. Ask God to help you bring destiny helpers who will see the secret within you, help you out of your pregnancy state, and help you push the greatness within you. God's will manifests even through the heaviest storms and dark times because anything born of the light always stands out. In situations where the enemy plots against you, the will of God still prevails. In circumstances where you find yourself lost, the will of God will find you. In places where you find yourself trapped, the will of God will set you free. God's will for your life is something you cannot escape. His will is part of who you are. Saul, who became Paul, couldn't escape the will of God for his life—a man who went from killing Christians to a man who proclaimed the good news of God (Acts 9:1–22).

As I matured in Christ, God started showing me a glimpse of what He wanted to do with me, through me, for me, but because God never shows us the whole picture at once, I still found myself wondering what His will for my life was, more so what is next after another and how and when I would get there. This is the thing about God. He will show you that one beautiful vision, but He will never show you the challenges or oppositions you will encounter through the journey. The walk to purpose is a walk of faith.

Through the journey, I've held on to questions such as—*Am I where He wants me to be? Am I doing what He wants me to do? Is He proud of me?* I realized with all the questions that it was not how, when, and what. It was about the who (me) and the journey—"How is my walk with God in this journey?" You see, it is not you but God who has the final say in your life, but it is up to you to accept His decrees and regulations.

I have chosen to pursue God's will for my life, and it is my job to surrender and obey Him so His will can prevail. Though His will for our lives is a specially mapped-out plan, we also have a part in bringing it to manifestation. Whether it seems good or bad, His will always prevail, just as in the lives of Joseph and many others in the Bible. No U-turns can shift us away from God's will. God pursues us and places us where we are meant to be. Getting there may seem challenging and sometimes hazy, but once that line is crossed, it all makes sense, and you start understanding why you faced certain trials along the way. Through the journey, the enemy will aim to stop you from reaching your destination, but you can always find hope in knowing that God fights for you.

As you draw nearer to God, He reveals Himself in extraordinary ways. He will constantly take you on a series of lessons. I call it spiritual school. These lessons will teach you things about yourself and the work you are to accomplish. Manifesting the plans of God for your life requires your utmost obedience and trust in Him. Will it be easy to get to your destination? No, but will He see you through to the finish line where you receive the crown of life? Yes! Trust Him to take the lead, even if what you face along the way is too painful to comprehend. Even when you feel like He is not with you, keep trusting.

Trusting Him shows an attitude of thankfulness even in your pain and uncertainties. Paul tells us to give thanks in all circumstances as it is God's will for us through Christ Jesus (1 Thessalonians 5:18). One may ask, "All circumstances? Even the ones that leave us shattered?" Yes! All circumstances. Part of surrendering to God's will is giving up your need to control every storm you pass through and simply looking up to Him in obedience and embracing every turn as it comes.

God created you for a purpose, for His glory, but sometimes we forget that and try to make things go our way, to do everything on our own, fight back, and reach for control in all things—but God desires for us to stand still and know that He is God (Psalm 46:10). When we direct our own steps, we miss the amazing plans He has for us. David knew this when He said, "You saw me before I was born. Every day of my life was recorded in your book. Every moment was laid out before a single day had passed" (Psalm 139:16 NLT).

The disappointments and heartbreaks happen when we try to control things on our own, shift God's plans, and insert ours. Though disappointments and heartbreaks allow us to learn and grow, we can avoid certain unnecessary situations and learn and grow spiritually through Christ when we obey His Word. Nothing good comes from trying to control what only God can navigate.

But the good news is that God never makes us feel rushed. He is patient with us, waiting for us to realize that real fulfillment comes from placing our utmost trust in Him. Do you think Jesus Christ enjoyed the harsh treatment He received on Earth? No, He did not! But He knew what He stood to gain was beyond what He was going through; for this reason, He kept enduring all the troubles He passed through.

The night before He was crucified, Jesus went to pray. His prayer revealed His emotional state toward what was happening to Him. He was tired, pleading for God to take away this whole predicament He was facing, but He knew that was not God's will for Him. So He said, "Yet I want your will to be done, not mine" (Matthew 26:39 NLT). This is what the apostle Paul meant when He said, "I consider that our present sufferings are not worth comparing to the glory that will be revealed in us" (Romans 18:8).

Can you stand in your storms and still wait for God to prevail without the urge to control things or quit? Just like Jesus, we must strive to hold tight, no matter how easy it will be to give up. God's will for your life comes with a price worth paying, one worth fighting for and enduring. Jesus endured to the end because He understood it was not about how He was feeling and what He was going through but what He was to accomplish. He said, "I have come from heaven not to do my will, but to do the will of Him who sent me" (John 6:38).

Everything in your life passes through God first. He knows what's best for you, and your part is to surrender in obedience and have faith in Him, no matter the storms. Even though the road to destiny may not always be smooth, the beautiful and comforting part is that God never leaves us to travel that path alone. James helps us understand that the crown of life is promised to all who love God and endure testing and temptations (James 1:12). What if what you are currently facing in your life is part of God's plan for you, whether good or bad, whether you agree with it or not? What if what you are going through is the transportation you need to take you to your destination? If you cannot handle the tests of time, you can't handle the surprises that await you when you reach your destination. As uncomfortable as it is to go through the storms of life, you must trust in God's plans for you and do your part in manifesting those plans.

Nothing we go through as children of God—the stress, worries, pain, hurt, and troubles—will affect us in Heaven. None of it will matter at home in the presence of our Father. Life is not about us. It is about the glory of God that will be revealed in us. It is about fulfilling the will of the Father. Paul understood this when he said, "My life is worth nothing to me unless I use it for finishing the work assigned me by the Lord Jesus—the job of telling others the Good News about the extraordinary grace of God" (Acts 20:24 NLT). We are here for His glory, for His will, not ours.

The route to the promised land requires you to obey God. "Can two people walk together without agreeing on the direction?" (Amos 3:3 NLT). You cannot walk with God unless you learn to agree with Him. It's hard to walk in your purpose if you choose your way over God's. It's hard to walk in your purpose if you do not believe in yourself or that you are worthy to accomplish the task God has entrusted you. Many are blind to the truth that our lives belong to God, and that He had planned it all for His glory, and because of this, there's always a conflict of will—what we want for our life versus what God wants for us. This is when life becomes a struggle—when we fight and ignore our calling, when our soul is starving, but our own will is focused on the desires of this world.

The reality is that many people live the life they choose for themselves. Amid it, they're struggling and blaming God for their struggles without even realizing that it is because they're not walking in the will of God for their lives. "He was pierced for our rebellion, crushed for our sins. He was beaten so we could be whole. He was whipped so we could be healed. All of us, like sheep, have strayed away. We have left God's paths to follow our own. Yet the Lord laid on Him the sins of us all" (Isaiah 53:5–6 NLT). This is what Jesus came down to go through for you. He had to endure this so you could draw near to God and follow His will for your life.

A Willing Heart

"I consider my life worth nothing to me; my only aim is to finish the race and complete the task the Lord Jesus has given me—the task of testifying to the good news of God's grace" (Acts 20:24). In His farewell letter to the Ephesian elders, Paul expressed that he considered his life worthless if it was not used for God's work. He aimed to focus on the task the Lord had given him –"testifying to the good news of God's grace." Telling others about the necessity of repenting from sin, turning to God, and having faith in Him is the job of every child of God. A willing heart knows this truth and is ready to give up all fleshly desires for the glory of God no matter what. We can see that Paul was willing. He had given himself up for God's work and found no interest in other things but in living his life in obedience to the call of God. God sees and knows your willingness to do His job. The desire to pick up your cross, take on the task entrusted to you, and do it wholeheartedly opens the doors for God to use you magnificently and supernaturally.

A willing heart can depend on a mustard seed of faith to get through life's challenges that come with the heaviness of carrying the cross. When you empty yourself and allow God to use you, He will use you. He will be there for you, equip you, and rebrand you for His glory. You can never take on the work of God without His first refining you. He will put you under strict training. Your result will determine how ready you are for God's task.

Some of us get distracted and sidetracked, making the training process harder and longer. The story of Job (Job 1:1–20) is an excellent example of being tested to prove the strength of our faith through endurance. Picking up your cross and following Jesus are never wasted, but how long can you keep holding on to that cross during a storm? Carrying it through life's most challenging storms will determine your readiness and finish line. A person with a willing heart is intentional in their walk with God and is focused on what He is doing in and through them. A person with a willing heart trusts God no matter what comes their way and remembers who they are in Christ. A person with a willing heart gives themselves up and clings to God; they are ready to sacrifice it all for the glory of God.

Purpose

When you know God's will for your life, when you are living in the fullness of why you were brought on this earth —you are living a life of purpose! Paul said, "We speak as messengers approved by God to be entrusted with the Good News. Our purpose in life is to please God, not people. He alone examines the motives of our hearts" (1 Thessalonians 2:4 NLT). "What is my purpose in life?" "What am I here for?" "What is next for me?" How many times have you asked yourself these questions? I believe you've wondered what your purpose is at some point.

You are not wrong for wanting to know, as we've all wondered what God's plans and purpose are as we journey through life. As the apostle Paul mentioned in Scripture, our first purpose as believers of Christ is to please God and draw people closer to Him. So, with that in mind, ask yourself, "How do I please God with my current situation? How do I please Him with the way I live?" "Is getting to know Him through His Word first on my to-do list, or is my schedule too swamped to fit Him in?"

Before making any decision, ask yourself the necessary questions: "Am I doing this to please God, man, or myself?" As a child of God, what do you think your number-one purpose in life is? Yes, we are called to something, and that inner hunger for more of God, that thirst you yearn to quench, that feeling of wanting more and doing more for Him in His kingdom, that call that never stops ringing until you answer—it all indicates that God is calling you, and until you answer, you will always wonder, repeatedly asking yourself the same questions.

How do we get there? How do we answer our call? Simple—surrender yourself for His, lose your will for His will. Paul said, "For me to live is Christ and to die is gain" (Philippians 1:21). Paul understood that if he died, it would be a gain for him as being with the Father is much more gain. But even if He lives on, living for Christ is dying to self and pursuing the work of God. To die to self is to resurrect in the Spirit, and to live in the Spirit is to seek God's will and live out the purpose by which you've been called. Once you realize that you are an empty vessel, ready to be filled with more, with all God has for you, your will to surrender will grow daily.

We exist for a reason, and most of us are lost, trapped in our minds, and roaming with question after question about our existence on earth because we've abandoned our first purpose in life. We've disconnected ourselves from God and connected ourselves with the patterns of this world. We must fulfill our first purpose, an ongoing activity, to be witnesses of Christ, proclaiming the good name of the Lord and winning souls to His kingdom.

God controls all things, including our destiny. Our day jobs alone can never give us the fulfillment we seek. Nothing we do will bring us absolute satisfaction if God is not involved. We must represent and proclaim Him even at our workplaces and businesses. The problem is that we usually forget and focus on our nine-to-five-day jobs. We focus on temporary fulfillment.

We unravel so many secrets to life through serving the purpose we've been called. Life is mysterious, and the only way to get answers is by walking intimately with the one who knows everything, including the beginning and end of your story.

Push! Survival of the Fetus

"Therefore, dear brothers and sisters, we have no obligation—but it is not to the flesh to live according to it. For if you live according to the flesh, you will die; but if by the Spirit you put to death the misdeeds of the body, you will live" (Romans 8:12–13). In this passage, Paul tells us that the Spirit of God gives us life and helps us stand firm in our pregnant state, and if we start living by the commands of our flesh, that life ceases.

One of the enemy's jobs is to ensure that he overshadows that spiritual part of you. He does that by getting into your mind with his lies. There is greatness inside each of us, and this greatness that God has placed within us requires us to go through all the stages of pregnancy. Before we get to "pushing," we must go through the three trimesters of pregnancy!

First Trimester

In the first trimester, you discover something within yourself and realize that God has put something unique inside you. The battle is strong in this stage because the enemy knows what God has planted inside you. You will get sick, your body may go through stress, and as the seed grows, you will go through a series of tiredness and pressure. The battle may seem endless and tiring, but it only means the enemy is threatened by what has been planted inside you.

This is the beginning—the beginning of something amazing! Paul said, "Our present sufferings are not worth comparing with the glory that will be revealed in us" (Romans 8:18). So even though there are battles along the way to the labor ward, the place you birth your greatness, even though the survival of your fetus is in jeopardy, the greatness that you will give birth to cannot be compared to the pains that you feel in these three trimesters of pregnancy.

Second Trimester

In the second trimester, you slowly get comfortable with whatever God has put inside you. You walk in it, embrace it, embody it, and identify it. This is where you will start feeling the love and presence of this greatness within you. It becomes something you pursue. It becomes something you meditate on, something that excites you. Something you can't wait to give birth to, something that you constantly go to God to reveal more of because the thrill of this greatness has become a solid part of you and who you are meant to become. It has become the reason for your joy, the reason you exist. The reason you keep going and never give up.

Third and Last Trimester

In the third trimester, you will start going through things like what you experienced in your first trimester. This is where God has fully helped in developing your greatness. This is the stage in which you are to birth your greatness. It is time to *push,* but the enemy becomes even more threatened, and the battle worsens. This is the stage at which the enemy works in all avenues. It is when he tries all his tricks to ensure you are kept in this stage for longer than planned.

Many people are still walking around the world, still pregnant with their greatness, because somehow the enemy has kept them captive in that position, and they're unaware of it. But that is not your story. It is time to *push!* The enemy does not want you to push, so he tries many tricks to ensure you are distracted, worn out, and stranded. He does anything to prevent you from pushing and birthing your greatness. At times, his games become the focus in your life instead of pushing, and the need to push becomes something you find yourself putting in the back seat.

One of Satan's biggest ways to distract us is by playing games with our minds (a topic I will address later in the chapter). Paul tells us not to copy the behavior and customs of this world but to let God transform us into new people by changing how we think. Then we will learn to know God's will for us—and God's will for us is good, it's pleasing, and it's perfect (Romans 12:2). The first place Satan seeks is your mind, and it is also where we fight our greatest and most challenging battles. Satan knows that if he can direct and weaken your mind, he will be able to keep you from pushing out your greatness, but as a child of God, you know the narratives can change—but only if you depend on God to help free you from whatever keeps you stagnant. What are you allowing in your thoughts? What are you allowing the enemy to use against you to keep you captive and in your labor ward? What are you allowing the enemy to use against you to keep you from pushing?

I want you to note that Satan is real, and ignoring his existence is to put him one step ahead of you. As children of God, we should not tremble because our God is also real—the God of all creation and, above all powers and principalities, who has already won all the battles for us. Why do you think Satan tries so hard to divert your attention? It's to keep you from living the life you are destined for, in that pregnant state, in that labor ward, to keep you distracted from pushing and birthing the beauty within. God is saying it is time to push, and Satan says, "No, never. I won't allow it." What are you also saying? Whose words are you going to follow? Whose words are you going to meditate on? And whose words are you going to let motivate your actions?

God says you are a fighter, you are victorious, you are a conqueror, a warrior. Satan says you are a failure, that you can't do it. Whose words are you going to believe? To win the race of life, you need to reach a point at which the voice of God becomes the forefront of your life. Winning the race of life is when the Spirit of God in you overshadows the urges of your flesh. Paul said, "We have no obligation to do what our sinful nature urges us to do" (Romans 8:12). We have the power to overcome and defeat. We have the power to rise above the strongholds. When we feed our fleshly desires, we kill the spiritual aspect of us, but when we starve our flesh as Paul tells us to do, we resurrect the spiritual part of us. And when that spiritual aspect of us is awakened, we can gain the strength to *push*!

Overcoming Fear and Walking in Your Purpose

God told Jeremiah, "I knew you before I formed you in your mother's womb. Before you were born, I set you apart and appointed you as my prophet to the nations." Jeremiah said to the Lord, "O Sovereign Lord, I can't speak for you! I'm too young!" The Lord replied, "Don't say, 'I'm too young,' for you must go wherever I send you and say whatever I tell you. And don't be afraid of the people, for I will be with you and will protect you. I, the Lord, have spoken!" (Jeremiah 1:5–8 NLT). Fear is man's worst enemy. It keeps us in places that question our ability to rise. When we think of the purpose by which God has called us, we often link it to the wrong places—in our jobs, relationships, ethnicity, titles, and so on. We look around and wonder why others are living a life of purpose, but for some reason, we are stuck, standing in our own way. Now, my question to you is, How are you pleasing God in this very moment, right now, with everything He has given you? Are you using what He has given you to please Him?

Satan has one reason for attacking you, and it all comes down to the fact that he wants to prevent you from walking in the fullness of God's glory and experiencing the fullness of joy and abundance that is promised to you. His ways of doing this are many. He has so many tactics, and one of them is fear—fear of uncertainties, fear of making a mockery of yourself, fear of what people will think, fear of failing, fear of what you may have to sacrifice, and so on. Whatever fear you are currently dealing with that prevents you from walking in your purpose, God wants you to break free of it. He wants you to start walking in His fullness. He has given you everything you need to walk in that fullness and has given you the power to fight off any hindrances.

God's plans for you are good. Knowing who you are in Him is the basis of that plan, knowing where you stand in His kingdom and how seriously you take your relationship with Him. You were created for great things but hesitate to take a step even when the opportunity comes around. Why is that? Because you fear what might happen if you take that step or that you don't think you are good enough to be the one to take that step. Greatness can be achieved only by going for it, even if you're afraid of what's ahead or what you will uncover. Satan uses fear to remind us of everything that could go wrong if we leap forward. What he does is to cause you to believe that the only way to your freedom is by keeping yourself trapped, by staying in that safe zone. He cripples you and causes you to sit. He does not want you to live a life of purpose and will use fear, among his other tactics, to ensure you're stuck.

The Word of God tells us that Satan is the father of all lies (John 8:44). What is a lie? It is something that does not exist. Fear is a lie—it is simply an illusion. It does not exist! Fear questions God's hands in your life. It questions His plans for your life and the very essence of God, which is *love,* but the Word of God tells us there is no fear in love, but perfect love drives out fear (1 John 4:18). Fear tells us we can't trust God. It tells us that God will abandon us, that we are in this walk of life alone, and that we face uncertainties alone, which causes us to doubt God's power.

The Word of God tells us that Peter was walking on water but started sinking because of fear (Matthew 14:30). Gideon hesitated in fighting against the Midianites because of fear and self-doubt (Judges 6:11–17; Judges 7:1–25). The disciples feared the wind and storm, forgetting the power of the one with them in that boat because of fear (Matthew 8:23–27). Pharoah and his army were behind the Israelites just before God parted the sea. They were consumed with fear because they did not see a way (Matthew 14:11–14). That is what fear does—it clouds your judgment.

David said, "I sought the Lord, and he answered me and delivered me from all my fears. Those who look to him are radiant, and their faces shall never be ashamed" (Psalm 34:4–5). Who do you turn to when you feel afraid? Who do you go to with your feelings of fear? David said to seek God. The good news is that when you go to God with your fears and ask Him to help you deal with them, He will help you remove them and transform your life.

One day, after a short devotion, I was curious about what was keeping me stagnant and what was keeping me from moving forward when it came to my destiny. I asked God to show me, and He gave me a dream in which I saw myself in front of a short bridge. People were passing on this bridge—passing by me and crossing this bridge effortlessly. However, when it got to my turn, I was still standing there, afraid to cross. When I managed to step onto the bridge, I found myself staggering in fear and fell on the bridge. Then, instead of getting up, I crawled my way across. Fear can cause a delay in where God is taking you. The Spirit of God told me this when fear was imminent. He told me to see fear as a red traffic light that causes you to park in traffic for a long time. This red light is simply an illusion. It is fake and does not exist, but the enemy makes you think the light is red when it is green. It is okay for you to go, but because you believe you see a red light, you are scared to go, causing you to stay in parking mode. You refuse to step on that accelerator, and the people not consumed by fear pass by you, and you're still sitting in traffic. Your children might even pass while you're in parking mode.

This is what happens when we allow fear to control us. It keeps us from taking that leap of faith. Crawling your way into your destiny is not what God wants for you—that is the spirit of delay you've allowed to take residence in your life. What should take a month to accomplish will take a year or even longer.

In the second part of the dream, I saw myself at a playground with familiar faces around me. I was on top of something. It was shaped like a webbed dome or something of that sort, and I had to get down from this thing, but I was afraid to and called the people around to help me. No one was listening to me. They pretended they couldn't hear me. So, I was left to either find my way down or sit up in fear. In the end, I managed to get down on my own, and suddenly, I saw these people coming around me cheerfully, cheering me on for making it down. Another thing fear does is place you in your comfort zone, and many people are stuck in that zone because they doubt their capabilities. They believe they don't have the power to walk the road to "purpose" or the ability to rise, and the only way is if someone is holding their hands.

When you are in your comfort zone, your sense of power diminishes, and you start thinking you need someone else's power to help you reach your destination. But the only power you need is the power God has given you. When God sees that you are striving and trying to walk in the fullness of His glory, He sends you helpers who will help you along the journey. If, because of fear, you are parked and sitting there in comfort, you will drive away all the helpers God sends you. The Israelites in Egypt made this mistake. They were so comfortable in their lowly position in Egypt, and many did not appreciate their journey to purpose or greener pastures. They blamed Moses and said that he had brought them to their deaths. They did not realize the abundance God wanted to give them. They saw Moses as a torturer rather than a savior because they were not used to the journey of walking with purpose. So many of them gave up before getting to the promised land (Exodus 14:5–29).

The same concept goes for each of us. Many people give up in fear before they get to experience God's glory in their lives. If you're not ready to grasp that vision for your life, you will see anyone God sends your way to help you as a burden rather than a helper. Your readiness will be determined when God sends you a "Moses." Your readiness will be determined when you get to "Mount Sinai." The enemy creates destruction to discourage you from moving into your promised land. Some of this destruction may be worrying about what people think—fear of their criticizing you and rejecting you, having people around you who may not believe in God's vision for your life, or supporting you the way that they should. But that's okay because God gave the vision to you and trusted you with the task, and your job is to make sure it is accomplished; your job is to make sure you are walking and not sitting.

We are all called for different purposes, and being called requires us to be set apart. The secret is that once you know God's purpose for your life, you approach and walk confidently. How do you walk confidently in your purpose? By having faith in God, who has called you, believing and embracing the purpose He has called you to and believing in yourself to get the work done.

When God asked Moses to free His people, the Israelites, from Egypt, Moses questioned his ability to get the work done and his worth. He said, "Who am I to appear before Pharaoh? Who am I to lead the people of Israel out of Egypt?" But God said to him, "I will be with you" (Exodus 3:11–12), and that's the same thing God said to Jeremiah: "I will be with you" (Jeremiah 1:8 NLT). And that is what He is saying to you right now—"I will be with you."

Like Moses, you may fear what is next for you and fear taking a step because of your confidence in completing your task. You can do it! God may lead you on a different path than you are comfortable with because being called to walk in your purpose does not come with comfort. It is a sacrifice you must make. This path may seem challenging, but you can rest knowing that God will never lead you to a place without providing what's needed. He will never call you and abandon you halfway.

God chose Moses specifically to lead His people out of Egypt. God has also chosen you for your specific purpose, and He did so because He trusts you and expects you to embrace and walk confidently in that purpose. He trusts you to get the work done! Do not give the enemy the power to use fear to stop you from confidently pursuing your God-given purpose. Please do not allow him to hold you back, and have the best part of you. Do not allow him to win.

Battlefield

In his letter to the Romans, Paul said, "Do not conform to the patterns of this world but be transformed by the renewing of your mind" (Romans 12:2). Through the storms of life, I have learned that the hardest battles happen within our minds—the first place the enemy attacks and where we fight our greatest battles. But the narratives can change for those who look to God for help.

The Word of God tells us to have renewed minds so we can see the will of God for our lives—His good, pleasing, and perfect will. When we conform to the patterns of this world, our thinking becomes clouded, which results in a crooked way of living. Conforming to the patterns of the world allows the words of the enemy to permeate our thoughts and lead us instead of the Word of God.

As you go through life's challenges, you must guard yourself by taking note of the things you feed your mind or allow to take space in your mind—because what goes inside your mind will determine and influence what comes out —how you act and approach things. If you give way, Satan will play with your mind to keep you repeatedly reliving senseless moments to keep you distracted. The things he puts in your mind may seem so real that if you do not seek God for discernment, you may buy what he sells and start living your life contradicting the plans of God.

How do we win the battle of the mind? In what ways can we defeat the strongholds of our minds? By inviting God in daily, making an effort to think uplifting thoughts, things that matter, and paying attention to the things you are accepting or the things you fixate on. Satan aims to block you. Many have fallen for his tricks time after time, forgetting that they have the power as children of God to beat him at his games. The battle against your mind is real, and Satan is constantly prowling around, seeking ways to fill your mind with lies to gain access to destroy what God has prepared for you. You can command him to leave your personal space, overcome and win this battle, and live the life God has called you to— pleasing and perfect!

The Bible often speaks about our thoughts and our tongues. The tongue has the power of life and death (Proverbs 18:21). What we think and confess with our mouths shapes who we become. Changing the way we think changes our perspective and our actions. The Word of God tells us that "God gives perfect peace to all whose thoughts are fixed on him and trust in him" (Isaiah 26:3 NLT). What flows through our minds can direct us on either the right or wrong paths. We acknowledge Satan and his lies when we believe the negative things he puts in our minds, and doing so only leads to wrong actions and a wrong path—one of destruction and one God has not called us to. Acknowledging God in all we do—how we think, what we say, what we believe, and how we act and approach the matters in our lives, will lead us to a straight and fulfilling path.

The enemy can only triumph over you if you allow him to cripple you with lies. God wants you to live a life of freedom, peace, a prosperous future, and a life that illustrates His love. All the enemy needs is a tiny space to invade and deceive. How do you defeat the enemy in his game of deception? How do you break free from the stronghold keeping you captive in your mind? By inviting God in every single day. You must be intentional about this, to invite Him every day and ask for His help.

As a child of God, you must recognize the difference between the enemy's lies and God's truth. How do you do this? Knowing the Word of God reveals the truth, the way, and the life! (John 4:6), so when the enemy's lies start consuming your mind, you can immediately differentiate between the two and resist. Paul advises us to think of "whatever is true, whatever is noble, whatever is right, whatever is pure, whatever is lovely, whatever is admirable, excellent or praiseworthy" (Philippians 4:8). Who is worthy of our praise? Our Lord Jesus Christ! (Psalm 145:3). He is worthy of our praise in all situations. "Fix your thoughts on what is true." What is the truth? Our Lord Jesus Christ! (John 14:6; 16:3). His words are true and set us free.

Through Christ, there is clarity. We must keep challenging ourselves to do better, to think better, and to act better. This is what is expected of us as children and ambassadors of God, and this is how we can break through. I've come across so many young women who carry the fear of not being good enough or not worthy enough for God's plans, feeling inadequate and unqualified. Though I have been there and understood exactly how they felt, it also saddens me to hear how sometimes we can allow our storms to make us forget or overlook the deep and purest love of a merciful and compassionate Father. Through the blood of Jesus, we are made righteous, and God shuns no one who seeks Him in repentance. He embraces and guides. Through Him, you are victorious and not a victim. You possess the power to shut down negative thoughts because the Spirit who raised Jesus from death lives in you (Romans 8:11). Because of this truth, there is nothing we can't conquer in this journey of life.

The battle of the mind can be draining and tormenting, but remember that the enemy fights the hardest against those who stand to destroy his works. You have something amazing within you. You are a threat to Satan; he will stop at nothing to see you go down. You have God—that is why you are in this wrenching battle, but this is also why Paul tells us to rejoice in our afflictions (Romans 5:3) because the cost is nothing compared to the prize we stand to gain at the end of that battle.

The enemy is afraid of you, and you must realize and accept this truth to defeat him. Your strength to fight is limited, but God's strength takes over your weakness (2 Corinthians 12:9–10). When you feel weak, drained, and tired mentally, you can turn to the promises of God as a reminder to keep pushing, keep fighting, and gain the hope that will bring you back to God's strength. With faith as small as a mustard seed, you can always find your way back to the presence of God, where safety, strength, and help are guaranteed. The more your thoughts are fixed on God, the more you will attract great things into your life, and the clearer your visions will become, giving you better chances to recognize the enemy's lies.

Voices of Contradiction

As Jesus prepared to go to Jerusalem, He told His disciples that He would suffer terrible things from the elders, the leading priests, and the teachers of religious law. He told them He would be killed but on the third day would be raised from death. Peter took Him aside and reprimanded Him for saying this. "Never, Lord! . . . This shall never happen to you!" (Matthew 16: 22). But Jesus turned to Peter and said, "Get behind me, Satan! You are a stumbling block to me. You do not have in mind the concerns of God, but merely human concerns" (Matthew 16:23). Jesus said this not because He thought Peter was evil but because He immediately recognized the enemy's voice in what Peter said. Remember that only the enemy's voice will reprimand us for serving our purpose. The death of Jesus was meant to happen for our salvation.

Imagine how the story would have turned out if Jesus had listened to Peter, as Peter was one of the people closest to Him. This is relatable to our journeys in life; we often listen to certain people's voices through advice or gossip. We believe what they share or say because they are close to us, and we cherish their words or opinions. But the hard truth is that just as God can use a person, the enemy can also influence someone. He also has ambassadors who work for him to bring down the kingdom of God. It is up to us to know the difference between God's voice and the enemy's, to realize when the enemy is trying to speak through those around us to contradict God's purpose in our lives.

God has given us His Word to know Him, for us to familiarize ourselves with His heart and voice. What better way for the enemy to get through to us than to use a familiar face or voice? The enemy draws out his tactics, but God's plans surpass his smartness. Whether these voices come from our loved ones or strangers, we must realize, rebuke, and resist them immediately. Paying attention to secondary voices will cause you to be redirected from where God wants to take you.

What if the terrible things that happen to you along the way are God's way of freeing you from a burden? What if everything you're facing is part of God's plan for you this season? What if you were meant to have that car accident to draw you nearer to witness His divine power and faithfulness in your life and heighten your faith in Him? Yes, it is the enemy's will for us to fail, be destroyed, and die, but it is God's will to experience resurrection in things that are meant to kill us. That is why God takes what the enemy means for bad and uses it to show His sovereignty—this is how we become a witness of the glory of God.

What if God wants to teach you that you shouldn't depend too much on the people around you for what you should rely on Him for? In the case of Jesus, Peter saw what would happen to Him as a problem, but because Jesus knew it was His purpose, He knew that the voice through Peter was a voice of contradiction rather than one of concern. The deceptive voice of the enemy can indeed come as a voice of concern. The devil's sole purpose is to steal, destroy, and kill, but God's primary purpose is to give us life in full (John 10:10). The enemy's voice causes confusion and disunity and causes us to judge one another and reject others, second-guess who we are in Christ, and second-guess the power of God. His voice leads us on a crooked path, on a path of destruction, but the voice of God brings fulfillment and revelation to those who recognize it.

Appointed to Reign

We have many reasons to boast as children of God, but I would love to focus on the fact that, number one, you were made in the likeness of God, and number two, He appointed you to rule over all living creatures (Genesis 1:26–27). Do you know what this means?

It means God has given you the authority to rule over the serpent. When the enemy rises against you, remember you can command him to leave. The serpent does not have power over you, as God has given you dominion over him. We are reminded of this also in the words of Jesus: "I have given you the authority to trample on snakes and scorpions and to overcome all the power of the enemy; nothing will harm you" (Luke 10:19).

God first showed His trust toward us through His relationship with Adam and Eve, trusting them to look after the Garden of Eden. He blessed them and sent them to fill the earth and to have sovereignty over the earth, the fish in the sea, the birds in the skies, and all other animals (Genesis 1:28). God blessed them with plants throughout the earth so they could have food to eat, having nothing to worry about in terms of provision (Genesis 9:3). After the first fall of man, God never forgot about His children. He still looked out for them and never turned His face from them, and to prove His deep love, years after the fall of man, He sent His Son to save humanity (John 3:17).

How does it feel to know that God placed you in charge of all living things, to have sovereignty over the earth, the fish in the sea, the birds in the skies, and all other living creatures? He did not give that authority to the fallen angel (Satan) but to you and me. And though Satan had access to God's powers, his was limited. You have access to something Satan did not yet gain access to. God has appointed you to rule over everything, including your life challenges. You were born to reign! You are with Jesus, an heir to the kingdom of God; therefore, the same Spirit who worked with Him and raised Him from death is always with you and gives you the power to reign—a power that only you possess.

Why fear the arrows thrown your way or the terrors at night? You have dominion. What lives in you is bigger and more powerful than in this world (1 John 4:4). Take on your authority. Reign over the sea, over the fish, over the wild animals, over your enemies, and reign over your storms. Claim your power, claim your place of sovereignty, and accept the position God has trusted you with. You are a ruler over Satan. You are a ruler over your storms, and you are a ruler over all living creatures. Nothing has power over you on this earth unless you give your power to it.

The storms and all the unpleasant situations are like mist in the air, here one moment, gone the next (James 4:14). You are prepared for the storms of life more than you realize. God has given you all the necessary tools to overcome them. You have it in you to rise above the chaos and claim victory. Rise and take ownership of every power given to you! "He who raised Christ from the dead will also give life to your mortal bodies because of His Spirit who lives in you" (Romans 8:11). This is your confidence.

17

AUTHENTICITY

———— ⌒❧⌒ ————

Authenticity is a love language—only the
genuine understands its tongue.

"Don't just pretend to love others. Love them. Hate what is wrong. Hold tightly to what is good. Love each other with genuine affection and delight in honoring each other"(Romans 12:9–10 NLT). Authenticity has become rare today, so much so that it has become foreign to many. It has become the act of many flatteries and giggles. It is more of "Who will sit with you when times get hard?" "Who will still see your heart and goodness despite your mistakes?" This is what many of us are lacking in our relationships today.

Growing up and observing people around me, I have noticed that you are considered authentic if you tell people exactly what they want to hear and compliment them. It has become easier to place authenticity in the back seat because walking on eggshells with others seems to flow much more smoothly than getting in deeply with them and allowing them to see us as flawed. How many of you can say that those you consider to have close relationships with you will see you as they do now if they discover the flaws you hide to keep up?

Just as the Pharisees were quick to judge and throw stones at Mary Magdalene (John 8:1–11), we also are quick to see the flawed parts of others, forgetting that we are not particularly innocent. This is why it is difficult for the majority to engage in authentic relationships. The fear of being judged and misunderstood by others keeps us from being ourselves, and instead, we put up walls. As believers, we were made to engage in relationships with one another. No matter how often we've been hurt in our past relationships, we never fully close our hearts to wanting that authentic, godly relationship.

One may ask, does this even exist in today's world? Is it possible to have authenticity in our relationship with God and people? I would say no through the lens of this world, but through the lens of Christ, there is a way, and anything is possible. We may have many people to speak to and chat with on social media, but we aren't so fortunate when it comes to the authenticity we all crave to have around us. As believers of Christ, we should offer authenticity regardless, even if we are not receiving it in our relationships, giving rather than expecting, and through that, God will bless you with better than you expect. God watches over His people, frees them from where they are not meant to be, and leads them to where they belong.

The act of authenticity starts with us—we can't expect what we do not offer to others. We must learn to be authentic no matter what, instead of what Pastor Rick Warren refers to as a "surface-level relationship," which consists of fake conversations and flattery, in which nothing real, deep, and meaningful is shared, in which feelings are ignored, and pretense becomes the new normal. In this type of relationship, there is fear of sharing your deepest emotions and pain with another because of fear of judgment and betrayal.

We all wish to have genuine, deep relationships with people but sometimes end up in the wrong ones, where misunderstandings and confusion arise. I often struggled with this in the past: placing people on a higher pedestal than they deserved. I tried to figure out where I honestly stood in the lives of those around me, those I opened my heart to. But over the years, the closer I got to God, the more He showed me the hearts and true motives of those I came in contact with. God helped me understand that He has always been and will always be there for me. He helped me see my importance and that I never have to wonder where I belong in the lives of those who are meant to be in my life.

I am grateful to a Father who always ensures I do not end up where I do not belong. At a point in my life, I became withdrawn from the crowd and the community I once saw as family, not because I did not like them but because I allowed God to lead me to where I was meant to be. I allowed His discerning Spirit to guide me.

I have concluded that authenticity is rare through my years of seeing through and studying people. It is a blessing from God to have at least one godly confidant in your life who will see you and cheer for you, a divine voice who will see in you what God has designed you to be and help you cultivate that greatness, one who will point out your strength when you are weak, who will bring you back to reality when you are drifting off in despair. This may sound like I am describing Jesus, but it is possible to have such relationships and be that to someone else.

Over the years, the Holy Spirit has helped me realize that we do not have to wait for what we desire to come to us. We must instead make the first move in being authentic for others to benefit, and through that, we attract like-minded people. It is hard to recognize something we are not used to. We keep falling into broken relationships because we have not had authentic relationships. When you stay true to yourself, you will recognize when you are surrounded by anything outside that radar. It is time to say no. Time to say to yourself, "I deserve realness; I deserve to have what I know God wants for me." It is time to stop settling for flatteries and empty giggles.

I used to carry the mentality that I could have a gut-level, heart-sharing relationship with people simply because they were Christians, sat in the front pews on Sunday mornings, stood in the front of the church with a microphone in their hands, led worship, and sang with angelic voices. But life lessons taught me that was an infantile way of thinking. Over the years, I have realized that even though we were all created in the image of God, we are also different in many ways. This is the beauty of authenticity, to be different yet blending in harmony and meeting on common ground, laying bare your heart with others—regardless of having different opinions and perspectives. Asking God for wisdom and discernment about whom you can have gut-level conversations is the answer to avoiding future confusion and problems.

Christ demonstrated serving each other authentically by washing His disciples' feet (John 13:1–17). He did so with love and gladness as an example to all. Nothing about Him is false or make-believe. He is not ashamed to identify with you, no matter how much He hates your sinful ways. He is never ashamed to claim you as His own. And He wants you to have the same attitude toward others. He wants you to "be completely humble, gentle, patient, bearing with one another in love" (Ephesians 4:2).

We may not be able to tell everyone about Christ, but we can show the world who Christ is through our actions. When we do so, we look to no one for praise, applause, or honor. We do not go to church every Sunday morning because we are perfect. If that were the case, the death of Christ would have been for nothing.

We do not need permission from each other to walk as Christians. It's a personal choice we make individually. We can't be authentic with one another if our relationship with God is short-coming. The Bible offers many stories about pure relationships; the most important is our relationship with God. Time after time, He's proven His undying love for us and goes beyond for us. Not only should we be authentic in our dealings with each other, but also in our relationship with God. That is where our authenticity begins—when we are real with God and go to Him in honesty. The Word of God tells us, "God is spirit, and his worshipers must worship in the Spirit and in truth" (John 4:24).

We don't love others with the flattering kind of love, laughing together but judging each other in our minds, or the "many compliments" type of love. Instead, we love each other with the kind of love you show even when it is hard to, the kind that rebukes with love. King Solomon referenced this in the book of Proverbs: "You can trust a friend who wounds you with his honesty, but your enemy's pretended flattery comes from insincerity" (Proverbs 27:5–6 TPT).

Your honesty with God will determine how real you are in your relationships. The relationship between you and God is unbreakable, incomparable, and undeniably pure. No mind can comprehend the love God has for His children. His love enables us to love one another with authenticity no matter what. Suppose the way you treat others is determined by secondhand stories, flaws, or the level of value you place on them. In that case, you might want to assess your authenticity as a Christ-follower. The thought of Christ dying for us and continually pursuing us over and over should make us strive to love others with no conditions, motives, pretense, and pureness and selflessness. What if God would tell you He loves you only because you read the Bible and pray, and His love ceases the days you do not? How would this make you feel? How does knowing God pursues you regardless of your unfaithfulness make you feel? Will this help you pursue others irrespective of their imperfections?

When a relationship has no purpose, problems become the focus. When your reason for being in a relationship with another is to gain something for your benefit, it lacks the essential ingredient to keep it flowing even through the darkest times—love! Our relationship with others should be intentional. There should never be any other reason we love our fellow brothers and sisters in Christ other than that they belong to God.

High-Performance Standards

As Jesus and the disciples continued to Jerusalem, they came to a certain village where a woman named Martha welcomed him into her home. Her sister, Mary, sat at the Lord's feet, listening to what he taught. But Martha was distracted by the big dinner she was preparing. She came to Jesus and said, "Lord, doesn't it seem unfair that my sister sits here while I do all the work? Tell her to come and help me." But the Lord said to her, "My dear Martha, you are worried and upset over all these details! There is only one thing worth being concerned about. Mary has discovered it, and it will not be taken away from her" (Luke 10:38–42 NLT).

The story of Jesus' visit to Mary and Martha's house teaches us that trying to be perfect distracts us from what matters the most, causing us to stress over things that should not be a priority. When we strive to be perfect, we make it about us and how we want others to see us, but God does not care about that. He is already aware of all our flaws and is not looking for us to be perfect. That is impossible! He is looking for a heart that seeks Him, yearns for Him, and is willing to yield to His will. We were created not to attract traffic to ourselves but to God. God sees us through the eyes of grace. We don't have to work hard to be seen by Him.

Sometimes, we are so focused on what to do to make God proud when all He wants is for us to spend intimate time with Him. We try so hard to be perfect because we think it is what will make God accept us. Mary saw it as a priority to sit at the feet of Jesus, listening to what He was saying, but Martha was more focused on pleasing God with her cooking. Take little children, for instance. You may think buying them all the material things they love will make them happy, but what makes them happy at the end of the day is knowing that Daddy and Mommy are right beside them. That is where their happy place is.

It is the same for Christ and us. He loves nothing more than for us to be in His presence. We can do everything that makes Him happy—read our Bibles, sweep the church, sing in the praise and worship team, and play the drums as loudly as we can—but if we never spend quality time with Him, all those things are meaningless!

We get so consumed with all the domestic chores that we forget that the primary purpose of our existence is to make the Creator our priority and not the creation. "Wherever your treasure is, there the desires of your heart will also be" (Luke 12:34).

No matter how busy life gets, we must never forget that resting in the presence of God and spending quality time with Him makes Him the happiest, not our race to perfection to please Him. He does not expect us to be perfect. He knew you were imperfect when He sent His Son to die for you. It is not your role to prove to Him that you are good. It is your role to prove to the world that *He* is! This should be your priority.

18

LET GO AND LET GOD

Letting go may be hard, but letting God is worth it.

"Since we are surrounded by such a great cloud of witnesses, let us throw off everything that hinders and the sin that so easily entangles. And let us run with perseverance the race marked out for us" (Hebrews 12:1). Through life's journey we tend to carry on lots of loads that hinder our walk with God. Letting go of an old habit, an addiction, a relationship, a career, and so on can be very hard, but as followers of Christ, we are expected to throw behind us everything that hinders our walk with Christ, everything that slows us down, things that steal our attention from God and threaten our destiny.

God's aim is for us to experience His gift of freedom and peace while pursuing Him and His will for our lives. Freedom is not easy to attain on our own, but through Christ, we have the freedom to move forward and the peace that transcends all understanding to move along. Forgetting what we can't control and straining toward what is ahead is not easy, but all things are possible with the strength we have through Jesus Christ. Let God change your heart toward what you are drawn to that steals your attention from Him. Allow Him to help you refocus and shift things around. You are destined for much more than what is keeping you hostage.

Sometimes, we seek God for answers and a change in our circumstances. However, it's not about your problems leaving you but you simply walking away from them. We get so tied up in our messes that we forget the only way to get out of them is to walk away. We stand in those messes, afraid to move while at the same time asking God to help us move when He has already given us all we need to make that move.

Look within you! You have the same Spirit of Christ who raised Him from death. Look within you and tap into that power. The point is to get to where you can freely let go of your problems, the things that distract you from your task. No matter what they are or how things may look, take a bold step away from them. God cannot do His job in carrying our burdens if we cannot trust Him enough to step away and let go. Holding on to expectations causes damages that are hard to repair. Let go so that you can move; let go to free yourself from limitations. Let go to dim all other voices so you can hear God's the loudest. Let go so you can become all God has destined you to be.

No one knows you as well as God does. No one sees you in a complete light as He does. He created all of us for specific tasks, and right now, whatever you are still holding on to is keeping you from fulfilling that task. The more we let go and cling to Him, the more we discover our potential and who we are in Him.

A Time to Grieve

Throughout Scripture, we see the occurrences of death and grief. In the Old Testament, we see that when Jacob got the news that a wild animal had eaten Joseph, he broke down and mourned the loss of his son and refused to be comforted by his family. "All his sons and daughters came to comfort him, but he refused to be comforted. 'No,' he said, 'I will continue to mourn until I join my son in the grave.' So his father wept for him" (Genesis 37:35).

We also read about David and Bathsheba mourning the death of their baby boy (2 Samuel 12:14– 24) and the death of David's older sons, Absalom and Amnon (2 Samuel 13:23-38; 18:32-33), and also mourned when he learns about the death of his best friend, Jonathan (2 Samuel 1:25–27). As he went through such excruciating times in his life, David turned to God for comfort and gave us a verse that we lean on in the dark times in our lives. He said, "Even though I walk through the valley of the shadow of death, I will fear no evil, for you are with me; your rod and your staff, they comfort me" (Psalm 23:4 ESV). This encourages believers in times like these—to have no fear as the Lord is with them. Jesus said, "Blessed are they who mourn, for they will be comforted" (Matthew 5:4).

I once heard a story about a couple who wanted the fruit of the womb, but each time the woman got pregnant, she suffered a miscarriage. This happened about six times or so. Finally, she carried her baby until the thirty-eighth week. When it was time for delivery, she gave birth to a ten-pound stillborn baby. As I listened to the story, I began placing myself in this woman's shoes, and if I could tear up as much as I did over her loss, I can't imagine how she herself must have felt and the pain she had to endure through her loss.

Nothing prepares us for such terrible times, whether we lose our loved ones through childbirth or accidental or natural causes. As we go through life's busy schedules, storms, and turbulences, nothing in this world can prepare us for the trauma of losing a loved one. The Word of God tells us, "There is a time for everything and a season for every activity under the heavens" (Ecclesiastes 3:1). King Solomon lists some of the things we pass through under the heavens; he mentioned "a time to weep and a time to laugh, a time to mourn and a time to dance" (Ecclesiastes 3:4). God has made the time for losing, even though it is not a time we all look forward to. But I encourage you to find comfort in knowing that if you are a child of God, to die is to unite with God.

This is the truth Paul realized in his own life when he said, "To live is Christ, and to die is gain" (Philippians 1:21–23). For Paul, if he died, it was a gain as he got to be with God, but if God kept him alive, it was also a good thing because it would give him more time to keep doing the work of God. So, Paul saw both as win-win situations. The good news for all of us is that God promises to comfort us so we never face such wrenching times alone.

No one knows what tomorrow holds, but God blesses us each day with new mercies. We are to move boldly in it. God wants us to make the best of each day and enjoy the life He has given to us. The season of grief can make one feel abandoned, anxious, stressed, and so on, and these feelings may manifest through how one acts. It can make a person feel like there is nothing to look forward to, creating a sense of hopelessness. This can affect a person's physical, mental, and spiritual health.

Grief is experienced not only when a loved one passes away. Any form of loss can bring about grief in a person's life. Though there are many reasons for experiencing grief, the number-one reason for grief is the loss of a loved one or other meaningful relationships. Many of us live life burdened and stressed by our challenges. We worry about yesterday's storms instead of enjoying the thirty minutes of sunshine today. We worry about the possibility of going through the storms tomorrow instead of enjoying what is in front of us. Jesus tells us, "Don't worry about tomorrow, for tomorrow will bring its own worries. Today's trouble is enough for today" (Matthew 6:34 NLT).

Each day is a gift from God. Even in chaos, we must learn to focus on the giver of all things, including our lives. We must learn to enjoy today's gift in God's presence because we never know when the time for mourning will come. Solomon said, "No one can bring us back to see what happens after we die" (Ecclesiastes 3:22 NLT). If you are reading this and have lost a loved one, I want to remind you to cling to God's promises as an anchor of hope. Embrace each season as it comes, knowing that God is with you every step, whether rain or shine, sad or happy times. God's warmth, love, comfort, and embrace are not limited. They are available for all who seek them. Cling to Him and find rest in His arms. He is closer to you than ever in this trying time. You must believe that all things are working for you, even in this time, and that God has not forsaken you.

Losses and grief are not a time of punishment from God, but rather, as believers of Christ, we should realize that they are a gift of eternity— a gift of something much bigger and greater on the other side. We may feel God has failed us when we lose a loved one, but even in these times, God wants you to know He loves you very much and is with you.

"Now Elimelek, Naomi's husband, died, and she was left with her two sons" (Ruth 1:3). Who can forget the story of Naomi and what she went through? She lost a husband and both her sons and was left all alone. You would think that was the peak of it all. She also had to go through famine and lacked so much that she felt God had abandoned her. 'Don't call me Naomi,' she told them. 'Call me Mara because the Almighty has made my life very bitter. I went away full, but the Lord has brought me back empty. Why call me Naomi? The Lord has afflicted me; the Almighty has brought misfortune upon me" (Ruth 1:20–21).

Though Naomi felt this way, going through all these mixed emotions, she didn't realize that all she went through was paving the way for something greater ahead. God had a plan for her life. And even though it was a painful and dark time for Naomi, God knew of a different story. We may see darkness, sorrow, and pain in such a season. Maybe you are feeling discouraged and losing faith in God's love for you and what He has planned concerning your life. Perhaps you are feeling sad and angry at God for a loss. You feel as though He has abandoned you. You ask Him, "Why?" and feel broken. The Word of God tells us, "Whoever believes in Him . . . will not be disappointed" (Romans 10:11 AMP).

This is the time to trust God the most, rest on His promises, and remember that something much bigger is in the works for you. Even in your mourning, know that you are blessed. God's warmth and comfort are not far (Matthew 5:4). God's promises are our great amour. We must rest in them, especially when we're experiencing grief.

Don't go through grief alone. Don't go through happy times alone. In every season of your life, acknowledge God, and remember that He has not and will never let you face such times alone. He is never deaf to your cries or blind to your storms.

Healing

They say time heals all wounds, but without God in our healing process, time will continue, and we'll still find ourselves returning to the same places of hurt. Whether it is an emotional, psychological, or physical wound, the severity of it depends on what or how it was inflicted on us—but the diminishment of it depends on how we allow God in the healing process.

At some point in our lives, we all have gone through one wound or the other. Though they may be in different areas and at varying levels of severity, we all need a Saviour in our healing process.

The healing process can be much more painful than the wound inflicted. And even after we are completely healed, sometimes we are left with a scar that reminds us of our wounds. This scar can bring on old feelings of pain or feelings of strength, depending on how you've allowed yourself to heal. The strength to stare at our scars and feel empowered, safe, joyful, fulfilled, and unbothered will depend on our willingness to allow God to strengthen us and to accept His peace through it. Healing can be painful, traumatic, and messy, but the good news is that we have Jesus, who can relate to our pain and is there for us. God works in mysterious ways, and when we depend on Him in times of our weaknesses, He gives us the strength to push through the difficulties.

Most of us go through life with hidden wounds from which we never really heal. We pretend and put up an act because the uncomfortable feeling of having to go through the healing process is too much for us to bear. Healing means facing our wounds; those not ready to do that would rather hide or cover up their wounds. They deceive themselves into thinking that they are healed. The pain becomes their comfort because that is what they are used to—and the healing process is seen as a threat.

Yes, we all go through the unexpected. To move mentally, emotionally, spiritually, and physically in good health, we must decide whether we want to be healed. We were created in such a way that we constantly need to be connected to Christ, especially when there is a glitch in our system. When we disconnect, we shut down; when we connect, we rise to full function. The problem is that most of us run away from the source. We may run away for different reasons, but the number one reason is that we find it hard to accept God's love for us. We run due to shame, embarrassment, disappointments, a painful past, and so on. We would rather ignore them than deal with them, thinking, "If I'm hurt and broken, what could God find of value in me? If He allowed this to happen to me, He must think I am worthless." Resist such thoughts. They are not of God.

God cares about His children, and that includes you. No one has felt pain more than what Jesus came down to experience on our behalf. If anyone understands your wounds, it is He. When we cover up our wounds without allowing them to heal, we will keep experiencing the same pain over and over. Covering it up doesn't mean the wound is gone. It just means you can't see it; if you can't, you don't have to deal with it. The mistake is that this can keep you from moving forward. When you think you are moving on, the pain will resurface, and you will start limping, and eventually, you will start feeling pain as if the wounds were fresh again.

The worst even happens when someone brings up the topic of how your pain was inflicted. If we are not healed, we will blow up and break down in pain again. The real test of a healed person is having joy in their heart and no pain whatsoever at the mention of their wounds.

As I went through my healing process, one thing I found to be soothing was aligning with God, letting go, and trusting Him to take control of the situations I couldn't change so I could rest in Him. I realized that the moments when I felt as if God were far away were not because He had left me, but because I was not seeking Him as I should in my broken moments, and because of that, I found myself drifting back, playing scenarios in my mind over and over, which made the pain worse than it initially was. I fixated on the "what ifs"— "Maybe if I had not passed on this road,

I would not have ended up here." "Maybe if I had gone a certain route, I would not have been trapped in this." If this happened to me, does that mean God hates me as much as those who inflicted the wound? Being disconnected from God in times when I should have gone to Him made me question His love for me and His ability to help heal. I started feeling alone, and the way others saw me was the same way God saw me, and I broke down, feeling as if I had come to my last stop.

As I allowed God in, I began feeling His unfailing, nonprejudiced, unconditional, non-judgmental love for me as I freed myself from the captivity of my thoughts and people's opinions. I started feeling whole, confident, and peaceful in Him again. So the secret to our healing is not about covering up the wounds and pretending they never existed, but instead accepting to walk in those wounds with God side by side, accepting His gift of love and peace and the truth of who you are in Him.

Today, I urge you to remain in Him and trust Him to walk with you in your healing journey. Give Him what you cannot bear, and He will care for you.

Peace amidst the Storms

"I am leaving you with a gift—peace of mind and heart. And the peace I give is a gift the world cannot give. So, don't be troubled or afraid" (John 14:27 NLT). Aside from the gift of the Advocate, the Holy Spirit, Jesus left us with another priceless gift— peace! Many grew up believing we can acquire peace only when we have no problems. But that is the world's way of thinking, and it's far from the truth from a believer's perspective.

Jesus set an excellent example for us when He was on earth. He endured many problems, but He always remained peaceful no matter what He went through. The devil works hard to steal our peace, but the apostle Paul tells us not to be intimidated by the devil

(Philippians 1:28). When the devil throws his best at you, and you're still standing, this signals to him that he can't handle you. How do you stand still in times when you should be falling? By trusting God and accepting His gift of peace. We are called to live in peace (1 Corinthians 7:15).

It is not the will of God for us to burden ourselves with the problems we face. The peace of God helps us stand still in hope and allows us to see the steps ahead with a clear mind. Paul said, "The peace of God, which transcends all understanding, will guard your hearts and minds in Christ Jesus" (Philippians 4:7).

There are two types of peace—peace as the world gives and peace as God gives. We all strive to have the peace of God in our lives but struggle to grasp it, not because it is out of our reach but because we allow the worries of this world to burden us, stealing our joy. God promises that His covenant of peace will never be shaken in our lives (Isaiah 54:10). This means that His peace is certain, even amid the greatest storms.

Are you living your life as a true believer in the Word of God, or does the slightest sound of thunder threaten and get you to lose your calm? Accepting God's peace amid the storms is up to you, or the enemy will capitalize on your worries and cause more damage than your current situation. True peace is enduring problems and challenges with a sound mind, knowing God has everything under control. The peace of God is a gift to humanity, given to us by Christ because He knew that if we would need anything in this world to get us by, having peace of mind would be it.

Your peace can easily be stripped away from you if you place it into the hands of your circumstances, job/career, money, people, places, or things, but the peace of God is not as the world gives. It transcends all understanding. The only way to achieve such peace is by placing your utmost trust in God. We do not have a problem-free life, and chances are we will never have that in this world. It was not one of the promises of God to offer us a problem-free life, but it was a promise of His to be with us through the problems we pass through. The strength required to bear our crosses comes from Christ. He loves us too much to leave us empty-handed, knowing of the issues we will face.

This world gives us no reason to live peacefully. Scripture reminds us to submit to God in whatever we do, and He will provide us with peace, even in the middle of chaos. He will make our paths prosperous (Job 22:21). This world can offer us luxury and good living. We can be well put together and still battle with the lack of peace. We can have all we've ever hoped for—good relationships, careers, and all the financial stability in the world and still go to bed turning and tossing in the middle of the night. The world knows of a peace that takes effect only in the absence of troubles, but God's peace is effective even in the worst storms.

When we remain peaceful during storms, it is hard for the enemy to get through to us. The story of Jesus calming the storms is a good reminder that we do not have to fear the storms because if God is by our side, He will comfort us and calm our storms (Mark 4:35–41). When you forget that God is always by your side, whether rain or shine, it makes sense that His peace will also be thrown in the back seat.

How do we attain peace when we constantly face hardships? You must never forget that the man in our boat is for you. When you call on Him when things get out of control, accept His peace, and know He is working for you. It makes sense to find no reason to stay calm during the storms when all we see is bad news when we turn on the television. Leaning toward the faithfulness of God and remembering His promises for us will get us through.

Jesus Christ alerted His disciples in the book of John of the trials and sorrows we will face on earth, but there is good news for us—Jesus Christ has overcome the world (John 16:33). And because of this, we can enjoy His peace today and know that our battles have already been won. God wants us to have it all. His peace is sacred; we must seek and accept Him to enjoy it. You can't find real peace without accepting Jesus as your Savior. He is peace and the light that shines in our darkness. He is "the calm" amid the storms. "He offers not carnal or limited things but the supernatural kind—peace that works above human understanding. Jesus Christ could have left us anything He wanted, but He chose peace. He did not leave us money or material things but something more valuable to help us hang on to hope.

I grew up in a Christian home, where my uncle, I lived with, was the pastor of my childhood church. However, I realized in those days that I struggled with a busy mind because I always felt something was missing. As I grew older, I realized nothing was missing; I didn't know how to stabilize my mind by focusing on what mattered. God was right there, and I was looking in the distance for Him. Every problem I encountered seemed to shift His peace to the back of my mind. I was easily distracted by all the things that were going on around me, but God never gave up on me. He has always been there as a shield.

Hearing stories of my childhood from my mom always brings me to tears—the many battles and storms she had to endure with me, Baby Esther. I thank God for my life, for keeping me close and in perfect peace, never letting go, never giving up on me, and waiting on me until I got my priorities straight. I have always been the type who keeps so much in and wants to figure everything out, stressed about tomorrow and crushed by yesterday's incidents. Everything has changed since I surrendered all my life's battles to God, making Him first in all I do. I gave Him my worries, and He gave me His peace. I now worry less and trust Him more. I grab onto this peace that transcends all understanding. It is mine, a gift I did not deserve, but He gave it graciously. It's mine because I decided to let go and let Him step in for me.

One thing always stands out when I think about all the people I have crossed paths with over the years: people come and go, but God has always been there, loving me through the ups and downs. Dear Child of God, I pray for the same peace in your life today. It is the best feeling in the world. I want you to taste His peace the way I have so that you can attest to it and praise Him for it. I pray for you to seek it. As you go through life's journey, believing that you have no one, I pray you realize that you always have God. He is always there.

My dear friend, don't lose sight of Him. Keep your eyes on Him, place Him over everything else in your life, and He will change your life in a way you never thought possible. "I pray that God, the source of hope, will fill you completely with joy and peace because you trust in him. Then you will overflow with confident hope through the power of the Holy Spirit" (Romans 15:13–14 NLT). Today, I encourage you to choose His gift of peace, which surpasses all understanding amidst the storms of life.

By His Wounds We Are Healed

"He was pierced for our transgressions. He was crushed for our iniquities; the punishment that brought us peace was on him, and by his wounds, we are healed" (Isaiah 53:5 NLT). Normally, death is a time to mourn when the departure of a loved one breaks us and turns our worlds upside down. But Easter holds a different meaning to death. It is a time to rejoice, as Christ's death represents the birth of new life for you and me. He died with our sins and was resurrected with the gift of eternal life. What a beautiful gift! It's a gift that reconciles us to the Father. What an amazing day to rejoice! This day—the day our stories turned around for good, the day the stains of sin were removed from our history forever, and we were set free from webs of shame.

As we rejoice over the gift of hope, light, and freedom through the blood of Jesus, let's also remember to be thankful that God gives us love and forgiveness repeatedly, no matter where we find ourselves. Even though we have the gift of salvation through Jesus Christ, we sometimes fail to do what is pleasing in the sight of God. But because God is merciful and gracious, He offers us new beginnings each day to get our lives right. What a merciful God! He is a God of second chances.

Jesus Christ sacrificed Himself for you, knowing the pain He would endure. The penalty of sin has been wiped out for us, not because we are so good and worthy but because we serve a God who is. He was pierced for our sins.

What are you doing today that speaks of your appreciation for what Jesus did on the cross for you? Are you paying it forward, or are you holding out on others? Today, we can rejoice that death could not hold Him captive. Even in the grave, He is still sovereign. He is still running things and orchestrating everything to work in our favor. We can rejoice that on this day at Golgotha, Jesus Christ exchanged our brokenness, ashes, and flaws for His beauty. He purchased us with His blood and called us His own.

We were once broken and powerless, but we no longer must look in the mirror and see faults. Today, I want you to carry these words with you when you feel so drained, are too weak to stand, and have no idea where your strength will come from. I want you to remember that Christ came and rescued you at the right time, and there is nothing else He will not do for you.

19

AT THE MENTION OF HIS NAME!

⸻ ❦ ⸻

Everyone who calls on the name of the Lord will be saved.
—Romans 10:13

When our loved ones call us by name, what happens? We respond and go to them. The name of the Lord is not like our own. His name is a fortified tower that the righteous can run to and feel safe in during times of trouble (Proverbs 18:10). His name is above all other names (Philippians 2:9). Paul tells us, "Everyone who calls on the name of the Lord will be saved" (Romans 10:13), and in verse 14 he asks, "But how can they call on him to save them unless they believe in him?" Anyone who calls on the name of the Lord must first believe He is the Lord, who came down to earth to redeem us from our sins. But Paul further says the only way people can believe in Christ is if they hear about Him, and that can happen only if you and I do our job of telling them about Christ.

As children of God, we know to call on the name of the Lord and be saved—this is one of our advantages. But can we say the same for those who do not know His name is a tower for safety? Our responsibility as ambassadors of Christ is to ensure that all people know they have access to safety in times of trouble by dwelling in the name of the Lord, which is a fortified tower. Nothing associated with the Lord's name comes back void. He is not dead. He is very much alive, and so is your victory.

Sometimes, we may feel God is not hearing us when we call on Him, but that's not true. What happens is that with faith as small as a mustard seed, something amazing and extraordinary happens at the mention of His name. You must call Him with intention and have faith. Everyone who calls on His name must accept Him as their Lord and personal Saviour. At the mention of His name, the mountains in your way shift, and the opposers tremble. His name is a weapon for warfare—He is the Word, and the Word is a sword (Hebrews 4:12), and as children of God, we can't go to war without the sword of the Spirit. We can't fight the battle against the enemy without going in the name of the Lord.

David said to the Philistine, "You come against me with sword and spear and javelin, but I come against you in the name of the Lord Almighty, the God of the armies of Israel, whom you have defied" 1 Samuel 17:45). The name of the Lord is a mighty weapon that has the power to defeat any strong-holds. Whether in your home, marketplace, shower, church or wherever else, speak his name— silently speak His name no matter where you are. His name should never depart from your lips. Call on Him in times of trouble and in your joyful times. He rejoices with us during our glorious moments, just as He sympathizes with us during our breakdown moments.

Throughout the Bible, we find many stories in which God's people didn't need a physical weapon to fight against their enemies but went in the name of the Lord and, through the Lord's guidance, won every battle without laying a finger on their opponents. We see that with the story of Gideon and the Midianites (Judges 7:1–24) and many more. We are no exception, as we can face the enemy without needing armies, spears, javelins, and physical armor for protection. None of God's people has ever called on His name, and nothing happened. His name is our weapon. Lift your voice and call on His name.

When the Lord Is Your Army

"The Lord told Gideon, 'With these three hundred men, I will rescue you and give you victory over the Midianites. Send all the others home'" (Judges 7:7 NLT). God gave me this verse on the seventh day of the seventh month. I read it and felt His Spirit speak to me. Today, through that same story, God wants to remind you of the promise He made to Gideon and how that promise also stands for you—He will give you victory over your enemies.

When God appointed Gideon to lead the Israelites into a battle with the Midianite army, Gideon did not know how that would be possible. Still, the Lord assured him he would be with him and give him victory over the Midianites. He revealed this through someone else's dream and ensured that Gideon walked in at the right time as the man told his friend his dream. When he heard this, Gideon trusted God's plan to help take down the enemies (Judges 7:13–15).

Usually, to go into a battle, you need a large army to take down the opposing team, but this was not the case for Gideon and the Israelites. God knew that if the Israelites faced the Midianites with all their soldiers, they would believe they had won the battle with their own strength. He selected three hundred men, far fewer than what the Midianites had (Judges 7:2–8). On the day of the battle, Gideon gave each of the men a trumpet and an empty jar with torches inside (Judges 7:16–22). This may sound odd, as this is not usually how anyone would face a battle. But with God, nothing ever is normal. His ways are far beyond the human mind's comprehension.

All the Israelites did was blow their trumpets, smash the jars, and shout, "A sword for the Lord and for Gideon!" Without a single weapon, they terrified the Midianites, who ran, cried, and fled the scene (Judges 7:20–23). By the sound of their trumpets, the Lord caused the Midianites throughout the camp to turn on each other with their swords.

This is the point God wants to make to you in this story. For God's glory to shine in your life, there must be a shortage of something. His power works best in our weaknesses and lacking seasons. God goes ahead of you and fights for you to give you victory. When He is your army, the only effort required of you is to trust and obey Him. How hard could that be, right? David said, "Though a thousand fall at your side, though ten thousand are dying around you, these evils will not touch you. Just open your eyes, and see how the wicked are punished" (Psalm 91:7–8 NLT). When you trust God and do as He says, you never have to fear the troops that come against you. You never have to worry about who will stand and back you up. God is the only one who can help you defeat your enemies. When God fights for you, He can do in a second what a thousand soldiers cannot achieve in hours. When He is behind you, the enemies turn up confused and distorted and wonder how you are still standing amid all the blows they have thrown your way.

No matter what God's plans for your life are, He will reveal them to you one way or the other. He does this so you will lean on Him and trust Him through the process. Because He is on your side, nothing but victory is your result. All that is required of you is obedience. Gideon obeyed and did exactly as God said. He could have said, *Okay, I'm not sure if God will back us. I'm not sure if I should trust Him. I should face the Midianites with my large number of soldiers instead of listening to God to go with just three hundred men.* But no—he chose to trust the Lord.

What about you? Are you trusting God through your battles, or are you looking for your own gathered army to back you up? I don't know what you currently face in life, but I know that we serve a mighty God who constantly fights for us day and night to give us victory. God wants to assure you that you need not worry about the many battles that wage against you. He wants your trust and obedience because when He is your army, no amount of soldiers can defeat you.

Ultimate Protector

One beautiful Sunday afternoon during an online church service, the preacher asked what our "No matter what, I will not give up" prayer was. Out of curiosity, I turned to my husband and asked what his was. He replied, "No matter what, I will never stop praying for God to protect my mother." His mother is back home in Ghana, West Africa. Because he is not there to assist her how he would want to, he always feels uneasy regarding her well-being, as the world has become unpredictable. I asked him if he thought his presence near his mother would make a difference. Would being in his mother's presence assure him of her safety?

I asked that question because I used to battle with the fear of not protecting those I love, those under my responsibility. When I first had my firstborn, I checked on him more times than I could count to ensure he was breathing—I am sure every parent can relate to this. I used to think I would be the type of parent who would creep outside their children's school windows to check if they were okay. As funny and silly as it sounds, that was my mentality to protect my loved ones. Whenever my husband would step out of the door to go to work, I prayed for his safety—but then would turn to worry, wondering if he was all right until he messaged me, "Babe, I'm at work now," and would worry about his trip back home until he stepped back inside the house. I had the mentality that not being around those I loved would keep me away from helping them if something happened to them and that I needed to be with them all the time to ensure their safety.

This reality and the old way of thinking changed when I learned to surrender to God. I realized that my strength was limited, that I was mere human, and that it was not my job as their ultimate protector. A weight lifted off me as I learned to hand over to God the things that kept me spinning in fear. We can always ask God for protection, but it doesn't change the fact that He still provides it by default. The divine protection He has on us and our loved ones is beyond our presence in their lives. Our presence does not make the difference; God's presence does. Knowing that He is a shield around His children should be enough for us not to worry. Whether or not we are around those we love, it doesn't change God's promise to protect them. He is our ultimate protector. We can be around those we love, and something could still go wrong, or we could be absent, and they would still be protected under God's mighty arms. As children of God, we are used only as vessels to carry out God's missions.

Have you ever encountered someone choking with no one around to help, and you happened to walk in just at the right time to save the person? It might not be in that same scenario, but the point is that God places us in the center of moments like these for a reason: to be a blessing unto another or vice versa. We may see incidents like these as coincidences, but I see them as part of God's saving plans. It is never by our efforts but by the power of God through the Holy Spirit, who moves with us wherever we go, giving us the ability to overcome life's many hiccups.

Today, I can enjoy His unexplainable peace because I've learned to give Him all the control. I've learned to surrender so He can do His rightful job in my life and the lives of those I love. God's protection is a natural dome that hovers over His children. Because of this natural protection, we can go to various places and make it home safely. We can't promise protection to our loved ones because we do not always control life's events. We can only make the best of what is presented. Knowing that we have a Father who looks out for us and works beyond what our strength can handle should cease our worries. Surrendering to God gives us the peace of mind to live joyfully and in gratitude daily.

When put into the lion's Den, Daniel did not need rescue from a brother or a friend because they would never have been able to silence the mouths of the lions; it would have been a messy situation if attempted. Daniel was unbothered because He knew God was protecting him (Daniel 6:22). The three brothers, Shadrach,

Meshach, and Abednego, could not save themselves from the blazing fire. God's presence protected them (Daniel 3:8–25). When we are alone and need a rescuer, we must remember God's promises to protect us. God's protection can come in many forms; sometimes, that protection may seem like a problem to us. Sometimes, it may look like an end to a story, but if we could open our eyes and see His handwork, we would realize that what seems like an end is the beginning of something magnificent. Though, at times, God may not get us out of the fires or the dens, we can rest assured and find comfort in the fact that He is always with us and will always be right next to us, holding our hands through it all. Rest in the Lord today, and let go of the need to make sure everything aligns with your thinking.

20

GOD THE HOLY SPIRIT

The walk with the Holy Spirit is a divine journey of power.

"He has identified us as his own by placing the Holy Spirit in our hearts as the first installment that guarantees everything he has promised us" (2 Corinthians 1:22 NLT). Before ascending into heaven, Jesus, the Son of God, promised us the Holy Spirit, who would advocate for us and show us the true way of life. Who is the Holy Spirit? He is the third person of the Holy Trinity. God in three persons usually reveals Himself as the Father, Son, and Holy Spirit. And though all three are one, they appear to serve different roles in our lives: to help us birth our purpose, to protect and help us walk upright as children of God, and to accomplish God's good work so we can inherit what is promised to us.

Jesus, who came down as the Son to give His life for our freedom (John 3:16), now must leave to prepare a place for us in our Father's house (John 14:3). Before He left, He said to His disciples, "If you love me, obey my commandments, and I will ask the Father, and he will give you another advocate to help you and be with you forever" (John 14:15–16). God is a God of His word; He provided an advocate to help us navigate life correctly. The Holy Spirit's job is to support, teach, and convict us, remind us of God's Word, guide us on the right path, help us accomplish the tasks entrusted to us by working through us, and nudge us of what is wrong and right. He is our power source. We often do not acknowledge Him enough as we should, but He is a person we must accept in our hearts. To walk with the Holy Spirit is to walk in power.

The Holy Spirit helps us in times of weakness. He speaks and thinks on our behalf when we can't think for ourselves or connect our words sensibly (Romans 8:26–27). He is an eternal gift. Jesus taught His disciples about the characteristics of the Holy Spirit. He said, The world cannot accept or see the Holy Spirit because the world does not search for Him or recognize Him, but as children of God, we will recognize Him when He comes upon us because we know Him as He lives with us and in us (John 14:17).

Jesus says, "I will not leave you as orphans; I will come to you. Before long, the world will not see me anymore, but you will see me. Because I live, you also will live. On the day you realize that I am in my Father, and you are in me, and I am in you. Whoever has my commands and keeps them is the one who loves me. The one who loves me will be loved by my Father, and I too will love them and show myself to them" (John 14:19–20).

Jesus Christ came down to serve a purpose: to save us from ourselves, from the bondage of sin. Then He leaves us with the Holy Spirit, who will never depart from us, a friend who will make us feel safe when the storms of life are too much to handle. He will distribute to us the gifts of the Spirit and help us cultivate these gifts in us to edify the church for the glory of God (Ephesians 4:10–13). I want you to find comfort in this truth today—God will never and has never left you, and He is always by your side. Every believer's mark is that they have the Holy Spirit in them.

The evidence that a person carries the Holy Spirit speaks in times of circumstances. The Holy Spirit makes us more like Jesus. The Spirit hovers over us, teaching us the wisdom to live in a broken world. God kept His promise never to leave us, and the Holy Spirit is proof of that promise. He is a friend who is always with us to help us fight life's battles, guiding us to live fruitful lives and become the best versions of ourselves.

Dreams and Visions

"God works in different ways, but the same God does the work in all of us" (1 Corinthians 12:6). Before the earth was formed, you were first a child of God, whom God knew and had plans for before you were conceived. Throughout the journey of life, I have realized that before God does something in the lives of His children, He reveals it to them. He places a strong desire in their hearts as a form of direction.

God can show someone a revelation that pertains to another person. If you are someone who sees many visions or a dreamer, you will know that the revealed things can sometimes be about a total stranger. As we all carry and possess spiritual gifts, the enemy targets our very place of spiritual giftings and ministry. So, as children of God, we must be vigilant, stay alert through prayers, and be consistent in our seeking. The enemy fights hard to keep our minds busy on the things that can easily keep us away from the things of God, blocking us from potentially hearing from God. You must look out for the enemy and train your mind to resist him. This is the only way to manifest greatness. Fight to focus on the right things, make the presence of God your dwelling place, and glue yourself to the things of God—this will help you gain the rest needed to pursue your purpose.

We can't hear from God if our minds are far away from Him. Our brains can focus on only one thing at a time and often focus on our busy schedules. Pay attention. Be still. Getting to that place of productivity takes discipline. It is so easy to be consumed by the worries and the storms of life, but to be focused and walk on the right path takes strict dedication and intentionality in doing what is required.

Concerning the battle with the Midianites, God instructed Gideon about what to do and revealed how He would give him and the Israelites victory over the Midianites. As noted earlier, He did this through a vision from another person's dream. God ensured that

Gideon heard of it at the right time, which pushed and gave him confidence in taking on the task he had been given (Judges 7:13–15).

God reveals things to us not so we would boast, be careless, satisfy our curiosities, or be ignorant about them. When God shows us a vision, we must listen to His commands and guidance in fulfilling His plans. God reveals to redeem through the Holy Spirit, but for that redemption to occur, we also have a hand to play in the manifestation of it. He reveals things to us because He loves us and wants us to know His plans, equip us for what's ahead, and be ahead of the enemy.

God does not reveal things for us to sit and do nothing about them. Many prophecies are late in manifesting in our lives because we fail to get up and do our parts. As a child of God, you know that prayer is your weapon. Prayer with works equals results. Because your faith without action is dead (James 2:17). Pray to manifest it and break down the bondages concerning the visions of God for your life. God is always speaking to you and alerting you of the direction to take. The enemy works hard to derail you but can never blindside you if you follow God's voice.

God wants us to be on guard, alert, and "sober-minded" as the enemy lurks around, looking for the children of God to destroy (1 Peter 5:8). The Word of God is a prophecy for your life. Read it, be it, and live it. Doing this allows you to see things clearly and become a sword in the spirit. The moments of revelation through visions, dreams, and the Word of God assure us of God's plans for our lives and reveal the dangers ahead. Stand in prayer, take up your sword, and prepare for battle. He reveals so that we can view things in our lives not as they seem but from a spiritual standpoint—His standpoint. He reveals this because He trusts us and wants us to know He controls everything, including our destiny.

Pay attention to what God is showing you and where He is leading you. Dwell in His presence always. Daniel said to King Nebuchadnezzar, "No wise man, enchanter, magician, or diviner can explain to the king the mystery he has asked about, but there is a God in heaven who reveals mysteries. He has shown King Nebuchadnezzar what will happen in the days to come. Your dream and the visions that passed through your mind as you were lying in bed are these" (Daniel 2:26–28). Only God can reveal to us the mysteries of life. Through the Holy Spirit, power is boundless. Wisdom comes from Him, and He gives it to all who seek it (James 1:5).

For His Glory

> Then he spit on the ground, made mud with the saliva, and spread the mud over the blind man's eyes. He told him, "Go wash yourself in the pool of Siloam" (Siloam means 'sent'). So the man went and washed and came back seeing! His neighbors and others who knew him as a blind beggar asked each other, "Isn't this the man who used to sit and beg?" Some said he was, and others said, "No, he just looks like him!" But the beggar kept saying, "Yes, I am the same one!" (John 9:6–9 NLT)

One of the mistakes many believers make is giving credit where it is not due, giving themselves glory for what God has done. We face certain things in life so God's glory can be shown. One day, as Jesus and His disciples were walking, they saw a man who had been blind from birth. His disciples asked Him if the man was blind because of his or his parents' sins. Jesus answered. 'Neither this man nor his parents sinned,'" But this happened so that the works of God might be displayed in him" (John 9:2–3). He said, "As long as it is day, we must do the works of Him who sent me. Night is coming when no one can work" (John 9:4). God did not send us into this world to scatter in emptiness. My reason for being created is different from yours. We each carry different destinies. That is why what works for one person might not work for another.

We may at times find ourselves in predicaments when we wonder, "Why me?" and whether this predicament happens to be something that has been in our life since birth or decided to appear in the middle of our life, Jesus Christ helps us understand in the story of the blind beggar that such incidences are there so that the glory of the Lord will be displayed in our lives. There is a reason we are to be grateful in all things (1 Thessalonians 5:18)—trusting God in whatever situations we find ourselves in because He holds us in our problems.

In this story, the man had been blind since birth for the glory of God to be displayed. Maybe the task in your life is to be barren, as in the story of Sarah and Abraham (Genesis 17:1–27), so that God can work His miracles in your life for those around you to see how powerful our God is. With God, the blind man sees, the lame walks, the barren woman gives birth, and the captives are set free.

I am not in any way saying that it is amazing to go through seasons of lack, such as having a physical defect or not being able to conceive. But in the context of this story, the blind man's situation and healing were in such a way that God could reveal His power in his life. The story teaches us that we can trust God to do the impossible in our lives, regardless of how long we've been sitting in the waiting room.

Maybe you currently lack financially, and for the longest time, you have not caught a break in living life comfortably. You can be encouraged that God used the blind man's circumstance to bring glory to His name. He can also use yours for His glory. The blind man's neighbors and others who knew him as a blind beggar asked each other, "Isn't this the same man who used to sit and beg?" (John 9:8). They were in total disbelief and couldn't believe it was the same man they'd known all these years to be blind and begging.

Your current situation is not something that God is not aware of or is surprised by. You may not be sent to hold a Bible and preach before a congregation, but you may be sent for a different purpose. It is not only the pastor who, through Him, God's glory is displayed;

it is also shown through the person seeking healing. We all play a part in bringing glory to His name.

See your problems as a privilege for God to show Himself in your life. It may not feel like a privilege in the storms, but if we could lift our heads and see things beyond the natural, we would see it as an honor to be the one God chose for His glory. When we pray for God's glory to show in our lives, we don't get to decide how that will play out. I am sure that people did not see the favor in Mary's situation of being a pregnant virgin, but it was the biggest favor and honor to be the one to birth the world's Savior (Luke 1:26–56; Matthew 1:18–25), but the Word of God tells us that Mary was blessed because she believed what God said He would do and never shredded the task (Luke 1:45).

Believe that you are here on earth for a reason that counts in His kingdom. Take pride in this. Just as He sends us, He also anoints and gives us strength to withstand. I once heard a story about a pregnant woman whose doctor said she had lost her baby because she had contracted the coronavirus. She was asked to push out the deceased baby, and when the day came for her to do so, she pushed out a lively, healthy baby girl. If this is not the mighty hand of God, I do not know what it is. This cannot be a coincidence or magic, but the hand of God at work in a person's life. God does whatever He pleases, and in this situation, it meant raising a deceased baby in the womb for a watching world to see His mighty hands at work.

God has the final say, not the doctors or your storms. No matter what the reports say after that medical checkup or your problems, I want to encourage you never to lose hope—because if God has not signed off on it, then it is not final. He holds the power to change your story.

Do the Wicked Go Unpunished?

"Why doesn't the Almighty bring the wicked to judgment? Why must the godly wait for him in vain?" (Job 24:1 NLT). This is a question I have wondered about in life but have had the privilege of shining light on in my ministry. So much goes on under the sun that the human mind cannot understand. Some of these things can leave us questioning God's intentions. So many terrible things happen in this world that we are drawn to ask, "Does God leave the wicked unpunished? Do the dark plans carried out by wicked people go unnoticed by God?"

Sometimes, you cannot help but wonder when you see the wicked moving around freely without consequences for their actions. We wonder why God is slow in acting toward the wicked and not punishing them for their crimes. We are tempted to give up on God's judgments. Concluding that maybe, just maybe, He allows the wickedness to slide. He is slow to anger (Nahum 1:3) and merciful, so He must have overlooked the acts of the wicked. But the Scripture repeatedly affirms that God does not allow the wicked to go unpunished. His Word let us know that though He is slow to get angry, He doesn't let the guilty go unpunished. His being slow to get angry does not change His sovereignty.

In his book *The Wicked Will Not Go Unpunished*, Dr. D. K. Olukoya stated, "Everyone has the power to choose his or her sins, but nobody has the power to choose the consequences of those sins. Every sin has a consequence or punishment assigned to it." The wicked, indeed, do not go unpunished. There is nothing in the world that goes unseen by God.

The book of Ecclesiastes helps us understand that when a crime is not punished fast enough, the ones committing it may feel it is all right to continue doing wrong because no one sees or holds them accountable. It further explains that "even though a person sins a hundred times and still lives a long time, those who fear God will be better off. The wicked will not prosper, for they do not fear

God. Their days will never grow long like the evening shadows" (Ecclesiastes 8:11–13 NLT). We might seek to see the results of God punishing those who wrong us or the wicked in our own time, but He does everything at the right time.

David said, "Though a thousand fall at your side, though ten thousand are dying around you, these evil will not touch you. Just open your eyes and see how the wicked are punished" (Psalm 91:7–8 NLT). This is a verse of protection for the children of God, who trust God to act. As believers, we must sit still and wait for God's judgment. We must endure and persevere, regardless of how hard it is to watch the grins on the faces of those we find guilty of atrocious acts. We must wait as the enemy continues planning their attacks. When we trust God, a time will come when all we will have to do is "see how the wicked are punished." The book of Peter also mentions how God looks out for His people, rescues them from man's wicked plans, and places judgment on the unrighteous (2 Peter 2:9).

I believe that as God gives us many chances to repent, we must also trust Him many times, even when it seems that He is pardoning man's wicked acts. His time to act is perfect, and ours is not. It is the human tendency to act quickly without thinking about the consequences. Many times in the Bible, we notice that whenever it is affirmed that the wicked will not go unpunished, it is also confirmed that the righteous will be delivered (Proverbs 11:21). There is a time when the darkness will reign (Luke 22:53), but not for long. These are times when God shows up and takes His glory. When you are about to lose all hope, and the enemy thinks he's won, God sends you a big blessing to remind you that He is the God who answers by fire and that your prayers have been heard.

God's Word stands. He is a God who has so much compassion toward humanity and gives us all the time needed to turn from our sinful ways and turn to Him. The book of Ezekiel makes this clear: "But if wicked people turn away from all their sins and begin to obey my decrees and do what is just and right, they will surely live and not die" (Ezekiel 18:21 NLT). Many of us use the time of freedom God gives us to commit more sinful acts, forgetting that God sees all and that every action births a result or consequence. The Word of God tells us that God watches both the righteous and the unrighteous and punishes all according to their actions. No one walks away free from their crimes. God sees every crime and punishes it in His time, not ours. Trust Him to bring justice to your situations at the right time.

A Jealous God

Some time ago, my then six-year-old son asked, "What is an idol?" As I attempted to explain what an idol was, he interrupted me. He said, "The invention you made is cool, but do not love the invention more than God." I was so stunned and speechless that all I could say was, "Yup, anything you love more than God is an idol." I felt his words in my spirit, and I knew those were not his words, but God had explained them to him in a way he could easily understand. Scripture makes it clear to submit only to Him:

- He is a consuming fire, a jealous God (Deuteronomy 4:24).
- We must not have any other god but Him (Exodus 20:3).
- Those who turn against Him will be punished, and their children down to the third and fourth generation will bear the consequences as He is a jealous God (Deuteronomy 5:9; Exodus 20:5–6).
- He doesn't want to share His praise or glory with idols or anyone else. He alone deserves our glory and praise (Isaiah 42:8).
- Though He is slow to anger, He is provoked to anger by our detestable acts (Nahum 1:3; Deuteronomy 32:16).

- He is a jealous and avenging God. He takes vengeance on His foes and unleashes His wrath against His enemies (Nahum 1:2).
- Among God's many names and descriptions, *jealousy* is one of them (Exodus 34:14).

God repeatedly makes His jealousy known to us. We are His beloved, and He wants us for Himself and does not desire to share us with any other gods or give His praise and honor to any other gods. Society has this idea that being jealous is a terrible thing. As we can see, God Himself identifies as a jealous God. It is not wrong to be harmlessly jealous, as it is a way of expressing our emotions.

Sometimes, jealousy rises only when our love or actions toward someone are not reciprocated. We then watch that same person give that love and attention to another person or something we may feel is much less deserving of their attention. This is how God feels when He looks down on His people, who are to worship only Him but give their attention and praise to an undeserving object that neither moves nor speaks nor has the power to create. One of my favorite scriptures in the bible is when the psalmist described idols. He said, "They have mouths but cannot speak, eyes, but cannot see. They have ears, but cannot hear, noses, but cannot smell. They have hands, but cannot feel, feet, but cannot walk, nor can they utter a sound with their throats. Those who make them will be like them, and so will all who trust in them" (Psalm 115:5-8). How can we turn away from a God who saves and turns to idols made by human hands and cannot function?

God is the creator of all things and expects His creation to acknowledge and give Him praise, for He deserves more than our praise. As David said, "Let everything that has breath praise the Lord" (Psalm 150:6). This is God's right—for His creation to praise Him and worship only Him, but at the same time, He does not force us to obey His commands.

Now, when we come to the body of Christ, though you and I are entitled to show emotions, does that give us the right to act on them incorrectly? To chase after another person's achievement and envy what another person has? Or command that another person be indebted to only us and no one else? Jealousy becomes a problem amongst the body of Christ when it becomes why we harm each other.

As children of God, wanting and being envious of what someone has, to the extent of plotting evil against them, is not what God wants for us. God has called us to live in peace with each other (1 Corinthians 7:15; Romans 12:18). Human understanding differs from God's. The way we go about things can be destructive, and only God has the power to destroy what He has created. God created us and has every right to act on His jealousy for us. He does whatever He pleases. But because we are so limited in our way of doing things and living in a world that mainly lives to satisfy the desires of the flesh, sometimes we take our emotions to another level.

"The Lord takes his place in court and presents his case against his people (Isaiah 3:13). God created us for Himself. To be witnesses of who He is. He has every right to take His own people to court and present His case when they turn against Him. This court is known as "Judgment Day." As we grow closer and closer to God, we learn that the most important things in life are not acquired under people's wings but in God's presence. "For jealousy makes a man furious, and he will not spare when he takes revenge" (Proverbs 6:34 ESV). We must realize as children of God that just as we feel jealous when our efforts are not reciprocated or noticed but rather given to another, in the same way, God feels disappointed, jealous, and saddened by us acknowledging other things or gods. Eventually, this provokes Him to anger.

It is no surprise that God makes it known throughout the Bible that He is a jealous God, and we are to bow down to no other but Him. It has been made clear to us. What we do with such commandments is solely up to us, but we must be prepared to face the consequences of disobeying God's commands. What would happen if we chose to worship any other gods? Destruction! When God sent Jonah to go to the city of Nineveh to warn the people to stop their evil ways, or else He would destroy the whole city, Jonah first disobeyed and tried to hide from God, but he later listened after facing a heavy storm and spending three days and nights in the belly of a huge fish (Jonah 1:1–17).

The consequences He faced warn us of what we stand to face when we turn against God's commands. As we draw nearer to God, may we develop a heart that obeys His commandments and love and compassion toward others. May God help us avoid all the things that distract us from Him. He alone deserves our attention, praise, and honor.

21

OVERCOMING DISTRACTIONS

Submit to God, and you will have peace;
then things will go right for you.
—Job 22:21 NLT

Webster's dictionary defines *distraction* as "an object that directs one's attention away from something else." This object can come into our lives in so many forms. As children of God, we have been advised in the Word of God to focus on pure and trustworthy things (Philippians 4:8). Even as believers of Christ, we may find ourselves thinking of things that are not praiseworthy from time to time. This is a trap, and since God has given us the power of self-control, we are to immediately recognize such thoughts and speak life and positivity against them.

Compelling yourself, focusing on your goals and dreams, and working hard to bring them to fruition is the most incredible feeling anyone could have. Look at your achievements and be proud of how far you've come. But is this always easy? Not always. Have you ever decided to do a certain project, only for something else to happen and bring that project to a halt? Yes, I've been there. These forms of distractions are ones that we cannot control because no one can control the natural causes of life. But we can take what happens and work around it, no matter the distractions; giving up on our dream is not the answer.

Some distractions are not our fault, but what about those we can prevent or resist? For example, suppose you know that social media distracts you from progressing in your daily planned goals. In that case, you can discipline yourself by reducing phone use, especially when working on a project.

When God created us with a beginning and an end, what happens in between depends on what you do with your time and how you allow God to help you get to the end of your race. You would think that because we belong to God who knows our beginning and end, and because He is powerful over all things, we get to live life smoothly from beginning to end. But if anything, being a child of God makes us a target for great distractions.

I believe that all humans can concentrate if they decide this is what they will do. Being distracted by our chaotic schedules, daily activities, and unnecessary things can delay us. Through the detours, confusions, battles, storms, and ups and downs, we're given a chance to either feed into our distractions or challenge ourselves in walking regardless of the storms that disrupt life's journey. Along the way, the many trials you will face will challenge you in more ways than you can imagine. You will face many distractions that will threaten your peace and shift your focus if you allow them. But the good news is that God has given us the spirit of power over all adversities (2 Timothy 1:7).

We must remember who we are through life's journey and never lose why we started that project. Those who find refuge in the Lord will constantly have renewed strength through life's most unbearable moments. Pay more attention to the things that build you and motivate you.

How can you help yourself overcome the distractions you face in life? Here are some that have worked for me :

- *Identify where the distractions are coming from.* If your distraction is a place, make a personal effort to remove yourself from that place. If it is a thing or an act, exercise self–control over your choices and actions. If it is people, cut off the time of gatherings and spend more of that time in solitude with God. This will help with direction and narrow down the things clouding your space, giving you the clarity to shift your focus on the task at hand.

- *Determine where your distractions are aimed.* Are they causing you to stall the realization of your goals and dreams? Are they causing your mind to wander into unnecessary thoughts, preventing you from thinking about fruitful things? Remember: your number-one battleground is your mind. This is where the enemy is most likely to start. He places thoughts in your mind, drawing you away from what matters. You must train your mind to think of things that give life, fulfill, build, and give you confidence each morning with renewed hope. Paul reminds us of this in his letter to the Romans: "Do not conform to the patterns of this world, but be transformed by the renewing of your mind" (Romans 12:2). If we dwell on the things we go through or what is happening around us, we will never make it to the end of the race, and our minds will not get the chance to be renewed. There will always be distractions everywhere, but does that mean we should allow them to stop us?

- *Attack the distractions by feeding yourself with the Word of God daily and indulging in godly activities.* In other words, *"feed your focus and starve your distractions."* The best antidote for avoiding distractions from your life is reading and knowing the Word of God. God never stops speaking to us, no matter what we face. His word enables us to hear Him. Being consumed with distracting things can cause us to miss what He says. We must fight with the power God has given us to tackle all forms of opposition, including the things that hinder our spiritual walk.

Re-visiting the story of Job, the word of God tells us Job still stood by God. He continued focusing and leaning on God even though life gave him all the reasons not to. Along the way, he faced many distractions that could have caused him to give up. Even when Eliphaz had insinuated that Job's sufferings were due to his sins, according to him, God cannot benefit if a man is blameless. He believed God was interested only in punishing sin. Job never allowed those words to distract His mindset about God. Job stood by his focus, which was his personal beliefs about who God is and what He meant to him. He starved the lies and stood the test of time (Job 22:4–5).

The proof of God's presence in your life is not always easy; if it were easy, we would not need faith. Can you trust yourself to stand the test of time in your own life? Can you fight off the distractions that come along through the journey of life? When you stand firm in what you believe in without giving in to distractions and allow God to take control and allowing Him to refine the gold in you, the result will be a beautiful rebirth.

Following the Crowd

"Do not follow the crowd in doing wrong. When you give testimony in a lawsuit, do not prevent justice by siding with the crowd" (Exodus 23:2). As we journey through the storms of life, there will come a time when we may feel obligated to follow a certain crowd to feel important. But if there is one thing I have learned in life—that our worth is not found in whom we are connected to on earth but in who we are tied to in heaven. Anyone who finds you worthy based on whom you are connected to on earth is not genuinely seeing you through the eyes of grace.

Regarding how we identify with others, one of the most important questions we must ask ourselves is, "Am I part of the solution or part of the problem?" Do I treat and accept people based on how God sees them? We may not see or know the destinies of those we cross paths with, but would the way we treat them or identify with them be any different if we knew who God has destined them to be? Why can't we love and cherish others because they belong to and are loved by God?

The Word of God instructs us to practice what will make us blameless in the sight of God (Deuteronomy 18:13). Jesus Christ lived a blameless life on earth. He is pure and desires us to be just like Him. When we stand for Christ, we will never be tilted or fight to be part of a crowd to feel important. We will never shun others just to fit in with a certain group. Following the crowd is when we feel we must do as the world does to belong. We follow because we believe the crowd can get us to our destination. We follow to be a part of the "circle." We move in a certain direction because everyone else is moving in that direction, and we start looking down on certain people because everyone else is doing the same.

As God's children, He expects us to move differently from the world because we are set apart (Deuteronomy 7:6–11). We can not follow two masters. We must allow God's wisdom to lead us. We don't do what everyone else is doing; we don't act on what others are saying or doing, but we must choose to do what we know is right in the sight of God.

Are you part of the solution or the problem? Are you the one who stands in for the one being stoned, or are you amongst those throwing the stones? Are you condoning people's bad behavior toward another with your silence, or are you speaking up to bring peace and unity, even if it will cost you your circle? James tells us that if we know the good we must do and don't do it, we sin (James 4:17). Silence is as loud as your words, and sometimes, it speaks louder. Not saying anything for fear of losing your place in the crowd is a sin. When we follow the crowd, we condone. However, when we know who we are and how valuable we are, we will understand that we've been called to be different.

There are many ways of being a crowd-follower or crowd-pleaser. We often condone those we follow when we transfer our fear of Christ onto them— idolizing them instead of God. King Solomon said, "Fearing people is a dangerous trap, but trusting the Lord means safety. (Proverbs 29:25 NLT). To fear people to the extent of disregarding the Word of God is a dangerous trap. People can fail us; following them does not guarantee safety, but following God does. Fearing God is the best antidote to fearing people. It is better to be cast out by people than by God. Following the crowd means:

- *We lack self-confidence.* This makes us forget how God sees us. And we start placing our value and importance in the hands of people. We shy away from things we should address and lower our standards to comfort those we value.
- *We have no sense of direction.* We are lost, so we say, "Let me just do as they are doing; that might get me to high places as they seem to know what they are doing." As Christians, we are to be leaders— to lead the crowd. Every leader should know where they are going. How can we find direction? By mimicking the ways of Christ through the word.
- *We are easily shaken.* Moses was a man who led the crowd, and when the crowd complained in fear, he turned to God and followed instructions in leading the people of Israel. Depending on God kept him going no matter the hiccups. It helped him gain the wisdom in leading the Israelites. How would we accomplish such a task for God if we were rather *in* the crowd?
- *We suffocate our destiny.* Dreams and purposes cannot be discovered in a crowd. To see your direction clearly, you must be separated and focused. The crowd can prevent us from seeing and striving toward what is ahead. When we follow the crowd, we usually focus on what is happening around us. But when we set ourselves apart and are the difference, we gaze upon God and the task ahead.

Standing alone, feeling as though you have nobody to stand with you, may seem scary, but when you know where you are going, where you belong, and who directs your path, you can stand firm in everything. You discover your strengths and weaknesses by standing alone. But by following the crowd, those strengths dissolve; they become hidden and eventually lost, never to be discovered.

You have so much to offer to make the world better, and you cannot do this by hiding in the shadows of those around you. Be the leader; be the one to stop the norm and break the chains. Be the one to say no when everyone else is afraid to say it. And be the one who stays when everyone else walks away. Let God direct your steps as you refrain from being a follower. When you stand alone, you stand for something or someone, but with the majority, you stand for what they stand for and believe. Standing alone with God is better than following a crowd and losing out on what God has for you.

To Walk with God

God's utmost desire is for us to walk with Him side by side through faith—this has been made possible through Jesus. Through Him, we can go to the Father. Through Christ, not only are we able to walk side by side with God, but we are also given the privilege of dining with Him. He made this clear by setting His people, the Israelites, apart. Throughout the Bible, we see how faithful, merciful, patient, and protective God was over the Israelites; their constant complaint and disobedience provoked Him to anger, showing that they did not trust Him (Numbers 11–20).

Everything God did was orchestrated for the benefit of His people. Knowing this today, Satan goes after God's people with lies to turn them away from God. An example is the fall of man in the book of Genesis, chapters one through three. Satan disguised himself as a smart creature and approached Eve in the Garden of Eden to contradict God's instructions. This was the beginning of man's disobedience and disloyalty to God. The enemy had lured Eve into thinking that to disobey God was to gain knowledge and wisdom. Adam and Eve sinned by listening to the serpent. Because of this, when they heard God coming, they hid (Genesis 3:8). This was the beginning of a tainted relationship, which required the coming of the Messiah to save humanity, bringing back that innocent relationship we had with God from the start. God loves His people and desires to have them by His side. What is your walk with God like? Are you at a place in your life in which you would run and hide when you hear God's footsteps, or are you at a place in your relationship with Him in which you would run with joy toward Him? What does it mean to you to be walking alongside God? In your personal life, what has been the difference between walking with a person and walking with God? Are you in constant one-on-one, intimate communication with Him through prayer?

As you reflect on these questions and the depth of your relationship with God, you must know that walking with God is a personal choice that must be firm enough to beat all odds. When Adam was asked why he disobeyed, he said, "The woman you put here with me, she gave me some fruit from the tree, and I ate it" (Genesis 3:12). In our relationship with God, no one is responsible for our fall. "For we are each responsible for our own conduct" (Galatians 6:5 NLT). We can be tempted and pushed to the edge, but the will to hold on depends on how we allow God's strength to work within us.

Knowing that Christ is coming soon and judging by your walk with Him, are you excited by the thought of His coming, or are you nervous? God has never failed in His faithfulness to His people. Samuel referred to the Israelites as "God's special possession" (1 Samuel 10:1). This statement is proven valid throughout the Bible. God aimed to get His people to the land He had promised them. Walking with God means we forsake our will and surrender to His. It means looking up to Him to control the storms in our lives and allow Him to guide our steps.

Walking with God means involving Him in your everyday decisions. It means engaging with Him in conversations throughout the day and striving to be a better person. "Seek the kingdom of God above all things, and live righteously, and he will give you everything you need" (Matthew 6:33). This is one promise of God that has proven to be true in my walk with Him. By seeking Him, I gained the confidence and the assurance that He would bring to completion what He had started in my life (Philippians 1:6).

God showed His love and faithfulness time after time toward the Israelites, made ways for them through roadblocks, and provided for them wherever they lacked. I want to remind you that the same promises He made to them pertain to you today; whatever predicaments you find yourself in, you need not worry because God has set you apart. To walk with Him is to have victory in all aspects of your life; to walk with Him is to gain power through His Spirit; to walk with Him is to believe His ways are higher than yours; to walk with Him is to choose life in abundance; to walk with Him is to have peace that transcends all understanding. To walk with Christ is to depend on the Word of God as daily guidance. People no longer see the stain of sin on you but the presence of God in every room you enter. I challenge you today to start a journey with Him that will impact others to want to walk with Him, too.

Like Christ

Do you ever say, "When I grow up, I want to be just like you"? It's normal to want to be like those you admire, whether celebrities or not; there are reasons we wish to be like those we admire dearly. As a child of God, you are to imitate Christ's ways, representing the kingdom of God in the same way demonstrated through Jesus Christ when He was on earth. Jesus was a great teacher and leader; He taught His followers the right ways to live.

Today, however, we find this challenging as we constantly battle with our flesh, the weakest part of us. But "the one who is in you is greater than the one who is in the world" (1 John 4:4). We have the Holy Spirit and the wisdom of God to help us navigate our lives in a way that pleases God. The Word of God tells us that "whoever claims to live in Him must live as Jesus did" (1 John 2:6). When we accept Jesus Christ as our Saviour, we must strive to live a life that radiates His glory. To be like Christ is to love like Christ and act like Christ.

One thing I have learned to do over the years is that no matter what I go through and no matter where life takes me, I bring myself to reflect on who Jesus Christ is and what He endured for me. This helps me strive to be like Him when I shift in doubt. To be like Christ is to endure challenges and sufferings as Jesus did, to treat others according to what they mean to God and not our limited mind of them. Even when those we love do not show us love in the same way, we must still love and be there for them as Christ would want us to.

Being like Christ comes with a price—sacrificing yourself for the glory of God, forgiving and extending mercy to your neighbor, and giving to those you know have nothing to offer you in return. Love as Jesus Christ—not as it fits your taste but with no conditions and expectations. Love with intentions (Ephesians 5:2). Love is not feelings but action—as Jesus demonstrated.

Being unable to give love as He gives means we have not entirely accepted or felt His unconditional love for us. "Love your enemies. Do good to those who hate you. Bless those who curse you. Pray for those who mistreat you" (Luke 6:27–28). Jesus demonstrated His love by washing His disciples' feet and drying them with the towel wrapped around Him, even though He knew some of them would betray Him. He did this to teach us how we should treat one another. "Now that I, your Lord and Teacher, have washed your feet, you also should wash one another's feet" (John 13:14).

When someone misbehaves, and everyone sees him or her as bitter, troubled, faulty, or unstable, a faithful follower of Christ instead chooses to see pain, vulnerability, and a call for help or to be heard—and opens their arms to that person—a faithful follower of Christ who strives to be like Christ puts into practice the word of God.

It is usually so easy for us to open our arms to those who shower us with gifts and flattering words, but God wants us to open our arms to those who persecute us, those we can't relate to in any way. Christ calls us to be and do more. When you show authenticity, empathy, love, acceptance, and understanding toward someone, it could be the day you draw that person close to Christ. It could be the day you give out a taste of what God's love is through your actions.

When we practice this selfless act of love, we become more like Christ. Being like Christ is submitting to God's will for you. Jesus understood that the will of His Father surpasses the pain and shame He faced; He understood that the process of going through pain and suffering was part of fulfilling what has already been written (Luke 22:42). Just like Christ, we must endure knowing the pain, suffering, embarrassment, and trials we face are all part of preparing us for something great.

To be like Christ is to allow God to prune and refine you. To be like Christ is to forgive as He has forgiven you (Ephesians 4:32). The Word of God says, "Man shall not live on bread alone, but by every word that comes from the mouth of God" (Matthew 4:4). To be like Christ is to live by every word from God.

Self-Evaluation 101

"Examine yourselves to see whether you are in the faith; test yourselves. Do you not realize that Christ Jesus is in you—unless you fail the test?" (2 Corinthians 13:5). At some point in life, we all need to assess and monitor our progress —how we are doing and what improvements we need to make to improve our relationship with God and those around us.

How are your love for God and your love for others connected? You may say, "I love God dearly and always strive to do what is right in His sight. I have a good heart. God trusts me and loves me unconditionally." All that is amazing, but does your life reflect everything you say?

As I opened myself more and more to God's love for me and believed in His words over my life, I realized that the love I felt from Him enabled me to love others the same. The fear of God pushes me to do my best. At a point in my life, I decided to give myself time to reflect on important questions. Evaluating ourselves in our Christian walk is important. As humans, we are bound to fail God here and there, but recognizing our mistakes and rising above them shows our maturity and efforts to be the best version of ourselves. We accept that we are not perfect but try to do what pleases God because of our love for Him. He has been my source of comfort, and I want to get to the end of life and know that I made Him proud. So I turned to face myself, and some of the questions I needed to ask myself were as follows:

- *Am I accepting God's gift of freedom?* This changes the game forever. It enlarges the grounds we walk on and opens a new door of possibilities. It helps us realize that we no longer have to live in the bondage of what limits us but have the mindset that God's love has uprooted what holds us back.
- *Am I trusting in God's love for me?* Am I trusting enough to leave all my burdens at His feet? This question was necessary because how do I expect Him to believe in my love if I can't trust His for me? How is that even possible!? Long ago, the Lord said to Israel, "I have loved you, my people, with an everlasting love. With unfailing love, I have drawn you to myself" (Jeremiah 31:3 NLT). As I read these words, the Holy Spirit assured me that this word also pertained to me. He loved me with everlasting love, and it was time I started living my life as someone who believed in those words, no matter what I faced.

- *Are my words positive?* Are they in connection to my actions? I love God, and I know I do, but are those words proven by how I love and receive others, whether acquaintances, friends, or strangers? Is my love for Christ radiating through my actions and love for others? Am I showing grace and mercy to others as Christ offers to me? Are my words pleasing to God? Are they glorifying God? I needed to allow God to strip anything that stood in the way of my relationship with Him. "Wise words are like deep waters; wisdom flows from the wise like a bubbling brook" (Proverbs 18:4 NLT). Our words should be healing, encouraging, and not condemning and judgmental. When people speak to you, do they feel better or worse about themselves? Are we impacting with our words? Are we speaking well of others, even if they've wronged us, or are we complaining every chance we get? When we love God, our words toward others and ourselves should be of love and acceptance. Our words should only build and not tear down. They should console and not reject. If someone lies about you or misunderstands you and spreads false information about you, do you stand to their level in getting back at them in the same way? It's painful to hear negative words about us, but these are moments when we must practice what it means to have self-control and remain positive.

- *Am I faithful to God as He has been to me?* Saul, once the king of Israel, died because he was unfaithful to the Lord. He did not keep the word of the Lord, even consulted a medium for guidance, and did not inquire of the Lord. So, the Lord put him to death and turned the kingdom over to David, son of Jesse (1 Chronicles 10:13–14). Are we faithful to God in our walk with Him, or do we also consult with other things for answers and progress? I needed to make sure I was being faithful to God. This was important to me, as the faithfulness of God has kept me going through some of the most unspeakable times in my life. Today, I am reminded that no matter what I face in life, whether big, small or a blink-of-an-eye-type situation, I can count on Him as a source of strength.

- *Do I depend on my confidence, the confidence of others, or the confidence of God?* I needed to make sure my confidence was solely in Christ alone. The Word of God tells us, "Let us then approach God's throne of grace with confidence, so that we may receive mercy and find grace to help us in our time of need" (Hebrews 4:16). One of the biggest mistakes I used to make was to put my total confidence in people. Through God's undying love for me, I have developed a sense of security and comfort, knowing I can go to Him with all I am and never be judged for it. I placed all of me at His feet, and not once did He shun me and turn aside from me. He made me feel wanted, valued, and important and showed me His promises. As the world around me pointed out my flaws and painted me to be something I was not, God saw me for who I truly was —who He created me to be. He saw my heart! And I felt His love and presence. My confidence in people faded. I now confide in the only faithful friend I know.

- *Is there something in my life that I need God to shred?* "It is God who works in you to will and to act in order to fulfill his good purpose" (Philippians 2:13). I needed a balanced approach—to face my flaws and ask God to work through me. In which area did I need God's intervention, and which area needed cultivating for me to grow more maturely in Him? I knew that my life was for Christ and not my own, and in thinking so, I wanted God to cleanse all parts of me that were not serving Him, all parts that were not pleasing Him, all parts that were stifling His Holy Spirit in me. "It is no longer I who lives, but Christ who lives within me" (Galatians 2:20 NLT)—to use me, to help me, and to set my feet on a straight path. I aimed to please Him, whose love for me was genuine and pure. I was in a race to win the heavenly prize He called me in Christ Jesus. To do that, I needed to allow Him to strip me of everything that could hinder me.

- *Am I showing gratitude?* God constantly showers us with His grace and mercy. Though we are undeserving of all His goodness, He freely pours and fills us up gracefully daily. I pondered, "He turned my sadness into laughter, and my ashes for His beauty"—a gift I did not work for—and it was vital to cherish that. So I asked myself, "Am I loving my life and living it in a way that screams, 'I'm grateful, Lord'? Am I loving and appreciating myself the way God wants me to?" Through the storms of life, one of the things we can forget about doing is showing ourselves love and appreciating our efforts in trying. We can't only accept and expect love from others; we must start with ourselves and then learn to extend it to others. We cannot give what we do not have. Loving ourselves and appreciating our efforts is one way of showing God we are grateful for His excellent work. It tells Him that we are thankful for how wonderfully and fearfully He has made us and given us the strength to thrive.

My utmost desire has always been for God to use me beyond my level of comfort. You need to face yourself and ask yourself some important questions at some point in your life. Allow the Holy Spirit to convict you, especially if you desire to be like Christ and be used for God's glory. We should not expect God to use us if we are unwilling to admit our flaws and work on being the best versions of ourselves or expect God to shower us with many blessings if we fail to recognize the blessings He has given us now. Assess your walk with God, scan all aspects of your life, and get yourself in good standing with Him.

22

A DIFFERENT PERSPECTIVE

What you see is determined by where you stand

"He has identified us as his own by placing the Holy Spirit in our hearts as the first installment that guarantees everything he has promised us". (2 Corinthians 1:22 NLT). Whether you believe in Christ or something else, you will face problems in life. But as a child of God, you are made to look at your problems differently than the world does. How are you looking at your problems? Through what lenses are you viewing what is happening around you? If you're looking at your issues outside the presence of God, it makes sense that you will have no hope of hanging on. Because in His presence, there's a guarantee of freedom, and the Holy Spirit is proof of that (2 Corinthians 3:17).

Do you see your struggles as a threat you need to prevent or as part of your story you need to embrace? Life is such that today, you may find yourself swimming in the pool of happiness and satisfaction, and tomorrow, you may be staring at a whole new story altogether. How do we hop from one emotion to another in minutes, days, or weeks?

Sometimes, life offers us no chance to rejoice for an extended period. But the apostle Paul advises us to rejoice regardless of problems and trials. Through that, we develop endurance, which helps build strength of character. This gives us confidence. He assures us that God loves us and has given us the Holy Spirit to fill our hearts with His love (Romans 5:3–5). We have a good reason to view our struggles from a different perspective than what they present. Because of whom we belong to, we can see our struggles as a gift rather than a problem.

How we view our struggles matters. See your struggles as a necessary part of your journey—to help you grow and live in total reflection of who Christ is. For instance, if you step into a spot where you get cut by a sharp object, you can focus on the part where you learned never to put yourself in that position to be cut again instead of being upset about being cut. This helps you look at a challenging situation in a good light. You focus on the lessons you gained from your predicaments rather than the pain they cost you.

Every storm we face is a lesson that can turn into beauty. What we go through breaks us in the physical realm so we can mature in the spiritual realm. It's an awakening moment. We can endure many struggles and pains and still stay the same at the end of the day. There is always one inflicted pain that turns everything around, and God knows when that turnaround is needed for the next level.

We may not see the light while walking through the tunnels, but once we reach the end of those tunnels, His plans and purpose will be evident in our lives. We will see why we need to go through certain unfavorable routes. We have hope in Christ, which is why we can look at our storms in the light and never have to fear. God is always by our side, changing our situation for the better.

Out of Reach

"From his abundance, we have all received one gracious blessing after another" (John 1:16 NLT). How often have we searched for that one thing day and night, asking God to show up when what we've been searching for was right with us? The same goes for the many blessings we constantly ask God for. Our blessings are not out of reach. We already live in the blessings of God. Our minds are usually fixed on familiarity, so we search and search, failing to see what is in front of us because God's way of doing things differs from what we are used to. We do not see these God-given blessings because we are distracted by the wrong things in life and are looking elsewhere for them.

Look at it this way. God sends you a boat. You refuse to see or enter it because it is not what you expected; instead, you are still waiting, praying, and crying to Him for what He has already provided for you. You are waiting for your idea of what your boat should look like.

Let's look at another scenario. God has given you a mate in the form of the school mascot who is less popular. You say to yourself; *This is not who God wants for me* because he is not what you imagined your future husband to be like. You continue praying for a mate, hoping God will answer your prayers based on your expectations. When it doesn't go your way, you're disappointed and blame God for not answering your prayers. You pursue the school's quarterback instead, hoping he will somehow become who God has intended for you just because that is who you want.

Let's look at a final scenario. You were born with an extraordinary talent that can help you financially by cultivating it into more than it is. You constantly ask God for a financial breakthrough, and God whispers to you to do something with your talent, but you ignore it. Why? Your idea of a financial breakthrough is God reaching from the sky and dropping a huge sum of money or magically making things happen without effort. Funny as it sounds, that is not going to happen! The blessings are right around you.

Get close to God, and He will show you. He opens our eyes to these hidden blessings and favors. The closer we get to God, the clearer our visions become, and when you are able to see clearly, you will realize that God's blessings are not out of reach. We serve a God who knows what we need and gives us exactly that.

Just as God gives us breath and new mercies each morning, every new day comes with many other blessings that we can see only when our minds are focused on Him. God always wants the absolute best for us, but sometimes, we cause our misfortunes by refusing to tune in with Him. God wants us to remain in Him so we can hear Him better and have a better life.

Have you ever searched for something you thought you lost, for example, your car or house keys, only to realize that they've been in your pocket or on the counter next to you all this while? This is exactly what happens when we search for our blessings elsewhere instead of realizing they are right around us.

Identifying the Source

Google Dictionary defines "source" as a place, a person, or a thing in which something comes or can be obtained. "It's the devil's fault." We immediately point the finger at the devil for every negative thing in our lives—it's his fault. When is it *your* fault? When do we take accountability for our faults? Is it that the devil is much more powerful than we are, or do we love to justify our actions, making excuses for our poor decisions? Or is it that we no longer have the eyes to see when it is our fault or when God has allowed it to happen? There is a difference between knowing the things of the flesh that hinder us and doing something about it and knowing but choosing to ignore them. "If you live according to the flesh, you will die; but if by the Spirit you put to death the misdeeds of the body, you will live" (Romans 8:13).

Paul tells us that when we live to satisfy ourselves, our needs, and our wants, we will reap the consequences of those choices and actions—decay and, worse, death. See it this way: when you have a plant not being cared for correctly, it will eventually end up dead, and its fruit will decay. Harvesting good fruit is hard work. It takes being intentional and dedicated in the area you want to see bloom. If you want to see yourself rise, spend time teaching yourself, grooming yourself in the Word, striving to bear the fruit of the Spirit, meditating on a verse a day, and feeding yourself in the Spirit so much that you will know the difference between what is the devil's fault, what God allows to happen, and what is formed through your poor decisions or fleshly desire.

To be alive is to feed yourself with the right foods—spiritual food—the Word, prayer, bearing the fruits of the spirit. Yes, this is hard to do, but it is doable because God has not given us the spirit of timidity but of power (2 Timothy 1:7).

We all have a spiritual side—our identity in Christ—and a flesh side, which is the side the world inflicts on us. We are first spiritual beings. We were born the vessel in which God is pleased to dwell, innocent beings. Jesus said, "Let the little children come to me, and do not hinder them, for the kingdom of heaven belongs to such as these" (Matthew 19:4). God wants us to be like children, innocent, needing nothing! But as we grow, whatever environment (especially a non-Christian environment) we grew up in exposes us to things out of our control. These things stay in our minds, which the enemy later uses against us when we don't address and fight against them.

The Word of God says to train a child in how he or she should go so the child will not depart from it (Proverbs 22:6). Children mimic everything they see. So, imagine an innocent child growing up and being inflicted with so much negativity around them, from family, friends, and ugly life situations. What this does is create a certain wall or hold. It establishes the thought processes and how the person sees and acts. It can create ungodly fear and habits or keep the person in a bubble that he or she is afraid to come out of to experience a fruitful life. These are the fleshly things that the enemy can use against a person when not identified early.

We must know the source of what keeps us stagnant—identifying and recognizing our faults—the things we struggle with, or else the enemy can take those weaknesses and use them against us. When you become aware of the things you do that the enemy can capitalize on and use against you, you can turn to God's word and fight against it. The Word of God breaks all the strongholds and renews our minds. Paul said, "Those who live to please the Spirit will harvest everlasting life from the Spirit" (Galatians 6:8 NLT). Our identity is found in our Spiritual being. We often cause our predicaments when we ignore our weaknesses and live in hopes that they will disappear or that we can live through them. Our flesh will always cry out for what it wants, but the spirit trusts that God sees all things, knows all, hears all things, and moves for us so that His glory will be shown in our weaknesses.

When your flesh cries out for what it wants, and you answer to it when the time for facing the consequences arrives, do not give the enemy credit for it and say it is the devil's fault. Remember—that is what he wants to hear, that you acknowledge him. Rise, own up to your faults, and learn from them. It is *not* the devil's fault! Sometimes, it is the fact that we are ignoring the need to better ourselves in the spirit; the enemy then says, "Let me come in."

Ignorance causes us to walk past what we know is affecting us. We become like the Israelites who were too comfortable in their problems and would rather stay in them than travel on the road to purpose and abundance. We stay with what we know is affecting our progress because we are comfortable with predicaments. The Spirit of God constantly convicts us, but we refuse to confront our weaknesses because this is a part of us that we would like to have buried without facing. But then, simultaneously, we would be screaming for God to help us, yet we refuse to do what is required of us to break through.

Is the devil that powerful compared to you? It's not the devil's fault. It is your unwillingness to be pruned. When you are hit with the biggest storms in your life, as a child of God, you need to know the source of the storm before you draw out your battle plan. What if what you are going through is so that you can learn something? What if what you are going through is God allowing it for a purpose? Not everything is the devil's fault! We must pray for the spirit of discernment. The truth is, the devil cannot cause things in your life. He will fight you, yes. He will attack, yes. Every thief attacks to forcefully take what does not belong to them or kill and destroy to diminish something they are threatened by. God has given you authority over all living things, so has He also given you power over the enemy and your fleshly desires (Luke 10:19; Genesis 1:26). When the cross is too rugged to carry, it is okay to go to God and ask for help, but never turn to the devil and give him credit for making your cross heavy to carry, because that excites him.

Life's journey is not easy; Jesus did not have an easy life on earth. No matter what He faced, He never credited the devil but knew His power as the Son of God. He knew that the journey would not be smooth because of who He was and that there would be much opposition. He knew that not all would accept Him and what He represents. This should be an example for you. Take hardships as part of your journey, part of the process, and no matter what source your problems come from, when you lean on God, He will turn situations around for your good but do not focus on the enemy, giving him credit for your problems.

At a time when it was too hard for Jesus to bear, He went straight to His Father. He never lived a life of complaints, saying the devil did this and the devil did that. But He went straight to the source He knew He could lean on and from which He could receive the strength to carry on. Why would God allow His own Son to suffer? Was His suffering from the devil? Or was it that God beat Satan at his plans? When we go through a fraction of what Jesus went through, we start breaking down and pacing in despair. Why rebuke when you are the one who drove your car into your building? Why reprimand when God allowed it for a more significant cause? The devil came to kill, steal, and destroy (John 10:10). When something terrible happens in your life, and he is not the source of it, and then you give credit to him, you best believe he will be rejoicing over it. You are giving him credit he did not work for. Blaming the enemy for your predicaments is music to his ears because that's his purpose— to destroy you.

So a word of advice—don't put that smile on his face, but in all things, turn to God and say, "God, I may not understand what I am going through right now, but I am grateful because I know you are working for my good." Bless the name of the Lord in lacking seasons and in your seasons of abundance. Because regardless of where we stand in life, He is still God! When Jesus was tempted, the Spirit led Him into the wilderness to be tempted in the first place (Matthew 4:1). Has it ever occurred to you that some of the things you face are to test how strong your faith is in God? You cannot test God (Matthew 4:7), but He can test you. Because God is not a liar, He keeps His word. He does not need to prove His faithfulness; we do. After all He has done for you, what more can He do to prove that He has your back and is for you?

The Word of God says, "Then the devil took him to the holy city, Jerusalem, to the highest point of the temple, and said, 'If you are the Son of God, jump off! For the Scriptures say, "He will order His angels to protect you. And they will hold you up with their hands so you won't even hurt your foot on a stone" (Matthew 4:5–6 NLT). As we can see through these verses, the enemy knows the Scriptures and is quoting and using them to test Jesus. As a child of God, you should realize that it is an error if you don't know the Scriptures or do not use them in defending yourself against the enemy.

Do you know that the devil can't even test you without God's permission? Nope, he can't. There is nothing he can do that falls outside of God's dominion, and this God is on your side! He is in your boat. The sovereignty of God is unmatched, and even the devil knows—he acknowledged the sovereignty of God. He acknowledged the wall of protection God has around His children (Job 1:8–12 N), and if the devil knows it, why not you, a child of God? Why are you lacking such knowledge? We should not be giving Satan too much credit. The devil has no dominion over you. His power is limited.

Child of God, not every battle comes from the devil. We must learn to identify the source of our problem so that we are not taking unnecessary measures to fight the wrong battles. One thing you must keep in mind is that regardless of the source of your problems, know that "Everyone who calls on the name of the Lord will be saved" (Romans 10:13) and that everything works together for your good when you follow God's regulations (Romans 8:28).

23

DEFINING GOD

———————— ⌘ ————————

Creations reveal the power and the beauty of a sovereign God.

I was once asked in my theology class to define God, and I thought, *How can I describe the God who oversees why I can think and move? How does the clay describe the potter?* God is unchangeable, eternal, and indescribable; we are made whole in Him. No number of words can explain who God is, not even the many names He possesses. That is how sovereign and self-existing He is.

To me, God is the true meaning of *complete*. Before Him, there is no one. After Him, there is no one. In the book of Isaiah, the Lord Himself tells us that His thoughts are nothing like our thoughts and His ways are far beyond anything we could ever imagine, for just as the heavens are higher than the earth, so are the Lord's ways higher than ours and His thoughts higher than our thoughts (Isaiah 55:8–9). No one can second guess or question God (Romans 9:20). He is God by Himself, the only God. In search of wisdom and observing the burdens of human beings on earth, King Solomon concluded and realized that no one can ever find out what God is doing, not even the wisest of people (Ecclesiastes 8:16–17). He is a God who is fully man and fully God—this is how sovereign He is. God is—

> *Omniscient*—all-knowing. He is the God who sees all things. John says, "Even if we feel guilty, God is greater than our feelings, and he knows everything" (1 John 3:20 NLT). Isaiah tells us He makes known the end from the beginning, from ancient times, and what is

still to come (Isaiah 46:9–10). He is an on-time God. He knows and sees when He is to act and when He is to be silent, but even in His silence, He sees all and moves on our behalf. David said the Lord sits in heaven and watches over all. He examines both the righteous and the wicked (Psalm 11:4–11).

Omnipotent—all-powerful. He is not limited in His ways. When He speaks and acts, it leaves a mark for the world to witness. Because He is powerful, He works best in our weaknesses. His goodness is shown amid our storms. His power is not limited to our mistakes and shame. David said the power of God is absolute and that to understand Him is beyond what the human mind can comprehend (Psalm 147:5). David also said, "The Lord merely spoke, and the heavens were created. He breathed the word, and all the stars were born" (Psalm 33:6 NLT). He is powerful and strong; nothing is complicated for Him.

Unchangeable. "I am the Lord, and I do not change. That is why you descendants of Jacob are not already destroyed" (Malachi 3:6 NLT). He is a God who remains the same today, tomorrow, and forever, so His promises for us still hold no matter what. He does what He says He will do. God has many characters, but one thing He is not and can never be is a liar. His Word is sure, and as seasons and times change, we can always depend on this unchangeable God, who holds on to us. This gets me thinking each time: *Where would we be without Him? What has He not done for us?*

Omnipresent—present everywhere. He is the only God who can go before us and at the same time be with us. David knew this when he said, I can never escape from your Spirit! I can never get away from your presence! If I go up to heaven, you are there; if I go down to the grave, you are there. If I ride the wings of the morning, if I dwell by the farthest oceans, even there, your hand will guide me, and your strength will support me. I could ask the darkness to hide me and the light around me to become night—but even in darkness I cannot hide from you. To you the night shines as bright as day. Darkness and light are the same to you (Psalm 139:7–12 NLT).

I know that sometimes life may leave us questioning the presence of God in our lives, especially when we face storms. But David attests that we serve an omnipresent God, and not even the darkness can hide us from Him. God is the giver of grace (John 1:14, 17). God is the essence of love (John 14:16). He is faithful and good, and His mercies endure forever (Psalm 136; Psalm 34:8). He is Yahweh. He is light—the light that shines in our darkness. John said, "In him there is no darkness" (1 John 1:5 NLT). He is Jehovah Jireh, our provider (Genesis 22:14); Jehovah Rapha, our healer (Exodus 15:26); Jehovah Nissi, our banner (Exodus 17:15); Jehovah Shalom, our prince of peace (Judges 6:24). He is the Alpha and Omega (Revelation 1:8); He is the one who was and is to come (Revelation 1:4); He is the first and the last (Revelation 2:8), the beginning and the end (Revelation 21:6). There are so many attributes of God. In all His attributes, He proves Himself in the lives of His children. I can personally attest to His faithfulness in my life.

The incredible thing is that this powerful and indescribable God wants a relationship with us. David wondered this at a point in his life when he asked, "What are mere mortals that you should think about them, human beings that you should care for them?" (Psalm 8:4 NLT). We may not understand God's ways, but we are blessed to have such a God who looks out for us. When I was broken and left at a point where I questioned if He was truly there and saw what I was facing, He suddenly showed up. When He shows up, it is always beyond what I expect, beyond what my mind can ever comprehend. He is all we have in living a worthy life.

When God Reveals Himself

God reveals Himself to His children in so many ways. To mention a few—through the mind, history, nature, prophecy, and His Son, Jesus Christ. God reveals things that are impossible to get in any other way. Though He is a mysterious God, He has also shown Himself to those who seek Him to know Him and encounter Him. To know God is to be fulfilled. And the truth is that many Christians encounter God because they have His revelation. Encountering God is an experience that brings fulfillment to the lives of His children. This experience will never cause a believer's life to remain as it was. We can't know who God is if He has not revealed Himself to us. Encountering the supernatural is proof that God lives and moves in our lives. "We are his offspring" (Acts 17:28 NLT).

God reveals Himself through the works of His hands. He reveals Himself through His creations—you and I are part of that. He reveals Himself in the beauty of what He makes and the intricacy of what He creates. I believe that a glance at nature and the stature of the human being reveals the sovereignty of a beautiful God. His heart, love, and beauty are seen in His creation. The sight of creation should awaken a mood of praise and be in awe of the works of His hands.

Look at yourself in the mirror. What do you see? You are to see a beautiful likeness of God. David said, "I praise you because I am fearfully and wonderfully made. Your works are wonderful; I know that full well" (Psalm 139:14 NLT). Though God reveals Himself to us through creation, this is not enough for us to be saved because salvation requires accepting who He is through Christ—the willingness to accept Him and what He did for you, draw near to Him, and walk according to His commands. David wrote that God has shown Himself strong in the most powerful ways in the lives of His people.

God revealed Himself as the Creator, Saviour, and Ruler of the universe in the times of Abraham, Isaac, and Jacob (Joshua 24:2).

When God threatened to destroy the nation because of the sins of the Israelites, Moses begged Him to spare the people because that would bring dishonor to His name (Exodus 32:12–14). Through their obedience, He causes His people to triumph. David won the battles over his enemies because he listened and walked in the ways of God (1 Chronicles 14:8–17). Whenever nations disobeyed God, they experienced hardship —plaques, locusts, and setbacks in war (Exodus 10:4–5; 2 Kings 17:7–23). This is how and why God revealed Himself to the Israelites and the nation—through His mighty power at work. God's sovereignty is displayed for the betterment of His people when they listen and obey. And His wrath is revealed through destruction when they turn their backs on God.

God reveals Himself to us in our conscious minds, the part of our minds that judges our attitudes or actions, that lets us know if what we preach matches what we do and pushes us to do what is right. Our consciences are the image of God in our souls, revealing both the existence of God and, to some extent, the nature of God. Our consciences reveal God in that they differentiate between right and wrong and hold us responsible for the wrongful actions we take. When Christians set themselves up to walk in the will of God, they do what is right; they allow God in their consciences to lead them, refraining from doing what is detestable to God.

God reveals Himself through His acts to His chosen people, who are meant to deliver His Word. He reveals Himself through His performed miracles, which happen in the lives of His children daily. This brings me to the gift of prophecy. God reveals Himself through prophecy, in which His children learn His mind and thoughts about life events. The book of Joel foretold that both sons and daughters would prophesy after God poured out His Holy Spirit on all His children (Joel 2:28). This was true on the Day of Pentecost when the Spirit of God rested on all. They immediately started speaking in other languages (Acts 2:17–18). A prophecy that comes from the wisdom and presence of God is determined by whether the ones who uttered it live a life that is in Christ. What are that person's teachings? Is his or her life godly? The *false* prophets in the Old Testament were known to be drunkards (Isaiah 28:7), opportunists (Micah 3:11), liars (Micah 2:11), unfaithful (Jeremiah 23:14), and deceitful (Zephaniah 3:4). *True* prophets of God are convicted by the Holy Spirit. They are drawn away from living lives contrary to Christ's ways. Before a prophecy is viewed as genuine, we must ensure that there is no possibility of it being from our human thinking or intuition.

This brings me to the greatest revelation of all time: God revealing Himself and His mighty power through His Son and the resurrection of His Son, Jesus Christ — the living Word of God. The Bible is not simply a book you study—it is one that we must become and live. Meditate on the Word and become it, not merely memorizing it or knowing where verses are from but becoming the Word so that others may read you and gain the hope found only in Christ. Jesus's disciples learned from Him not simply because He was quoting verses but because He was *living* them. He was the Word made flesh (John 1:1). When we mimic Him and become the Word, we become a weapon. The Word is a weapon, sharper than the sharpest two-edged sword, cutting between soul and spirit, between joint and marrow. It exposes our innermost thoughts and desires (Hebrews 4:12).

Salvation is the acceptance of Jesus Christ, the living Word, and the power of God through Him. Salvation is given through Christ, and rewards are provided through our obedience. Your acceptance of what Christ did for you should be evident through your actions. Jesus dying for you is the beginning of your salvation. Accepting Him and taking Him as your Lord and personal Saviour and mimicking His ways is living by His finished work. You always have a part to play. Make sure you do not abandon your part.

Rewards in Work, Joy in Rewards

There is a reward in work, and there is joy in rewards. Whenever you win a soul for Christ, the reward you receive from God is mind-blowing! The devil tries to prevent us from serving our purposes because he aims to keep us from reaping those rewards. But remember that God desires to give us a good life, a joyful life.

So, child of God, do not give up no matter what! Keep walking in the fullness of His glory because rewards bring joy. This reminds me of a verse God gave me at a time when I was questioning whether to go on with ministry work or not, as I did not see the results that would lead to the vision He has shown to me concerning my ministry: "So, my dear brothers and sisters, be strong and immovable. Always work enthusiastically for the Lord, for you know that nothing you do for the Lord is ever useless" (1 Corinthians 15:58 NLT). This verse kept me pushing through even when things were not moving as I hoped they would. Our rewards always come from knowing we have a place prepared for us. We can look forward to this place that surpasses all other material rewards on earth. Sometimes, when we miss this truth, it's hard to keep the joy and continue doing God's work. When we see no progress, it can cause us to want to give up, but if we can fix our eyes on God and the task entrusted to us, we will yield an everlasting reward.

The apostle Paul took pride in his sufferings for Christ because they helped him preach the gospel. Nothing gave him more joy than bringing the church up in Christ and seeing them walk in their faith. The Word of God tells us that the joy of the Lord is our strength (Nehemiah 8:10). Going through challenging or difficult times can leave us feeling down and battered and, worse, tempted to give up, but we are reminded in the Word of God that the joy of the Lord gives us the strength to keep going, a strength that can be made possible only by dwelling in Christ and trusting Him.

Preaching the good news is supposed to bring joy to the hearts of believers because this is what we were made to do—witness Christ.

Our happiness is fixed in doing the work of God. King Solomon said, "The hope of the righteous is joy" (Proverbs 10:28 NLT). Joy is given to us. The Word says we have it inside us (Galatians 5:22). The Christian experience is not something that is going on around us but rather *in* us. "Christ lives in me" (Galatians 2:20 NLT). We must count our storms as joy and, most importantly, the work of God.

24

IN THE END, WE GROW

———————————— ⟨✕⟩ ————————————

*Out of your worst storms comes a shelter for many. Don't
just go through your storms; grow through them.*

The end of your story is determined by how well you've lived it
through your obedience to God. One of life's most beautiful things
is learning and growing through your storms so you can be a shelter
for those who need it. You've made it this far. You've come a long
way. You now know the will of God for your life and have vowed to
chase after it. As you move forward and pass through the storms of
life, let those storms refine you into becoming the *"you"* that only
God knows. No matter how raging the storm gets, never give up on
hope, or allow it to drown you.

Train your mind to resist anything not sent by God. Stay
embedded in the original story God has written about you. God
has chosen you for a great purpose. He has positioned you in a
way that will bring Him honor. Paul said, "Since we are God's
children, we are his heirs. In fact, together with Christ, we are heirs
of God's glory. But if we are to share his glory, we must also share his
suffering. Yet what we suffer now is nothing compared to the glory
he will reveal to us later" (Romans 8:17–18 NLT).

The boldness to walk in the glory of God can be hindered by the
storms around us, but as a child of God, I want to remind you again
that with God by your side, there are no mountains you cannot
climb. The boldness to walk in God's glory comes from knowing the
Word, but the confidence you gain comes from your understanding

of the Word. When you understand the Word, you trust, and when you trust, you gain fellowship with God.

Jesus came so you and I can access God to share in His glory. Sometimes you take a step only to realize it's been backward because of a lack of understanding of what you know, so if you have knowledge of God but lack understanding of who He is, you will have the boldness only to walk with Him, but you will lack the confidence to share Him with the world. We encounter God in remarkable ways when we know and understand the Word. Remember, as mentioned earlier in previous chapters, God never forsook the Israelites on their journey to the promised land. "The Lord went ahead of them. He guided them during the day with a pillar of cloud, and He provided light at night with a pillar of fire. This allowed them to travel by day or by night" (Exodus 13:21 NLT).

Knowledge is power, and power helps us walk in confidence. King Solomon advised us of this when he said, "Get wisdom; develop good judgment. Don't forget my words or turn away from them. Don't turn your back on wisdom, for she will protect you. Love her, and she will guard you. Getting wisdom is the wisest thing you can do! And whatever else you do, develop good judgment" (Proverbs 4:5–7 NLT).

The more I grow in Christ, the more I discover my hunger for Him and what He has called me to do. My greatest desire is to do the work God has entrusted to me, to guide people on the path God has set before them, by assuring them of their hope in Christ. It burdens me to see the future God has for so many people, yet they live a life that will deviate them from that future! God says, "I know the plans I have for you. . . . They are plans for good and not for disaster, to give you a future and a hope" (Jeremiah 29:11 NLT).

My burden is to help people realize God's plans for them and guide them on the right track to get in tune with God, who will then lead them to their destination. I have a burden to want to see everyone doing well. To see that people's situations are fixed and praise God for it, for them to know that God is not as limited as we are, for people to have no sadness, no sorrows, just joyfully thriving. To remind them that Hope lives. I want to see them be joyful in all circumstances and not allow what is happening around them to cause them to forget who God is and what He can do in their lives.

The storms of life have a way of shifting us, but understand this: those who trust God can never be shaken to the point of no return. It is always better with God—it is *always* better. Before we break through, God will test our strength in places where we struggle because He wants to ensure we're ready to handle what's on the other side. Our result will determine our next step. In the storms, we are blessed! Allow God to help you keep your focus above the waves.

What God Has Joined

Marriage is a beautiful union. Nothing is more beautiful than finding your God-given spouse and agreeing to start this beautiful journey hand in hand. As beautiful as that sounds, sometimes we encounter hiccups along the way. Two different individuals were raised in two separate homes, experiencing different upbringings. Undoubtedly, there will be clashes and bumps as couples grow together in one accord. Marriage is a covenant between the married couple and God. It is a spiritual commitment we make with God.

The secret to winning the journey and conquering the storms within this beautiful union is to place God in the center. Wherever God's covenant is, the enemy aims to break it. We are in a season when so many marriages are torn apart, and divorce is imminent because of how society views marriage. How we view this covenant with God determines how we approach it. Marriage is important to God. All relationships He gives us matter to Him, and He desires that we cherish and love the people He brings into our lives just as He loves us.

The Word of God tells us we love because His love was first demonstrated in our lives (1 John 4:19). Let me share what the

Holy Spirit says about the union of marriage. God led me to Luke 19:10—"The Son of Man came to seek and to save the lost." From this verse, He started talking to me.

We are all called to mimic the ways of Christ, and He came to save and seek after lost souls. The minute we pick our cross, we make ourselves fishers of men and ambassadors of Christ. Our job is to win souls for the kingdom of God. The number-one person or people to start with in drawing near to Christ are those closest to us, in this case, our spouses, who need a bit of push towards spiritual maturity.

I am speaking to the married man or woman at the point of a breakdown who feels there is no way out and his or her marriage has become a world of suffocation. You are in the middle of a road of questions, wondering why you are going through what you are going through. You married your spouse with the mindset of paradise, love, compassion, friendship, and fellowship with God. But, for some reason, the enemy has set out to put asunder what God has joined together. What was once a happy place has become a prison, and you are calling to escape. I know the skies look cloudy, and the temptations to leave increase daily. You've given it your all. You have faced mental and emotional trauma, cried out to God, and sometimes have sleepless nights, waking up with puffy eyes. At this point, with all efforts to make things work out, things are not looking good.

It may seem as if your spouse is not entirely trying to get to the level and capacity of your growth. Dear brother or sister, I know you have wanted to get your spouse to see you and to see things from your standpoint. You have been attempting to win them over to God, and the harder you pray and strive to love through the pain, the more things seem dull and hopeless. One season, you are hopeful; the next, you are hopeless. The Lord says this: "Divorce is not the answer." God is counting on you. He says your spouse is your first assignment. They may be lost and striving to get on the right standing with Christ. Your departure from their life will gain the world of darkness a soul, and heaven will lose one. We serve a God who came to seek and save the lost, a God who leaves the ninety-nine and goes after the one lost sheep. He called us out of the darkness into His marvelous light (1 Peter 2:9).

What if you are in each other's life for the sole purpose of saving one another? What if your job as an ambassador begins with those closest to you? You may be thinking, *What is that to do with the pain he [she] is causing me?* I do not have the answers to all questions. Still, one thing I know is that a man or woman who finds God's heart will hold yours in high esteem; therefore, our job is not to focus on the pain people cause us but on how we can help them find God's heart and live life with that heart.

Before I took the road of the union of marriage, one of the best advice my mother gave me was: "If you want to see changes in your spouse, you have to start with yourself." This advice has helped me in my personal life. Everything I expected my spouse to work on or did not like about him, I had to search deep within myself and realize that everything I did not want about him was what God used to work on me, to strengthen me, prune me, and make me the woman I am today. Your spouse being your first assignment as an ambassador of Christ is not only about you helping them find God's heart but also about your composures within the storms in your marriage. How are you handling yourself?

We endure pain to learn to resist the stones people throw at us. We go through loneliness so we can learn to appreciate our own company confidently. Loving and enjoying your own company is a form of natural growth and self-love, and enjoying the peaceful presence of God in solitude is a supernatural fulfillment that helps us grow spiritually.

I know that at this point, you are asking God, *Why? When will this season of pain and turmoil end?* But God says, *Keep loving through the confusion. Keep loving the way you've felt the love of Christ.* Most importantly, keep looking to Him, who makes all things better and beautiful in His time. The Word of God tells us that "if the husband or wife who isn't a believer insists on leaving, let them go.

In such cases, the believing husband or wife is no longer bound to the other, for God has called you to live in peace" (1 Corinthians 7:15 NLT). But If the unbelieving spouse wants to stay, you, the believing spouse, must allow him or her to, because as the Word says when you read further on, "Don't you wives realize that your husbands might be saved because of you? And don't you husbands realize that your wives might be saved because of you?" (1 Corinthians 7:16 NLT). Any union where two are joined from totally different backgrounds is not easy. If you do not place God at the center, you might divorce while your assignment or purpose by which God brought you two together goes to waste.

Many people think God brings a man and woman together mainly for lovey-dovey and to display affection. Sometimes, it's to join together to raise the children He gives you for His glory—to expand the future leaders in the kingdom of God. Sometimes, for you to come together with your spouse for a particular kingdom assignment, etc. Until we understand why God had joined us with our spouse, we will always be driven by the small blows of the enemy.

Our fight in life is not against flesh-and-blood enemies but against the powers of this dark world (Ephesians 6:12). Because of this truth, we must realize that the storms we face in God-ordained relationships are mostly tactics of the enemy to cause chaos and disunity, and then separation. The enemy plans to separate what God has joined together, and to do this; he first causes discord because he knows that a house is well-built when the builders are united and of one accord. "What God joined together, let no man separate" (Mark 10:9) —This verse speaks to the outsider trying to break a marriage and the couples within the union. We are each other's savings net. The joy in heaven when we win a soul is unexplainable, and your reward is incomparable. Child of God, your spouse is your first assignment!

A Revelation of Man's Relationship with God

I often hear conversations about how women are special to God. I rarely hear about a man's connection with God. Women are indeed special and, may I add, extraordinary beings. But let's look at men's connection with God. Before, the word became flesh and dwelled among men. He was "the Lord God, the Almighty— the one who always was, who is, and who is still to come" (Revelations 4:8 NLT).

During the creation of Adam, Jesus Christ existed and had a vital role in creation. Adam had a relationship with God, the Father, the Son, and the Holy Spirit. Before Mary was chosen to be the vessel that bore Jesus Christ, who came as flesh and dwelled amongst humans, there was Adam. I am trying to say that men have a special place with God. They are not far away from God. A man is God's best buddy.

When God wanted to create humans for Himself, He first made a man in His likeness. Even though a woman dwelled in a man, Adam was the first human to appear on earth. God's relationship was first with Adam. God saw Adam as a companion. A buddy for Himself. And when He saw this friend of His was lonely, He made him a suitable helper (Genesis 2:18). In this case, God brought out the woman within a man—this foretells why a man leaves his family and rejoins with his other half (the woman), and they become one again in companionship.

In the Garden of Eden, God commanded Adam not to eat the fruit of knowledge of good and evil (Genesis 2:15-17). God trusted Adam, His buddy, His companion, His friend whom He created for himself. He saw Adam as the head, gave him the instructions, and then made a woman for him. Adam was to look after the woman, protect her from the serpent, and see through to it that they do not fail God. But Adam failed in his task. He failed God, which was the beginning of a tainted relationship between man and God. God knew what Eve had done because He is an all-knowing God. But, when He came, He asked Adam, "Have you eaten from the tree whose fruit I commanded you not to eat?" and Adam said, "It was the woman you gave me who gave me the fruit, and I ate it." (Genesis 3:11-12 NLT).

Some men may think they are not close to God because the Son of God came through a woman. But they are God's first human relationship —outside Himself. God trusted Adam to be the head of the household known as the "Garden of Eden." He trusted man to be the protector and expected to love his wife as Christ loves him. This is why the word of God never said a woman must leave her parents and join with the man, but rather, a man shall leave his home and cling to his wife, and the two shall become one (Genesis 2:22-24).

A woman is dear to God's heart, and He sees her as delicate (1 Peter 3:7). To love his wife as Christ loves the church, a man must go through God. He must know and cultivate his relationship with God. He must remember that because of Christ, he can have that companionship he once had with God in the Garden.

My advice to every man: *until your relationship with God is established through Christ, you can never love your wife how she needs to be loved and cared for. Find God's heart because your wife's heart is hidden in His.* My advice to every woman: *before God hands you over to your husband, you first belong to Him. You must ensure your relationship with God is firmly established in service to Him alone. This will create a solid foundation on how to be of service to your husband.*

We all have a special place in the heart of God through Christ. Until we realize our place in the kingdom of God, we will always wander to find other means to feel whole and accepted in this land of the living.

Counsel through Proverbs

"I have observed something else under the sun. The fastest runner doesn't always win the race, and the strongest warrior doesn't always win the battle. The wise sometimes go hungry, and the skillful are not necessarily wealthy. And those who are educated don't always lead successful lives. It is all decided by chance, by being in the right place at the right time" (Ecclesiastes 9:11). Sometimes, we never know what we are capable of until we are given the opportunity. Sometimes, we never know we can fly until someone pushes us down from a mountaintop. Sometimes, we never know that we carry the words to heal many souls in a congregation until someone passes us a microphone. Sometimes, we never know that we can stand on our own two feet until those we hang on to let go of us.

Great things come from challenging and painful moments. Yes, a time will come when you'll be left alone in the middle of the road and forced to find the way out on your own but know in these moments that you are not alone, and God walks right with you. In these moments, ask God, *What is inside me that you want to help me birth this season?* The journey of claiming your heavenly prize, which Paul speaks of in Philippians 3:14, will not be easy. There will be many challenges along the way, but you can overcome these challenges with the help of God. There is only one of you in the whole world. Ensure you never lose sight of who you are and what makes you different. No matter where you find yourself, be different and stand up for what is true. Refuse to blend in.

At a point in life, it may feel as though you are doing life alone, but God is always there, guiding you every step of the way. Living life by your way of thinking will cause you to crash, but allowing God's wisdom to guide you will lead you on a straight path, for the Word of God tells us that even God's "foolish" plans are wiser than the human plans and His "weakness" is stronger than any human strength (1 Corinthians 1:25).

When the Israelites were being led out of Egypt to the promised land, God took them on the longest route. The Lord did not let them travel that route alone. He went ahead of them and guided them during the day with a pillar of cloud, and He provided light at night with a pillar of fire, allowing them to travel by day or night.

God did not remove the pillar of cloud or pillar of fire from its place in front of the people (Exodus 13:21–22).

Life's journey may feel long at times, especially in your waiting season, when you're waiting for God to grant you specific answers to your questions, but it seems that nothing is coming through—the Lord will always go before you, guiding you through the ups and downs, even in the questions. In every season, God has a solution to every obstacle. Get the wisdom of God, and get knowledge and understanding because when wisdom enters your heart, knowledge will fill your heart with joy, wise choices will watch over you, and understanding will keep you safe. Allowing God's wisdom to guide you in life will save you from evil people and those whose words are twisted (Proverbs 2:10–12).

As you go through life's journey, you may feel as though you are not noticed or that you are overlooked for your efforts, but know that there is time for everything under the sun (Ecclesiastes 3:1). Never allow what you see and feel to dictate you because life is more about what is unseen than what is seen. A day is coming when God will reveal you to a watching world. Until then, you must be okay with who the world limits you to be. Be okay with being talked about, be okay with being misrepresented, be okay with being rejected. Be okay with people viewing you according to their understanding of who they believe you are. Be okay with being the bad guy in the eyes of the masses. Be okay with it because life is measured not by how someone sees you but by how God sees you.

Not all situations you go through need your attention and retaliation because some are thrown your way to cause a distraction. Never allow the enemy's manipulations to cause you to lose sight of the bigger picture. Gain self-control because it is God's will that we all live a life of discipline and success to "gain insight into simple knowledge and discernment" through His wisdom (See Proverbs 1:1–16). King Solomon tells us to befriend wisdom and never turn our back on her as she will protect and guard us (Proverbs 4:6). Getting wisdom and developing wise judgment is the best thing you can do. Your growth in Christ is determined by understanding and obeying God's regulations.

The Word of God says to walk with the wise and become wise, but that befriending fools will get you in trouble (Proverbs 13:20). As a child of God, you must always walk in a way that speaks and represents who you are—a child of God! Always be friendly and good to everyone. Love everyone as you are obligated to do as Christ loves you, but be selective with whom you allow in your circle. Not everyone deserves a seat at your dining table because some are there to weaken the legs of that table. This is not harsh; it is simply learning to walk with wisdom and guarding your heart, as Solomon says, for it determines the course of your life (Proverbs 4:23).

Protect the vessel (you); you are expensive. Look for quality in life as it is better than quantity. It is not every visitor you open the doors of your heart to. Don't let life teach you easy lessons the hard way!

CONCLUSION

Fall Season

To the child of God reading this, keep this in mind:

In your journey to purpose, you will learn that many people will not agree with you along the way, and many more will not see you as God does, but that's all right! The vision is just for you to embark on. You are a voice to many who are counting on you. But know this: When people do not see you the way God sees you or do not know God's vision for your life, they may devalue you. When walking in your purpose, manifesting your gifts, and accepting God's will for your life. It will annoy a lot of people around you. Don't be discouraged by this.

When God starts revealing you to them, they will become speechless and bothered because initially, their level of value for you was based on their limited minds about themselves, which they projected onto you, so now that God is showing them who you are and that you are not what they thought you were, it'll begin to remove the mask they had on around you. This will help you see them for who they are. Next, they will naturally become distant. After all, they were around you because they believed you to be beneath them, but now that God has revealed you, they can't handle being around you since your light is too bright for them to comprehend.

This is how God shreds the dry leaves around you. Not only does He work on you on the inside, but He also shreds the outside. The process is challenging, as it is a season of letting go of those you once were attached to. Don't go after them. These people will never help you evolve. They will only suppress your growth to make themselves feel comfortable around you.

God says, "*Where I'm taking you, they can't come with you. Because they oppose who you are in me. I have your army, your audience, your supporters. Those that I have opened their eyes to see you as I do. They are the ones who will encourage and accept you and your evolvement in becoming the "you" that I created. Keep your focus on me and keep walking in your truth. I love you.*"

Dear Child of God, you are in your fall season, and God is bringing you fresh green leaves. Let the dried-up ones fall. Cheers to evolving! Cheers to growing through the storms!

ABOUT THE AUTHOR

Before getting to the season of answering her call, Prophetess Esther has gone through seasons of storms, which, through the power of the Holy Spirit, helped her navigate those storms, which brought her to this very moment in her life. She has endured the storms of life and grown and matured spiritually through them. She takes on the task of not only helping guide an individual's spiritual life, but she loves to encourage and advise many, helping them see the plans of God for their lives.

Esther was part of the choir and worship team at her previous church and served as a Sunday school coach at her current church. She is caring, compassionate, and, above all, a God-fearing wife and mother of three who takes God's work to heart. Her dedication attracts many to know her more and is a blessing to those who have crossed paths with her. She shares the word of God and prays with and intercedes for many, especially during difficult moments in their lives, where she motivates them to stay strong and trust God. Esther is loving, and her ingenuity and positive attitude allow others to confide in her. Her ministry, "Beyond Hope Ministries," has changed the lives of many through her words of hope.

Printed in the United States
by Baker & Taylor Publisher Services